W/D

D1492585

The Sea Angler's Guide to
Britain and Ireland

The Sea Angler's Guide to
Britain and Ireland

John Darling

LUTTERWORTH PRESS
GUILDFORD & LONDON

First published in Great Britain by
Lutterworth Press, Guildford &
London, in 1982

Copyright © 1982 Ventura Publishing
Ltd, London

Created, designed and produced by
Ventura Publishing Ltd, 44 Uxbridge
Street, London W8 7TG

ISBN Cased : 0 7188-2509-8
      Paper : 0 7188-2510-1

Filmset in Great Britain by SX
Composing Ltd, Rayleigh, Essex

Colour originations by D.S. Colour
International Ltd., London

Printed and bound in Singapore by
Tien Wah Press (Pte) Limited

The publishers have made every
effort to ensure that the information in
this book is correct at the time of going
to press, February 1982.
Any correspondence concerned with
the contents of this volume should be
addressed to Ventura Publishing Ltd,
44 Uxbridge St, London W8.

*Half title : A view of Lamlash and Holy
Isle from the Isle of Arran.
Page 2 : A good catch of large bass.
Page 3 : The season for rock bass
starts when the sea pinks are at their
best.
Page 5 : Hooking mackerel at sunrise
off the Kent coast.*

Foreword

As I seem to have a reputation for forecasting bad weather and even, by some, held responsible for it, I feel I must impress on anglers, if nothing else, that it is essential to seek meteorological advice before contemplating a fishing trip. I've seen many accidents not only on boats but also involving people being swept off piers, breakwaters and even beaches. The Meteorological Office is there to help – indeed, it wants to help. Offices are manned throughout the country, 24 hours a day, seven days a week, and for the price of a telephone call you can speak to a forecaster. Tell the forecaster when and where you are going and he or she will in turn give you a forecast. It's a free service, so make use of it. Even if there doesn't happen to be a Meteorological Office in your locality, there's always the telephone recorded weather service to turn to. The number for this and for your local forecasting office are in the front of your telephone directory.

By all means look at the television forecast or listen to the broadcasts from the London Weather Centre when you are planning the trip, but don't take them in isolation. With the time allowed, both types of forecast tend to be very 'broad brush'. Don't take the wind arrows you see on the television as gospel – they are intended to give general guidance over large areas, and will not give you local wind and sea conditions. The newspaper weather charts also suffer the same deficiency.

There are, though, certain things an angler can do for himself if all else fails, or indeed as a last-minute check on the forecast. Give the barometer a gentle tap, for instance. If it shoots down think twice before going: even more so if the cloud is thickening and lowering. Sometimes a rapidly rising barometer can spell trouble, too, as strong winds can come along just behind a depression. As a final piece of advice, do take a radio with you, as this will enable you to keep an ear tuned for the gale warnings and regular shipping forecasts (broadcast on Radio 4, 1500m/200kHz). If you hear a gale described as 'imminent', that means it will occur within six hours, 'soon' means between six and 12 hours, and 'later' means more than 12 hours away.

Anyhow, that's enough preaching from me. Enjoy this book, and I hope you have safe, fruitful fishing trips in, above all, ideal weather.

Michael Fish
London Weather Centre

Contents

Contents

Introduction

The Sea Angler's Guide gathers together a vast amount of information about the fishing around our coastline, both from the beach and from boats. Species, methods, baits and so on are outlined, together with a list of places where trailed boats of sensible size may be launched. Much of the coastline is described bay by bay, cove by headland so that the independent shore fisherman can make his own assessments, play his own hunches and, when they encounter success, he can feel justifiably smug.

Other anglers will find the lists of tackle dealers and other sources of information of great use. Tackle shops will always be clearing houses for up-to-the-second catch reports. Many dealers are also first class anglers. Visitors are advised to discuss their plans with knowledgeable locals in case they have overlooked a vital piece of information. After all a technique which works in one place may fail elsewhere. This book is designed to help you get it all right first time.

Top charter boats – especially those used for wreck fishing – are likely to be booked up many months in advance, so make your enquiries in good time. Some are listed here, but you will find many more listed in the angling press. Trailer-sailors are advised to contact local commercial fishermen, charter boatmen, coast-guards and tackle dealers before launching on to unknown waters. The British Isles offer a huge variety of sea conditions and it is essential to understand how the water reacts to different weather regimes and tidal conditions. This is a serious warning. Anglers are more interested in fishing and rarely have wide experience of boating conditions. Conditions that may be uncomfortable, but safe, back home may be quite impossible elsewhere.

Weather information may be obtained from numbers listed in telephone dialling code books and local airfields and bulletins from local radio stations. But the best person to consult for details of weather and tides is the coastguard.

When planning to use one of the launch sites listed, find out whether there are any pre-conditions and whether a fee is payable. Check on alternative landing sites and sheltered areas in which to ride out rough weather should the forecast have been inaccurate. Never leave without life-jackets and a full range of equipment for emergencies.

While bait collecting, think of the local man who makes his living from the beds, and remember that lines and hooks left by anglers can be a snare for sea-birds. If you leave the beach looking like a battle front, nobody will thank you and those who come after will be treated with animosity.

O.K. then. Take care, and may success go with you.

How to use the book

The coastlines of Britain and Ireland are divided into sections, based on counties, progressing in a clockwise direction as they appear on the map, starting with Kent. The sections are denoted on the map by black dots and the relevant page numbers are shown. Each section includes detailed information on the coastal topography and tides, species of fish to be caught and in what season, tackle dealers, boat launching facilities and charters, and the prime angling sites and bait areas. A numbered key (1, 2, 3 etc.) pinpoints the angling hot spots on the maps provided in each section, and bait areas are indicated by a lettered key (A, B, C etc.). Major roads are shown and advice on access given, but the maps should be used in conjunction with a good road atlas or Ordnance Survey map of the relevant area. Alternative spellings for place-names are given where two versions are commonly in use on available maps.

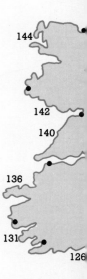

Channel Islands

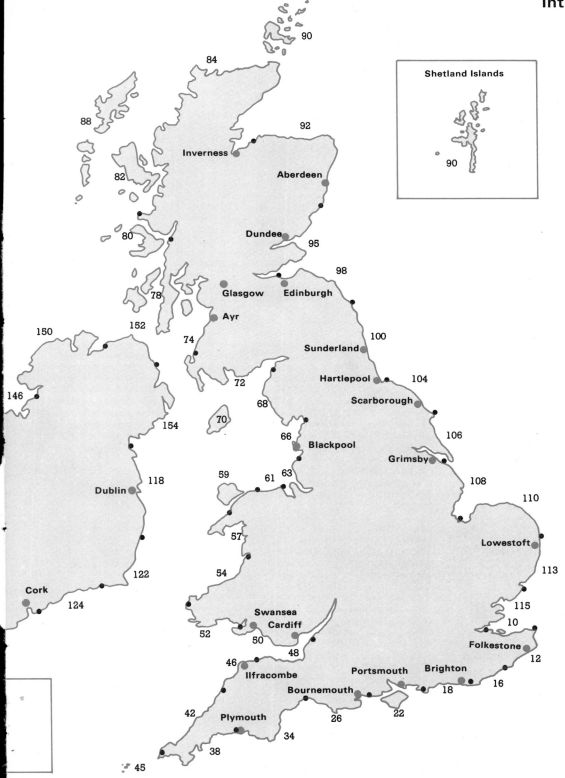

90

84

88

92

Inverness

82

Aberdeen

80

Dundee

95

98

78

Glasgow Edinburgh

Ayr

150   152

74

Sunderland   100

72

Hartlepool   104

68

Scarborough

146

154

70

106

66

Blackpool

Grimsby

Dublin   118

59   61   63

108

110

57

Lowestoft

122

54

113

Cork

124

115

Swansea

10

Cardiff

52   50

Folkestone

48

12

46

Portsmouth   Brighton

Ilfracombe

18   16

42

Bournemouth

Plymouth

22

26   34

38

45

Shetland Islands

90

Kent

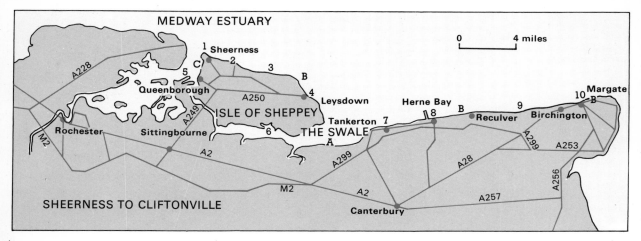

MEDWAY ESTUARY

0   4 miles

A228

1 Sheerness
2
C
3
5
B
Queenborough
A250
4
Leysdown
10 Margate
B
Herne Bay
A249
9
Birchington
ISLE OF SHEPPEY
8
Reculver
Rochester
Sittingbourne
THE SWALE
Tankerton 7
A
6
A299
A253
A28
A299
M2
A2
A256
M2
A2
A257
Canterbury

SHEERNESS TO CLIFTONVILLE

Caesar's legions landed here some two thousand years ago. Faced with an invasion of heating engineers, road builders and legislators, the locals painted themselves blue and hurled rocks at them before retreating towards London. Each year since then Londoners have been flocking to the north Kent coast in their thousands. So the beaches in summer tend to be crowded with tourists, sailors and powerboat enthusiasts. The best summer fishing is to be had from a boat offshore, while the shore fisherman is advised to operate early, late, or where the beach is less accessible.

Caesar landed here because the beaches are so flat. The high water mark generally consists of shingle, becoming sandier. Inside the Thames Estuary, and especially around the Isle of Sheppey, the foreshore becomes very muddy and is dangerous in some places. Areas of rock are extensive, patchy east of Herne Bay, but more frequent towards Cliftonville. Rocks are one of the features that attract fish around here. Deeper water near in also persuades the fish to come closer to the beach than elsewhere.

Shore fishing is for cod (but not a huge run, as in south Kent), whiting, dabs and flounders during the winter months; and for small tope, some thornback rays, huss and spotted dogfish, the occasional sting ray, bass, plaice, a few sole and thousands of silver eels in the summer months. Bass frequent the rocks early and late in the summer, spending the major part of their time hunting around the offshore sandbanks.

Much of the very best fishing is from

a boat because the beaches shelve so gently. Offshore, there are channels and sand-bars built up from sand and shell and one or two wrecks. Populations of fish out there are similar to those caught from the beach, but better in numbers and quality.

Visiting boat anglers should take care. The very shallow water reacts badly to winds from the north and east, especially when the tide is ebbing hard into the wind. Anything over force four sets up a dangerous, short wave pattern – very unpleasant and not safe for small boats. Weather details are available from Garrison Point (Tel: Sheerness (079 56) 3025).

Flood tides fill and ebb tides drain the Thames Estuary. High Water at Herne Bay is $1\frac{1}{2}$ hours before London Bridge. Inshore currents run parallel to the shore.

Club Headquarters: The Isle of Sheppey AA has a clubhouse close to the tackle shop at Neptune Terrace, Sheerness. Herne Bay AA has its headquarters at 59 Central Parade, Herne Bay (Tel: Herne Bay (022 73) 62127).

Onshore winds here bring the fish on the feed in both summer and winter. Overcast skies help, too, or dusk and dawn conditions, to reduce the light intensity in this shallow water. Launching is not advised during onshore wind regimes. Those with boats on trailers are advised that there are several public slipways and ramps, few of which can be used at all periods of the tide. Slipways exist at Queenborough (any time); Whitehouse ($2\frac{1}{2}$ hours each side of high water); Whitstable (3 hours each side of high water); Herne Bay (Neptune Jetty, 4 hours each side of

high water); Minnis Bay, Birchington (3 hours each side of high water); Margate Harbour (3 hours each side of high water).

1 Garrison Point   Very rocky with fierce tides. Some good bass fishing, especially for big ones. Good silver eels, dabs, scad, flounders and thick-lipped mullet in summer. Cod and whiting, in some years as far upstream as Gravesend, in winter. The pier is owned by the Medway Ports Authority and fishing there is restricted. Bait supplies are uncertain and hard to gather, so visitors are advised to contact Sheppey Bait and Tackle Shop, Neptune Terrace, Sheerness (Tel: Sheerness (079 56) 3665).

2 Barton's Point   Consistent for bass and eels in summer, though better in winter for cod and flatfish. Boat anglers are advised that there exists a no-go area around the buoyed wreck of the *Richard Montgomery* just offshore. Beware of large tankers and other commercial traffic that use the sea lanes. They cannot stop for small boats.

3 Eastchurch Gap   Some cliff here. Best results are achieved casting out a bit and at night for bass, eels and smooth hounds on crab in summer, cod and whiting in winter. This area is hard to get to and you risk being cut off by the tide, so survey the place carefully in daylight before starting to fish.

4 Leysdown   The fishing can be excellent, but shallow water limits operations to $2\frac{1}{2}$ hours each side of high water. Note that the private nudist beach at Shellness is accessible for neither fishing nor bait gathering.

5 Medway Estuary   This is the best area for flounder fishing using red river ragworm, especially when the fish are migrating early in the year. Plenty of silver eels and some school bass, especially at Stangate Creek. All West Minster and Queenborough walls are fishable. Boats can be chartered either through Sheppey Bait and Tackle, or through Stan Smith, High Street, Queenborough, Isle of Sheppey (Tel: Sheerness (079 56) 67304).

6 The Swale   Eels, flounders and school bass in summer, a few whiting in winter and the occasional cod. Like the Medway Estuary, the Swale is heavily populated by thick-lipped mullet in summer, for which specialist study and tackle are required.

7 Tankerton Bay and Whitstable Street   Good bass and flounders off Street on peeler crab all through tide, with flatfish and eels along the beach. Some cod and whiting in winter. Charter boats operate from Whitstable Harbour. Details of bookings from Ron Edwards at 50 High Street, Herne Bay (Tel: Herne Bay (022 73) 2517).

8 Herne Bay   Outcrops of reef provide good bass fishing all along this stretch of coast right round to Ramsgate. Spring tides in May, June and September see the best results at night with peeler crab. A few cod and whiting can be taken in winter; otherwise flounders, dabs, small tope and smooth hounds, and lots of eels in spring. Tackle and bait from Ron Edwards, 50 High Street, Herne Bay, Kent (Tel: Herne Bay (022 73) 2517).

9 Reculver to Birchington   Cod and whiting are caught during night tides from October to February, fishing around high tide. It is necessary to cast a fair way. There are bass in summer, some flatfish, and eels in abundance. Sometimes thornback rays come in here; long casts with very fresh herring produce a few early in the summer.

10 Margate   Plenty of rocky bays in the area around Margate and round towards Ramsgate. Joss Bay fishes well, has a large car park and less dangerous gulleys than others like Dumpton Gap, Kingsgate, Botany Bay and Foreness. Visitors are advised to go with locals until they know the layout of the reefs. Cod are taken from October through to June here, also bass in fair numbers throughout the warm months. Peeler crabs score best for both species – and the inevitable eels.

The harbour at Margate has silted up badly so that there is now no charter fleet there. Most of them have moved south to Ramsgate. For bait and information, contact Kingfishers Tackle Shop, 34 King Street, Margate, Kent (Tel: Margate (0843) 23866).

Bait Areas

A   Plenty of lugworm at Seasalter and Whitstable. Large brown blow-lugworm generally, dug by trenching, and a few cockles. Lugworm beds extend, patchily, round to Margate.

B   The north Kent coast, wherever there is some rocky or bouldery ground, will produce good numbers of peeler shore crabs from April to May, but fewer during the main summer months. Crabbing improves in September.

C   Plenty of harbour ragworm on mudflats at West Minster and Queenborough. Beware of soft mud while digging on the Isle of Sheppey.

Reward for a night on the beach, a good winter codling.

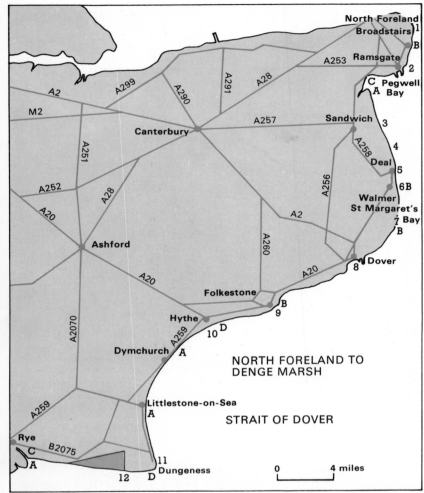

There are some dramatic changes in the shore line as one works south along this section of the Kent coast. The rocky ground north of Ramsgate contrasts sharply with the shallow sands at Pegwell Bay. The water deepens slightly south of the Stour estuary, round the broad sandy sweep of Sandwich Bay, a place many anglers visit if sou'westerlies at Dungeness make fishing impossible. Around Deal, the beaches are steeper still, of shingle, mixed rock and sand below the water line, which in turn becomes very reefy in the South Foreland area. This continues round to Folkestone, becoming sandier at Hythe, and more shallow again at Dymchurch before the dramatic depths and tides at Dungeness Point. The water is deep along Denge Marsh, but is shallower again at Camber and towards Rye Harbour.

The main fish species caught from the shore are cod, flounders, dabs, pouting and whiting in winter; bass, conger eels, small tope, mackerel, scad, garfish, small pouting and whiting, plaice, sole, some cod and some dogfish in summer. Many of the locals fish for sole and bass in summer, big dabs and large cod in winter.

Mullet are common in the harbours at Ramsgate, Dover, Folkestone and Rye and in the Stour and Rother estuaries. These are mainly thick-lipped, but thin-lipped mullet are found in the Rother and a few golden grey mullet are taken from the beaches.

Boats from Ramsgate, Deal, Walmer, Folkestone, Dungeness and Rye Harbour all provide good fishing in winter for big cod until late December when huge sprat shoals move in and blot out everything but small bottom feeders. Offshore grounds provide good tope, spur dogfish, flatfish, some rays and black bream and smaller species in summer. The wreck fishing can be very good for medium pollack and ling and for good cod in summer. The Straights of Dover have several large sandbanks, like the Varne, which also provide good cod and infrequent turbot fishing in summer.

Razorfish and lugworm make excellent bait for flounder fishing.

Slipways are available for those with boats on trailers at Broadstairs (4 hours before and after high water). Ramsgate harbour (not at dead low water); Deal Rowing Club; Dover (all states of tide); Folkestone (all times); Sandgate, behind the rowing club; Princes Parade, Hythe, and at Rye Harbour (not at dead low water).

The tides, especially to the north of Dover, run hard and in a confusing pattern. The visitor is advised to obtain expert advice for setting out. High tide times are $2\frac{1}{2}$ (Deal) and $2\frac{3}{4}$ (Dover) hours before London Bridge. Tidal streams are very complex.

There are thriving sea angling clubs at: Dover SAA, 14 Priory Road, Dover (Tel: Dover (0304) 204772); Deal AC at 13 The Marina, Deal; Deal and Walmer AA at South Toll House, Deal Pier.

1 North Foreland This is reefy ground interspersed with sandy bays, backed by cliffs. The best fishing is from the ends of rock fingers, especially where they give on to sand. Local knowledge is vital. Bass and cod are taken in May and June on peeler crab, bass and cod in September and October on crab, fresh squid etc and small congers on fish baits and edible peelers.

2 Ramsgate Most local species are to be caught from the piers, especially the south-western arm which gives onto deeper water. To the south, at Pegwell Bay, the water is too shallow for worthwhile fishing. There are booking agencies for charter boats at: 95 King's Street (Tel: Ramsgate (0843) 5294); Fisherman's Corner, 6 Kent Place (Tel: Ramsgate (0843) 582174) and Ramsgate Bait and Tackle, Westcliff Arcade (Tel: Ramsgate (0843) 53195).

3 Sandwich Bay Provides excellent surf fishing in winter for cod, but too popular with tourists in summer. Locals favour different areas. Two main access points are along the toll road at Sandwich, and along the road to the Chequers pub from Deal. Large whiting, some bass, lots of flatfish and the occasional ray are caught there. Long range casting is often vital.

4 Sandown Castle Good low-water area, especially in winter and after a summer blow for bass. Local yellow-tail lugworm, a variety of black lugworm, produces the most fish, though crab scores for spring cod and summer bass.

5 Deal A very long pier, ideal for angling, that produces plenty of fish when conditions are right. Mullet, bass, conger eels and cod are the most talked-about species there. Some nasty snags to either side, among the rocks, so obtain advice first. Night fishing is restricted. The beaches to either side of the pier are quite steep, shingle going on to rocky ground with a few sand patches. The Deal charter fleet – some 50 boats to around 27 ft – is kept to the south of the pier and launched straight off the shingle. There are several good tackle shops, one such, from which boats can be chartered, is Channel Angling, Deal Pier, Beach Street, Deal (Tel: Deal (030 45) 3104).

6 Walmer Species as for Deal. Plenty of car parking – and a pub – within a short walk of the beach. Deepish water close in produces the best results after dark. For charter boat bookings, bait and information, contact The Downs Tackle Centre, 29 The Strand, Walmer (Tel: Deal (030 45) 2811)

7 St Margaret's Bay The usual species are taken on worm, crab and fish baits. It is not easy to fish from here around to Dover because of the rocky nature of the South Foreland. Plenty of reefs to explore for bass, and to troll over in summer for bass, small pollack and mackerel.

8 Dover Some doubt about the future of fishing due to the new Hoverport. Plenty of mullet in the harbour, but access is restricted by bye-laws and the weather. A ferry boat is required to reach the Admiralty pier, and that may be cancelled in poor weather. Good fishing there, though, for big cod and bass and conger eels. Other species, too. Tides run very fast off the piers. Check out local details from Bill's Bait and Tackle, 130 Snargate Street, Dover (Tel: Dover (0304) 204542 day and Dover (0304) 206894 evening).

9 Folkestone The Warren, to the east of the town, is excellent for bass in summer and autumn, cod in winter. The pier offers mixed fishing – whiting, dabs, plaice, mackerel, small pollack etc. Some big cod are caught here in winter at high tide and also at dead low water. The rocky foreshore at Folkestone fishes well for bass in both calm and rough seas, especially when high tide occurs early on in the night. Edible crab is a favourite bait here, as are lugworm and white ragworm cocktails. Bait and information from Garry's Tackle Shop, 12 Tontime Street, Folkestone (Tel: Folkestone (0303) 53881); Wesley's Tackle & Bait Ltd., 252 Seabrook Road, Folkestone (Tel: Folkestone (0303) 38783).

Schoolbass are easy targets for fly-fishing tactics. Successful baits for bass include lugworm, king rag worm and crab. In the winter try slipper limpets and mussels, these become available to the fish after storms.

10 Hythe Plenty of small fish are caught from Princes Parade in summer when holiday makers take over the beach. Some good bass are taken here on dark tides. The best time is after a winter gale for good cod and large flounders, especially when razorfish are washed in. Access to the foreshore in front of the army ranges is restricted.

11 Dungeness Summer: large bass are taken on a variety of baits from the point, and are often caught in large numbers on lures and fish baits from the 'Boil', the power station warm-water outfall. Large shoals of mackerel appear at high tide. Fishing for sole is especially good at night. Sometimes tope and sting rays are taken, as are conger eels and dogfish.

Winter: The area between the beach opposite the offshore structure and the boats on the east beach is probably the best place in Britain for large cod on black lugworms, live pouting and whiting, razorfish and fresh sprats. Much bait is washed up after a big storm, the best time to fish.

Tackle and charter boat bookings from: The Point Tackle Shop, Allendale, Dungeness (Tel: Lydd (0679) 20049).

12 Denge Marsh and Galloways Access by road from Lydd. Species and seasons as for Dungeness. High water is generally the best time as the sea bed shallows off from the point towards Galloways, where sand is exposed at low water. Long-range casting is often essential. Some bass are taken from low-water surf on crab, squid or razorfish. Flatfish are more common from shallower ground. There is a run of plaice in March on shellfish baits.

Bait Areas
A Plenty of blow-lugworm at Pegwell Bay. Dig it by trenching, but moat diggings to keep out surface water. Keep an eye open for hover-craft. Lots of good black lugworms, which should be dug individually with a proper lugworm spade. Dymchurch and Dungeness, Galloways and Rye.
B Plenty of peeler crabs among the rocks in spring and autumn, also piddocks and rock worms here.
C Small harbour ragworm from the Stour and Rother estuaries.
D Storms often wash in large numbers of razorfish etc at Hythe and Dungeness.

FOR THE FAMILY
There are interesting places to visit and things to do all along the Channel Coast – from forest trails to Roman remains, exploring Romney Marsh, Dover or Rye, or taking a day trip by hovercraft or ferry to France.
Port Lympne Wildlife Sanctuary house and gardens nr Hythe. Tigers, wolves, elephants, rhinos on a hillside overlooking the sea. Zoo trek and art gallery.
North Downs Way walk part of this long footpath (the way is marked) with magnificent views from Downs and cliffs.
Richborough Castle nr Sandwich. Impressive remains of Roman Fort on the Saxon Shore. Interesting site museum.
Day visits to France (no passports needed) from Dover, Ramsgate or Folkestone to Calais or Boulogne. 7 hours in France.
Sandwich Precinct Toy Collection fascinating museum of early toys with 16 dolls houses, mechanical toys, Noah's Arks, etc. Open Easter–Sept.
Romney, Hythe and Dymchurch Railway 14 miles across Romney Marsh from Hythe to Dungeness lighthouse. Easter–Sept.
Dover The massive castle overlooking the Channel, Roman lighthouse and Roman Painted House are among Dover's many places of historical interest.

A superb 50lb female tope. Such fish are best put back alive after they have been weighed and photographed.

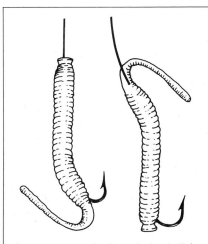

Lugworms may be threaded onto the hook from either head or tail. The fish could not care which, even though anglers hold partisan opinions.

Right: *The gurnard tribe walks over the sea bed on modified fin rays fitted with taste buds. Once skinned, this group of species tastes exceptionally fine.*

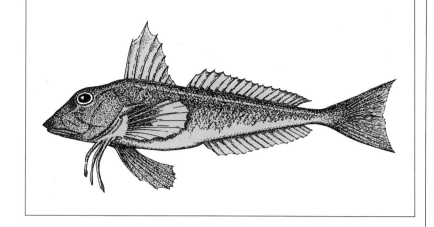

Below: *Centuries of erosion has formed extensive reefs beneath the Sussex cliffs. In some places they extend for over a mile beyond the low-water mark. Bass, cod, silver and conger eels frequent this habitat.*

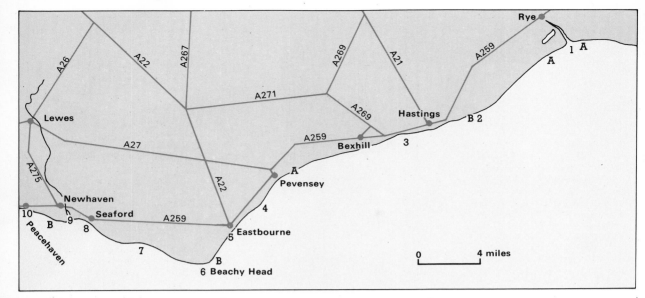

Thousands of years of erosion of the massive cliffs between Seaford and Eastbourne, Hastings and Winchelsea, have produced extensive reefs. In several places, these reefs extend for over a mile beyond the low-water mark. Much of the eroded material has been washed east by the tides and deposited along Winchelsea beach, Camber, and especially Dungeness, a promontory built almost entirely of shingle and still growing. By contrast, beaches to the west, between Brighton and Wittering, are very flat and virtually featureless.

Good-quality bass are common from late April to October, although some may be caught as late as December. Both black and red bream sometimes appear, though rarely in any size or numbers, except from West Sussex piers and beaches where reasonable bags of black-bream can be had. Cod are common between October and January, sometimes with a lesser run in spring. Tiny whiting sometimes reach plague proportions in summer, though better specimens appear in the colder months. Bait-size pouting are present for most of the year, better specimens being confined to offshore reefs.

Pollack, rarely exceeding 3 lb, form shoals around the piers in summer. Conger eels are common, especially round piers and reefy ground. Silver eels abound in the estuaries and over most reefs. Plaice are caught infrequently (a common, but sad, story nowadays), though flounders,

dabs and sole are relatively abundant. Indeed, the occasional turbot or brill is taken in September from the deep-water beaches. Mackerel, scad and garfish are common in fine summer weather. All three species of mullet are abundant, with most of the local rivers harbouring good populations of thin-lipped mullet.

Very few rays are caught inshore, even though thornback hatchlings are taken in shrimp nets. Spur dogfish and bull huss are taken in quantity offshore, though only occasional lesser-spotted dogfish are taken from the beach. Once they were very common at Dungeness, so this may relate to their breeding cycles. Tiny, beautifully coloured wrasse are frequently captured, but in prawn nets. Better specimens sometimes take crab baits fished from the rocks at Beachy Head.

The area boasts two thriving angling clubs, each with its own spacious headquarters building, bar, and boat-park right on the beach: Eastbourne AA, Royal Parade, Eastbourne (Tel: Eastbourne (0323) 23442); Hastings SAC, The Stade, Hastings (Tel: Hastings (0424) 430230).

Flood tides flow east and reverse on the ebb. Currents vary in strength with the length of the tide (spring or neap) and the weather. For high tide times, subtract 3 hrs from the London Bridge time for Dungeness, subtract 2 hrs 50 mins for Eastbourne and Newhaven.

1 Rye Harbour The water here is very shallow at low tide. In summer, mackerel, garfish and bass are taken from the gantry on the west side of the harbour. Bass also, on the early flood and middle ebb tides on crab and squid. Thick-lipped grey mullet are common in the harbour and taken on bread. Thin-lipped mullet are taken upstream of Iden Lock on harbour ragworm. In winter, cod, whiting and flounders may be taken from the harbour mouth and from adjacent beaches, but the water is very shallow along Camber Sands and Winchelsea Beach, making rod-and-line fishing hard work. Charter boats are obtained by contacting the individual skippers.

2 Pett Level and Fairlight Best in summer for bass, fishing peeler crab on flood and ebb among the rocky outcrops. Conger are taken on fish baits from similar ground and there are some smooth hounds and sole. Rarely worthwhile for winter cod and whiting.

3 Hastings and Bexhill Summer: some flatfish are taken on worm baits from open ground and piers, bass on crab from piers and rocky ground. Conger are caught from piers, as are mackerel, gurnard, scad and school bass on spinners and float-fished fish strip. Also pollack in fine, settled weather. Thick-lipped mullet are taken on bread from Hastings pier. Cod, whiting and flatfish are caught from the beaches in winter, but sport is best from the piers. No charter boats are available, but some private owners may take you out. Contact the main tackle dealer; Hastings Angling Centre, 33–35 The Bourne, Hastings (Tel: Hastings (0424) 432178).

4 Langney Point More fish are caught from here than from the surrounding shallower beaches of Pevensey Bay. A moderately shallow beach yielding flatfish in summer, especially sole, bass and mackerel. In winter, some good cod, whiting and pouting are taken. The best time is two hours each side of high water.

5 Eastbourne Pier Summer: bass are taken on live-baits and crab; mackerel, small pollack, scad and garfish in fine weather. Some flatfish, notably sole, dabs, flounders and the occasional plaice are caught on worm baits, thick-lipped mullet on bread and fish morsels. In winter, good cod and whiting are taken on worm and shellfish baits. Tackle shop: Tony's Tackle Shop, 211 Seaside, Eastbourne (Tel: Eastbourne (0323) 31388).

6 Beachy Head and Seven Sisters Famous for large bass on crab baits in the summer. Reefs extend from Eastbourne Pier round to Cuckmere Haven. Access is from Holywell; the footpath by the tea kiosk at the corner of Duke's Drive; the steps at Birling Gap (removed in winter): and the footpath to the beach at Cuckmere Haven. Rocky outcrops fish best, with low water and early flood a peak taking period, but bass change their timetables each season. Some conger eels to 40 lb are taken on fish and squid baits. Infrequent, but large, sole and plaice are caught from sandy areas amidst the reef. No worthwhile winter fishing, but the occasional bass is taken up to New Year and some cod in the spring, albeit patchy of late. The local bass specialist is the proprietor of the Eastbourne Tackle Shop, 183b Langney Road, Eastbourne (Tel: Eastbourne (0323) 20146).

7 Cuckmere Haven Unspoilt beach at its best. Very shallow, but bass are taken in surf conditions when the wind is not too fierce, and conger eels to 20 lb in the shallows during fine weather. Some flatfish, especially sole, are caught on worm baits. There are a few sea-trout, but more frequently seen than hooked. Thick-lipped mullet are taken on bread as far upstream as Eastbourne College Nature Reserve and thin-lipped mullet from there on up to Alfriston. Some golden-grey mullet can be taken in calm seas at the river mouth. In winter

there is good codding from time to time, and sometimes a good run in spring.

8 Seaford Shingle beach giving on to areas of reef and sand. Moderately shallow, but never uncovers at low tide. In summer, bass are taken on crab from rocks under Seaford Head and quite frequently from open beaches too. Live fish bait works well at high tide in calm weather for bass from shingle beaches and the sewer gantry. There are some flatfish, notably sole taken at night, and winter dabs. Mackerel, garfish and scad are frequent in fine weather on spinners and feathers. This beach is fair for winter cod and whiting. Nearest tackle shop: The Book & Bacca Shop, 8 Bridge Street, Newhaven (Tel: Newhaven (079 12) 3054).

9 Newhaven Minor port at the mouth of the River Ouse, with a small pier built on piles on the east side of the estuary, and a long, solid pier on the west side. Shallow, sandy Tide-Mills beach to the east is reached by a footpath starting at the Sealink terminal; an easily-missed track from the A259 Newhaven-Seaford road; and from the Buckle pub at Seaford. Summer: flatfish are caught here, especially sole and flounders, some bass in the surf, mackerel and garfish. Winter: codling, whiting and spring flounders. *Newhaven East Pier:* float-fished prawns and live pouting or mackerel catch bass close to the piles. Thick-lipped mullet take bread and golden-greys take harbour ragworm. Mackerel, garfish, small pollack and scad take spinners and float-fished fish strip at high tide. There are sole and flounders and some cod and whiting in winter. Thick-lipped mullet abound in the harbour, but fishing areas are limited by the marina and dock-side angling prohibitions. There

are good thick-lipped mullet as far upstream as Lewes, where thin-lipped mullet are common. The river boasts a good run of sea-trout, and some are taken on spinners from the piers and adjacent beaches. *West Arm:* the same species and methods as the East Pier. Mackerel are more common on the outside of the Arm. Good conger eels are taken from the lighthouse at the end, the only place where steps permit a safe landing. Charter boats available from the tackle dealer/central booking office: Harbour Tackle Shop, 107 Fort Road, Newhaven (Tel: Newhaven (079 12) 4441).

10 Peacehaven Reefy country, good for bass and some conger on crab and fish baits in summer. The beach adjacent to Newhaven West Arm is good for bass at high water on crab baits in rough seas. Additional access to the foreshore is by the steps at Peacehaven and Rottingdean. Winter fishing is rarely worthwhile, although the odd bass and cod are taken.

Bait Areas

A Good black lug, most easily dug on spring tides. Small patches of white ragworm. Beds of razorfish along extreme low-water mark. Queen cockles, slipper limpets and whelks sometimes washed in after storms. Good shrimping country, but beware of lesser weevers.

B Good crabbing areas. Plenty of shore crabs and some edibles at Fairlight and Peacehaven. From Beachy Head to Seaford Head, edible and velvet swimming crabs are more common and make more attractive baits. Some white ragworm under rocks, and plenty of piddocks. Rock-pool fish species and prawns in profusion.

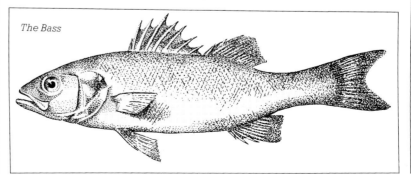

The Bass

Sussex

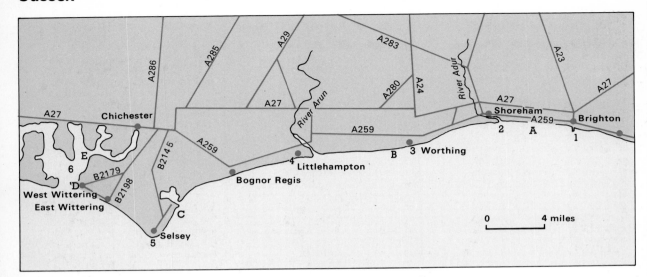

1 Brighton *Brighton Marina*, to the east of the town, has good fishing in summer from both arms. Small pollack and garfish, mackerel and scad are taken in settled weather. Plaice, flounders, dabs and pouting are taken on worm baits at the top of the tide from the east arm and on distant sand off the west arm. Fishing is not permitted inside the marina, even for mullet. Good bass are taken on crab, king ragworm and live fish from the west arm; also conger over 30 lb and some black bream. Breeding fluctuations have hit winter codding in West Sussex, though dabs, flounders and pouting are common. For information about the charter fleet, contact the tackle shop and central booking agency: The Tackle Box, Brighton Marina, Brighton (Tel: Brighton (0273) 696477)
Brighton Beaches: Portobello sewer outfall at Rottingdean sees good bass at all states of the tide on peeler crab. Likewise the Black Rock area, where squid also takes fish. Fishing is restricted on the piers – banned on the derelict West Pier, and reserved for Palace Pier club members from 1 April–31 September. Flat sandy beaches below the shingle line produce flounders, dabs, some plaice and sole, pouting and whiting. A popular area is behind the statue of King Alfred at Hove. There are some winter codling. Tackle dealers: Brighton Fishing Tackle Shop, 72 Beaconsfield Road, Brighton (Tel: Brighton (0273) 503426); Lagoon Bait & Tackle Shop, 327 Kingsway, Hove (Tel: Brighton (0273) 415879).

2 Shoreham Good summer fishing from the harbour walls, the river as far upstream as Beeding, and adjacent beaches. Fishing is no longer permitted around the power station. Bass are taken from the outside of the piers and inside the river, also sea defences at Southwick on crab, bunters, mackerel strip, squid and live fish. Some black bream, pollack and mackerel are caught from piers and beaches in warm weather. There are flounders, sole and some plaice. The area between Shoreham and Worthing has the best fishing for golden-grey mullet in the country, on cheese and harbour ragworm, plenty of thick-lipped mullet in the lower estuary and thin-lipped mullet well up-river. Winter fishing is only for small species, though good cod are taken offshore. Flounders are excellent in the River Adur on harbour

ragworm and peeler crab in January and February, but only on neap tides – the river has the third fastest tidal flow in the U.K. Tackle shop and central booking agency for the charter fleet: The Anglers Den, 35 East Street, Shoreham-by-Sea (Tel: Shoreham (079 17) 2014).

3 Worthing Flat, sandy beaches like these stretch right round to Chichester Harbour, placing the emphasis on special features that attract fish. Worthing Pier is the best place, though Goring Beach is noted locally for better size fish. Species are as for Shoreham. Good results are obtained from two hours after low to half ebb, the top of the tide is the best time. Evening fishing is most profitable for the majority of species, but golden-grey mullet bite well in warm, settled weather. There are thick-lipped mullet around the pier.

Peeler crab. When carapace is removed, new soft shell shows underneath.

Peeler crabs can be fixed thus to hook. Legs tied to hook disguise it from shy feeders.

A well-clad angler's lonely early-morning vigil to catch winter codling from the beach.

Sussex

Tackle shops : Hook, Line & Sinker, 80 Heene Road, Worthing (Tel : Worthing (079 17) 202025) ; Ken Dunman Ltd, 2 Marine Place, Worthing (Tel : Worthing (079 17) 39802).

4 Littlehampton The estuary is flanked by very flat, sandy beaches. Bass are taken from Climping beach in calm conditions at night and rough by day or night. There is a good run of sea-trout in the river, thick-lipped mullet in the lower reaches and some thin-lipped mullet well up-river. Very big bass are taken from the dilapidated wooden gantry on the west side of the estuary, on crab, squid and mackerel from low water to full tide. The current is very strong on the ebb. Some flatfish, especially winter flounders, are to be found in the river, and a few black bream from the gantry. Occasional large sting ray are taken from nearby beaches on lugworm, ragworm or mackerel strip. There is a public slipway at Fisherman's Quay – fee payable. Information on charter boats is available from : Tropicana, 6 Pier Road, Littlehampton (Tel : Littlehampton (090 64) 5190).

5 Selsey Area Some sting rays are caught from the Wittering beaches. Black bream are taken from June to September from Selsey Bill and Pagham Harbour area on a flooding tide. Bass dominate here, taken from shallow beaches in surf conditions on ragworm, lugworm, crab, squid and mackerel strip. Slipper limpet is a killer bait. At the mouth of Pagham Harbour crab, limpet and artificial lures should be used from one hour after high water until middle flood ; in Selsey tide race spinners (also mackerel etc) and from the east beach at Selsey crab and slipper limpets at high water. Winter fishing is for flounders and school bass when a storm has washed ashore slipper limpets and mussels, which die on beach and are washed back into sea during the following spring tides. There is some good night fishing for sole at Wittering.

6 Chichester Harbour Silver eels are a nuisance here. Plenty of thick-lipped grey mullet are caught on bread and harbour ragworm. Some black bream are taken at the mouth of Bosham Channel, down-tide of the shingle bars. Occasional smooth hounds are found in the channels. There are good plaice and flounders in the harbour. Baited spoon methods are best from a drifting dinghy, but shore fishing also scores. Some bass, mainly small, are caught from Wittering East Head, Cobnor Point and Dell Quay. Best baits are lugworm, king ragworm and slipper limpet. Mackerel are sometimes taken in the harbour, but a dinghy finds most fish. There are public slipways at Cobnor Point and Dell Quay. Tackle dealers : Russell Hillsdon, 46 South Street, Chichester (Tel : Chichester (0243) 783811) ; Daughtry's Tackle, The Hornet, Chichester (Tel : Chichester (0243) 783858).

One of England's most dramatic pieces of coastal scenery, the Seven Sisters cliffs.

Bait Areas

A   Black lugworm from West Pier beaches, Hove beaches. Harbour ragworm, peeler crab from banks of River Adur. Bunters from estuary drains.
B   Plenty of blow lugworm all through to Chichester Harbour and some cockles. Harbour ragworm, soft crab from River Arun. Bunters from estuary drains.
C   Some blow lugworm, plenty of slipper limpets, especially outside Pagham Harbour.
D   Plenty of slipper limpets, especially after a storm, and blow lugworm.
E   Peeler crabs under rubble in harbour. Blow lugworm and king ragworm from Cobnor Point, Dell Quay, and Itchenor. Bunters in drains. Sand-eels at Hayling Island.

FOR THE FAMILY
An area of outstanding natural beauty, with walking and riding on the South Downs, places of historic and prehistoric interest to visit, coastal towns for entertainment and shopping museums and country houses for a day out.
Brighton   see the Royal Pavilion – the Prince Regent's oriental-style extravaganza superbly restored. And there's always the pier, dolphinarium, Volk's Electric Railway, the new Marina, the 'Lanes', and all sorts of entertainments.
Chanctonbury Ring   nr Washington. Hilltop prehistoric landmark and magnificent viewpoint on the South Downs Way.
Arundel   impressive castle with fine interior and spacious park. Also visit Arundel Wildfowl Trust Reserve, and Potter's Museum of Curiosity for its amazing animal tableaux.
Bluebell Railway   an ideal family day out. Ride from Horsted Keynes through delightful country to the magnificent house and gardens of Sheffield Park.
Weald and Downland Open Air Museum   Singleton. Historic houses, forge, shops, etc re-erected in 40-acre woodland site. Nature trail and picnic sites.
National Butterfly Museum   St Mary's, Bramber. One of the world's finest collections, displayed in a 12thC house.

Fast boats like this one are becoming widely used by offshore wreck fishermen.

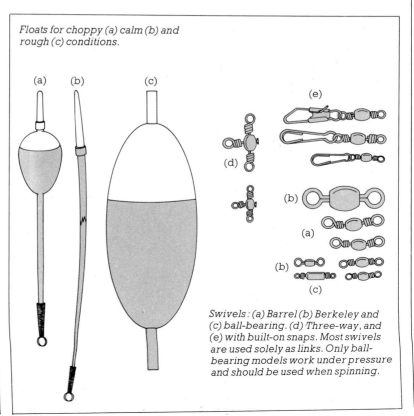
Floats for choppy (a) calm (b) and rough (c) conditions.

Swivels: (a) Barrel (b) Berkeley and (c) ball-bearing. (d) Three-way, and (e) with built-on snaps. Most swivels are used solely as links. Only ball-bearing models work under pressure and should be used when spinning.

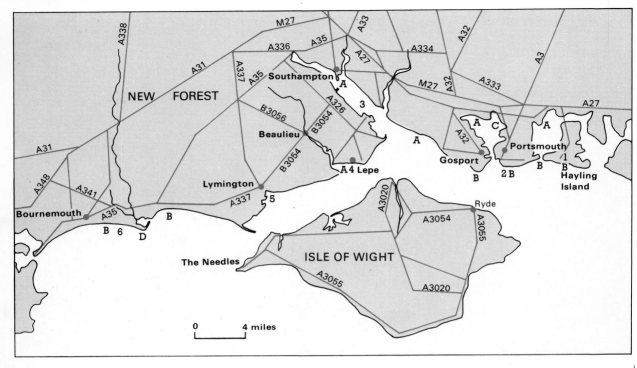

Much of this heavily indented coastline is comprised of sand along the outer reaches, with places like Bournemouth blessed with large, shallow sand-flats backed by low sand hills. More sheltered areas are somewhat muddy with patches of rubble-like rock. Despite fairly heavy pollution from extensive industrial sites and dockland, the bays and creeks of the Solent are rich in marine life and are nurseries for small fish. Sometimes baby black bream can reach plague proportions.

These attract the predators. Once Lepe beach was a favoured shore tope mark because big females would come in close when shedding their young. Catches of tope from the shore have dwindled in recent years, though there are still some good fish to be taken from boats.

Much of the mullet fishing has barely been tapped. The estuary creeks and little bays hold huge shoals of mullet in the summer, mainly of the thick-lipped variety, although some golden-grey mullet have been taken during fine spells off the sandy beaches fronting the open sea. Thin-lipped mullet are often taken on spinners at Christchurch.

From the shore, the most prevalent summer species are bass, silver eels,

Shoaling mackerel in a feeding frenzy.

flounders, dabs, plaice and dogfish. Some select places offer reasonable chances of getting the fast moving smooth hound or a very large sting ray.

Boat fishing offers the opportunity to catch a variety of species – bass, mullet, thornback and some small-eyed rays, tope, smooth hound, porbeagle shark, and the smaller species that are available from the beach. During the winter months, small bass, flounders, whiting, pouting and some cod make up the bulk of the catches, with some very good cod being taken offshore each year around the Needles.

Tides can be fierce around the Solent and Hayling Island. There is a double high tide along this coast caused by the tidal wave flooding first up the western Solent and later up the eastern Solent. High water at Portsmouth is some $2\frac{1}{2}$ hours before London Bridge time, at Lymington it is $3\frac{1}{4}$ hours before, and at Bournemouth 5 hours before – an indication of the confused tidal patterns in these parts.

Slipways, some of them public, are legion in this area with its naval and yachting traditions and sheltered bays. They are at Emsworth (3), Hayling Island (3), Portsmouth (2), Paulsgrove, Porchester, Fareham, Gosport (5), Lee-on-Solent (2), Warsash, Sarisbury Green, Swanwick, Hamble (2), Netley (2), Southampton (6), Eling, Ashlett Creek, Buckler's Hard, Lymington (2), Keyhaven, Mudeford, and Christchurch.

Weather information can be gleaned from the Meteorological Office at Southampton (Tel: Southampton (0703) 28844). Staff here can provide information for most of the south coast.

The largest angling club is Southsea SAC, 42 Granada Road, Southsea (Tel: Portsmouth (0705) 25508).

1 Hayling Island Flounders and bass are caught from Hayling bay, the flounders best from October to April. Bass prefer an onshore blow. Limpet/ragworm cocktails are most effective. Long casting is necessary during calm conditions, while rough water brings the fish in close. Between the Langstone Fairway and the Ferry Boat Inn is good fishing, especially for bass. The tides run very hard here – too hard for a small outboard to cope with (those with small boats beware), and the water drops to a depth of 30 feet only 10 feet from the beach.

The southernmost tip of the point is an excellent bass surf beach during the summer months.

2 Portsmouth Area On the Portsmouth side of the Langstone Fairway flatfish are caught by the outfall pipes behind the ECA buildings. The Winner Bank, some 200 yards west of the Frazer Gunnery Range is good for flounders, plaice and eels during the flood tide. Bass, flatfish and eels frequent a hole about 100 yards east of St George's Road, Southsea, though a long cast is necessary to reach them. Bass, flounders, plaice and eels are taken from the concrete blocks some 100 yards east of South Parade Pier, Southsea. Similar species are taken from the pier itself. The beach fronting Southsea Castle can produce good catches, especially bass, but it is very rocky, as is the sea bed around the mouth of Portsmouth Harbour which also has plenty of rubbish on the sea bed to trap tackle. Even so, the fishing there can be good for those who persevere. Calm conditions during the day are best for the flounders in Fareham Creek and around Porchester Castle. High tide is the worst time because by then most of the fish have moved out of the channels on to the mud flats. A hard frost is said to produce good fishing, the most successful baits being white ragworm and harbour ragworm. Charter bookings (for boats from Langstone Harbour), tackle and information can be had from Ed Jones at Ed's Tackle Shop, 6 Selbourne Terrace, Fratton Bridge, Portsmouth (Tel: Portsmouth (0705) 25210).

3 Southampton Water Southampton Water consists of a deep-water channel and a profusion of mud flats. Flounders, plaice, silver eels, mullet, bass, whiting and pouting, dogfish and the occasional skate are taken from this unlovely area. Southampton pier is closed and fishing from the docks is restricted to use by certain clubs on pre-arranged Saturdays and Sundays, although pensioners can fish from the docks provided they have a special pass issued by the dock authorities. No boats are allowed to anchor in the channels (which would, in any case, be suicidal since they are so busy), but along the edges. More details from Sea Angler's Supplies, 427 Millbrook Street, Southampton (Tel: Southampton (0703) 772958).

4 Lepe The mouth of the River Beaulieu is on Lord Montagu's estate,

so local anglers keep well away from the summer house behind the beach. There is good bass fishing to be had at the mouth of the river. At Lepe itself, some very large sole are caught each year fishing close in. To the west of the river, at Park Shore beach, the usual small fish are caught, but long casting in the summer months produces the occasional good bass, thornback rays and sometimes a good tope. Further west, past Sowley Boom, a large mudbank called Sowley Sedge is accessible around the low water period. It produces bass, large sting rays and sometimes a lot of smooth hounds. The smooth hounds take hard-backed crab because locals have difficulty finding peeler crabs. The sting rays take ragworm and the bass will eat peeler crabs imported from elsewhere, ragworm, slipper limpet and squid.

5 Lymington This is one of the ports used by boats fishing the Needles for large winter cod and off St Catherine's Point for porbeagle shark. Inshore, there are mullet, bass and the rest of the small species associated with this area. Nearby Hurst Castle offers very deep water close in, but big tides and drifting weed often limit fishing to short periods around slack water. In summer, bream, bass, rays, tope and dogfish are caught from here, along with plaice, flounders, dabs and the rest of the small fish. In winter some very large cod are taken from this deep water. Standard baits are worms, mollusc, fish and crab. Nearby, Barton beach and Milford beach offer similar fishing, but around the high water mark. Grapnel leads may be required in spring tide periods. Offshore, the landward side of the Isle of Wight offers excellent mixed fishing – bass, cod, mackerel, monkfish, tope, rays, conger eels and the occasional turbot, depending on whether open ground or wrecks are fished. Porbeagle sharks are scarcer than of late. More details and information can be obtained from local tackle dealers: Just Tackle, 1a Middle Road, Sway, Lymington (Tel: Lymington (0590) 682285).

6 Bournemouth area Hengistbury Head is a famous local mark for bass, conger, small pollack, mackerel and the usual small species. Christchurch harbour offers excellent sport with flatfish and also with good bass and mullet. The latter are partial to baited bar-spoons, with a little bit of ragworm fixed to the hook. Sandy

Bournemouth has a pier and there is also Boscombe Pier. Some good bass are taken on live baits among the piles, along with mullet. Plaice fishing can be very good from Boscombe pier during the summer months. Winter fishing along this shallow shore is viable for dabs, flounders, pouting and whiting. Some codling are taken during good seasons, but the general run is well offshore. More details can be obtained from Dave Swallow at Custom Tackle, 904 Wimborne Road, Moordown, Bournemouth (Tel: Bournemouth (0202) 514345); Davis Fishing Tackle, 75 Bargates, Christchurch (Tel: Bournemouth (0202) 485169) and Hales Tackle, 258 Barrack Road, Christchurch (Tel: Bournemouth (0202) 454518).

Bait Areas
A Plenty of good ragworm, dug with a flat-tined potato fork. Best time to start is two hours after the second high tide. There are several local places around Hayling Island and Portsea Island and up inside Chichester Harbour, Langstone Harbour and Southampton Water. Digging is restricted in front of Ministry of Defence establishments. Some smaller ragworm can be dug in Christchurch Harbour and on the banks of rivers.
B Although plenty of lugworm can be found in among the ragworm, the best lugworm digging, carried out by trenching with spade or fork, is in front of Hayling Island and Portsea Island and along to Bournemouth in the flat, shallow sands. Slipper limpet is washed up along these beaches in

fair numbers after an onshore blow.
C Peeler crab can be gathered near the pontoon to Hayling Ferry from Portsmouth, on the left of Ferry Road and at one or two other select areas inside the harbours.
D Sand-eels can be netted just off the Hayling Ferry pontoon in summer. Also from the sand-spit to the east of Christchurch Harbour. They can sometimes be obtained by digging in the sand or scraping with a sand-eel hook.

A mid-summer tope caught from an off-shore sandbank. Lepe beach was well known as a good tope area as the females used to swim close in-shore when shedding their young.

Isle of Wight
Extensive flat reef around Bembridge Pier, with sand inside the harbour, becomes pure sand at Whitecliff Bay. The foreshore here is backed by low hills which become taller and more precipitous at Culver Cliff, with reef along the bottom. To the west, Sandown Bay is very sandy, with Sandown Pier and Shanklin Pier protruding out over the flats. The sand turns to rock under the steep foreland on which Luccombe Village perches, with sand and a little reef running underneath, the land dropping away to Dunnose.

There are some cliffs and steep slopes separating the town of Ventnor from the sandy foreshore – and Ventnor Pier – such shoreline is also to be found at Woody Bay, Binnel Bay and Reeth Bay to St Catherine's Point.

Blackgang Chine to the west is very steep, with cliffs running westwards to Whale Chine where there is an access point, and on again to Atherfield Point. A small stream at Shepherd's Chine allows access to the sandy shore. Another stream has cut a valley at Grange Chine, and yet another at Chilton Chine. To the west there is a bit of cliff towards Compton Bay, behind which lie the downs.

There is reefy shore to the east of Freshwater Bay, with much of it, to Compton Chine, backed by cliffs. To the west of this horse-shoe bay lie the chalk cliffs that lead out to The Needles.

At Alum Bay there is a chairlift to the beach and the coast north from here is very steep, limiting access. Things get easier at Totland, where there is a pier. But the coastline becomes steep again around Colwell Bay and north east of Sconce Point, with the land falling away eastwards to Yarmouth.

There are two piers here, one on each side of the tidal creek called the River Yar. To the east, access to the shoreline poses few problems; the beach is mainly of sand. Bouldnor Cliff is steep and limits access to the foreshore, with the land falling away again towards the drowned creeks of Newtown River. There is a lot of mud – and mullet – inside here. Much of this area dries out at low tide. The National Trust owns all this shoreline as well as Bouldnor Cliff.

To the east of Newtown River the shoreline is very sandy, with the coast becoming steep around Pilgrims Path, then falling away again to the marshy mouth of the river that flows into Thorness Bay, rising again to fairly

---

FOR THE FAMILY
From east to west Hampshire's coast changes from the busy shipping scene around Portsmouth and Southampton to the popular coast bordering the New Forest. There are many interesting places to visit in its historic towns and opportunities for walking, riding, boating, birdwatching and ship watching.

Beaulieu 13thC Abbey and National Motor Museum, the world's finest collection of cars dating from 1895 onwards. Visit the maritime museum at Bucklers Hard.
Lymington popular sailing town with good swimming pool. Take a day trip by ferry to Yarmouth, Isle of Wight.

Marwell Zoo Park just south of Winchester. Unique collection with many unusual species in a lovely 250-acre park.
New Forest 145 sq miles of scenic beauty with famous wild ponies and abundant wildlife. Good centres are Lyndhurst and Brockenhurst.
Queen Elizabeth Country Park nr Petersfield. 1400 acres of woodlands. Picnic areas, nature trails, riding, grass skiing, hang gliding. Demonstration of farming going back to prehistoric times.
HMS Victory Portsmouth. Nelson's flagship in all its original glory. Museum has ships' figureheads and a panorama of his last battle.

steep slopes at Northwood.

Gurnard Ledge is one of a few reefy outcrops around here, but Gurnard Bay is sandy round to Egypt Point and Cowes at the mouth of the River Medina – another tidal creek, albeit a substantial one. There are extensive sands between the breakwater and Old Castle Point on the east side, with no access problems. There is more sand at King's Quay Inlet, with mud inside the inlet. The sands continue to the mouth of Wootton Creek, becoming more and more extensive to Ryde Pier. There are large flats here called Ryde East Sands which cut in towards Nettlestone Point. The land is fairly low-lying here but becomes a little steeper between Horestone Point and Node's Point, where there is an outcrop of reef. Outside Bembridge harbour a channel threads its way through the sands, with more sand inside The Duver (a causeway), much of which is heavily silted.

The Isle of Wight is reached by ferry from Southampton to Cowes, Portsmouth to Ryde and Wootton, and Lymington to Yarmouth.

Charter boats operate out from Yarmouth and Bembridge. Trailed boats may be launched from a number of sites around this popular sailing area. Ramps exist at Yarmouth, Cowes (several), Newport, East Cowes, Ryde, Seaview, Bembridge, Sandown, and at several sites on the Hampshire side of The Solent for boats wishing to make their own way across. There are also several locations where small craft can be dragged from their trailers to the sea's edge.

The island is subject to the Solent double high tide, this effect being less on the English Channel side. For tide times enquire locally at tackle shops, boat chandlers and tourist information bureaux. Local papers also publish times. High tide at Ventnor, for example is 3 hours earlier than at London Bridge.

Boats catch porbeagle shark, thresher shark, skate, tope, conger, turbot, rays, bream, monkfish, smooth hounds (mainly inside the Solent), sting rays and a variety of lesser species, including bass. Winter cod fishing off The Needles, baiting a double-hook rig with a large whole squid, produces very large cod. The shark fishing has deteriorated considerably of late, probably due to the severe over-kill for publicity purposes when the grounds were first discovered.

Nowadays it is advised that quick-release traces be used and the fish released unharmed.

Shore fishing is for small-eyed rays, thornback rays, dogfish, bass, pouting, whiting, sting rays, smooth hounds, plaice, flounders, dabs, black bream and a variety of small species. Cod are rarely caught from these beaches in winter. Long casting pays off over the flat sandy beaches. Short casting is all that the bass require when rock fishing. Visiting boat anglers may apply for temporary membership of the Ventnor Boat Fishing Club. This entitles them to use the club's outboard boats.

The Isle of Wight beaches are not easy to fish. For this reason no specific locations are shown on the map. The fish move about a great deal with the tides and the winds. As the island is small, seek advice from any of the tackle shops close to your point of arrival.

Details from : Isle of Wight Sea-Tac, 6–8 Wilkes Road, Sandown (Tel : Isle of Wight (0983) 403654) ; W. Bates & Son, 5 Spring Hill, Ventnor (Tel : Isle of Wight (0983) 852175) ; Don Sports, 21 Cross Street, Ryde (Tel : Isle of Wight (0983) 2912) ; A. P. Scott & Sons Ltd, 10 Lugley Street, Newport (Tel : Isle of Wight (0983) 2115) ; The Sports Shop, 74 Regent Street, Shanklin (Tel : Isle of Wight (0983) 862454) and Mr M. T. Sawyer, 27 Salters Road, Ryde (Tel : Isle of Wight (0983) 67611).

FOR THE FAMILY

Plenty for the family to see and do on this holiday island – sport and entertainments, walking on the cliff tops or in pleasant countryside, enjoying quiet beaches or lively and elegant resorts, visiting castles, houses, zoos, nature trails, museums and crafts centres.

Alum Bay cliffs of variegated sands (21 colours) and modern chairlift to the beach with a splendid view of the Needles. Pleasure Park.

Carisbrooke Castle Newport. Impressive Norman fortress with moat, in the centre of the island. Houses the Isle of Wight Museum and relics of Charles I.

Godshill lovely model village is a treat for small children. It also has a Toy Museum, and Natural History Collection, forge and old smithy.

Cowes besides watching the yachts you can visit Osborne House, Queen Victoria's home and a museum. Easter–Oct.

Robin Hill Country Park Arreton. A great variety of animals, and children's activities – pony rides, mini-dodgems, etc, in 80 acres of downlands. Barbecues, disco, etc, in summer.

Osborn-Smith's Wax Museum Brading. Has fascinating exhibits of island history in a 16thC house. Near Ventnor is a **Museum of Smuggling History.**

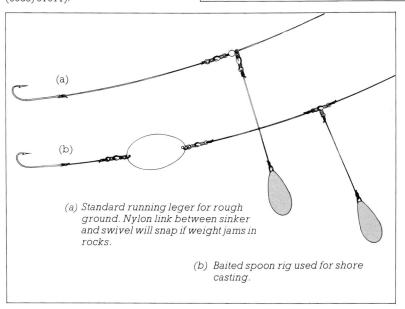

(a) Standard running leger for rough ground. Nylon link between sinker and swivel will snap if weight jams in rocks.

(b) Baited spoon rig used for shore casting.

Dorset

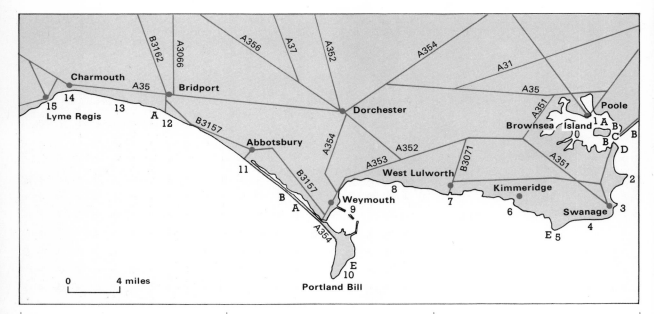

Dorset has some of England's most interesting shoreline, a variety of cliff and sand, flat yet not unfishably harsh. Poole Harbour is a huge tidal lagoon with the port on the north side and about 100 miles of shoreline indented by creeks. Outside the harbour, the beaches are flat, of sand, extending southwards to the featureless Studland Bay, beyond is the headland that tumbles to the Old Harry Rocks. A shallow reef forms the foreshore at Ballard Down, together with some sand, and the coastline becomes flat and shallow around Swanage Bay, with its virtually fishless pier, then reefs again at Peveril Ledge, with more rocks under the cliffs of Durlston Head and Anvil Point, then develops a shoreline of sand, shingle and boulders, with rock ledges between, towards steep-browed St Albans Head. North east of this headland lies picturesque, rocky Chapman's Pool and the cliff-backed country continues westwards to the tourist spot of Lulworth Cove and on past Durdle Door, the famous cliff arch, towards Bats Head and Ringstead Bay. The cliffs, with their accompanying reef foreshore, extend westwards to Redcliff Point, where the cliff country of the Isle of Purbeck effectively ends. Sandy Weymouth Bay runs south westward, past the built-up dockland at Portland Harbour, before the emergence of Portland Bill with its useful rock platforms and surging tide-race.

Once round this headland, the shoreline changes abruptly in character. The featureless stretch of Chesil Beach lies in an 18-mile long straight line towards the mouth of the river Brit at Bridport, backed at first by the Fleet, then flat salt marsh, and finally crumbling cliffs. Much of the coastal strip around to Lyme Regis is cliff-backed, stony and boulder-strewn shallow reef – bass country, where specimen fish are taken each season. This is also very picturesque country, with Charmouth and Seatown nestling among the downs, both on their tiny estuaries. Much of this area is protected by the National Trust.

The double high tide experienced around the Solent also affects this stretch of shore as far west as Durlston Head. The times for high water at Poole Harbour mouth are 5 hours and $1\frac{1}{2}$ hours before London Bridge. At Lulworth, high water occurs 5 hours after London Bridge, likewise Weymouth, Portland and East Chesil. At Bridport, high water occurs $4\frac{1}{2}$ hours after London Bridge and $4\frac{3}{4}$ hours after at Lyme Regis.

There are very strong tides off most of the headlands, especially Portland and at the mouth of Poole Harbour, with offshore tidal streams decreasing in strength towards Lyme Regis. The latter part of the ebb is very fierce at the mouth of Poole Harbour, as a vast area is draining through a small channel, and, of course, tide times vary inside to those outside.

Launching slipways, some public, are to be found at Sandbanks (Poole), Parkstone, Poole (3), Lilliput, Hamworthy (3), Wareham, Swanage (2), Weymouth (4), Bridport and Lyme Regis.

The main inshore species in summer are bass, silver eels, conger eels (from rocks), flounders, plaice, sole, dogfish, black bream, mackerel, garfish, wrasse, pollack, bull huss, some rays, dabs, spur dogfish and a few tope – however the major species found off Chesil beach are but lightly researched. Porbeagle sharks have been sighted close in there. Winter fishing is mainly for small species – small bass, silver eels, flounders and dabs. Deep water off Chesil attracts some very large cod, a few codling, and spur dogfish in winter. Obviously, similar species are to be found offshore together with rays, monkfish, turbot, and greater numbers of tope.

Charter boats operate out from Poole, Weymouth, Bridport, and can be contacted through advertisements in the press or tackle dealers.

1 Poole Harbour Custard paste is said to be the most effective bait for thick-lipped mullet off the various quays that project out into Poole Harbour. Locals either float-fish or leger with a swing-tip. Much of the Harbour's 10,000 acres of water is best reached by dinghy – and even then care should be taken lest a fast-ebbing tide leaves you stranded on a mud flat. Indeed, the mud here often has the consistency of sinking sand, so be wary. Bass, flounders, plaice and mullet are the most common species inside the harbour. Bass are caught on bottom tackle, float-fished baits and by spinning in the fast water between Sandbanks and South Haven Point.

With so much flat mud, points preferred for fishing are generally those where the ground allows easiest access ; such as at Poole Quay, Hamworthy, Salterns Pier, Sandbanks, South Haven Point, Shell Bay and so on. Flounders are caught all year round, except when offshore and spawning in February and March. Local ragworm is a popular bait. Night fishing offers the best opportunities for bass owing to the busy nature of these waterways. Early morning and late are the best times for mullet. Fish for them with a floating crust, after dark where a jetty is lit up at night.

The islands in the Harbour are strictly private, together with their beaches. Fishing is not permitted from private jetties and boatyards. No digging is allowed within 50 feet of any wall or jetty, and all holes must be refilled.

Boats can be chartered via the Derek Case Angling Agency, 5 High Street, Poole (Tel : Poole (020 13) 6597) ; also Les James Tackle, 19 High Street, Poole (Tel : Poole (020 13) 4409). Information is available from these or from P. G. Harvey, Poole Dolphins SAC, 6 Dale Road, Poole, Dorset (Tel : Poole (0202) 730931).

2 Old Harry Rocks After a long, sweaty scramble from Studland, departing just after half ebb, it is possible to take a few bass, good conger eels, small wrasse and small pollack from these rocks before the in-coming tides threaten drowning.

3 Swanage Fish from Swanage pier only if sufficiently experienced to persuade a bass or two to accept a live pouting fished close in to the structure, or for small pollack, mackerel etc at high tide during warm summery weather. Wrasse, too can be taken, some weighing just ounces. Black bream sometimes exceed 1 lb. Not very exciting. However, with less tourists, Ballard Ledge offers some good bass fishing for those who are familiar with graunch bassing, and some rays have been taken from sandy areas along here. More details from Swanage Angling Centre, 6 High Street, Swanage (Tel : Swanage (092 92) 4489).

4 Durlston Head to St Albans Head Lonely ground this, and not for the novice. It consists mainly of rock ledges from which one can fish on the bottom with standard baits for conger and big bass. Tope have been hooked from Peveril Ledge, near Swanage. Locals float-fish for smallish pollack wrasse and also for bass using crab, prawn, large red ragworms etc. Mackerel shoals move close in towards high water, especially early and late in the day. Some very good mullet have been seen browsing along here but so far nobody seems to have found the secret of hooking them.

5 Chapman's Pool Set among high cliffs, Chapman's Pool offers opportunities for crab, mackerel and squid fishing for bass and conger. Float-fished prawns, ragworm, live or dead crab and slim strips of mackerel will catch pollack from the rock ledges, while a spinner or a single feather fished paternoster style will also work. Crab and prawn also take the rather small wrasse here, and mackerel sometimes come in close. Freshwater Bay, a good walk to the west, has been a well-known fishing ground for bass, conger and rays.

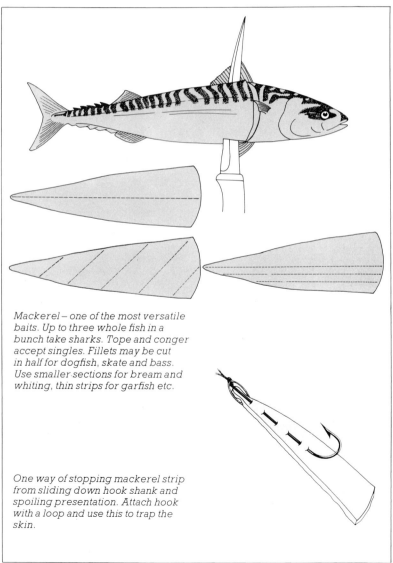

Mackerel – one of the most versatile baits. Up to three whole fish in a bunch take sharks. Tope and conger accept singles. Fillets may be cut in half for dogfish, skate and bass. Use smaller sections for bream and whiting, thin strips for garfish etc.

One way of stopping mackerel strip from sliding down hook shank and spoiling presentation. Attach hook with a loop and use this to trap the skin.

6 Kimmeridge One of the few villages in England to have an artificial trout fly, in this case a sedge species, named after it. The shore fishing around here is equally good as the local trout fishing. Bass visit these rocky shores, together with pollack, wrasse and conger eels. Between marks 5 and 6 (see map) extensive rock ledges project out to sea, offering opportunities for the adventurer. Some good rays have been taken from the less rugged parts of this shoreline on standard thornback baits, although frozen sand-eel is recommended as among the very best baits. The sunrise side of Broad Bench Point, to the west, offers deep-water spinning for pollack and sometimes mackerel and bass. Also wrasse on crab, prawn, lugworm etc, float-fished or paternostered. Note that the rock here is firm but often slippery, so wear cleated boots.

7 Lulworth Cove Not the place to come on a bright, sunny summer's day. Screeching kids and sun-worshippers are too heavy a price to pay to view this lovely scenery. But early morning and late evening sessions produce bass on crab and fish baits, especially towards the mouth of the cove. If you catch a bass with two heads, take it immediately to the Winfrith Atomic Research Establishment as it may have paid a visit to their outfall at Arish Mell Gap, itself inside a Ministry of Defence Danger Zone (gunnery range), where fishing is limited to periods when firing is not in progress. Along this stretch of coastline some rays, bull huss, bass, pollack, conger and wrasse are taken in suitable water conditions. However, much weed is piled up by storms during spring tide periods; this is visited by seaweed flies, and during the next spring tides mullet (and sometimes bass) forage on the maggots being washed out of the banks of rotting weed.

West of the Cove lies St Oswald's Bay, best fished in surf conditions, at night, for bass, using ragworm or crab. Unfortunately, dogfish sometimes take these baits. Conger eels frequent the reefs at each end of this sandy beach.

Further west, at Durdle Door (literally Devil's Door), a steep shingle beach has produced good catches of dogfish, with conger, pouting, bass and the occasional ray and tope mixed in among them. Tope fishing is not quite what it used to be, but this shoreline is favoured by them nevertheless.

8 Ringstead Bay Fishing for mullet from the rocks here has produced some excellent specimens of thick-lipped mullet. Otherwise, some bass, conger, pouting, whiting and similar small fish will be taken. Further west, at Osmington Mills, the fishing is not as good as the scenery. The bottom is rugged, a mass of boulders in most places, although selected rock ledges do produce species similar to those listed above.

9 Weymouth and Portland Harbour Weymouth's sandy bay offers fishing mainly for small species, though bass are to be caught when there is a fair surf running, especially at night. Daytime in summer sees too many tourists disporting themselves along this sandy shore. The harbour is also very busy in summer, which makes mullet fishing more productive early, late, and from quiet areas. The former record thick-lipped mullet came from here. There are restrictions to the fishing from the piers, but there are fishable jetties and walls from which flatfish can be taken, also pollack, mackerel and scad on float-fished ribbons of mackerel skin, spinners and flies.

Bowleze Cove has reefy ground which attracts night-hunting bass which will take peeler crab and, especially late in the year, mackerel and squid strips. Newtons Cove offers similar ground, with the occasional conger also taken. Pollack are sometimes caught, but they are not as good as the ones taken near the Portland Race. Details from Tuck & Discount Tackle, 52 Fortunes Well, Portland, Dorset (Tel: Portland (0305) (820527).

10 Portland Bill Very big bass appear here early in May. From then until late October, specimen bass are taken right the way through, with fewer coming ashore during the latter part of July through to early September when they move out to chase sand-eels, sprats and mackerel in the fast, confused tide race off the end of the Bill.

Much of the ground consists of rock ledges. Bass are taken from these on crab, fish strip, squid, dead fresh-caught wrasse and similar bait. Conger eels abound, when the water is calm, and pollack, mackerel and garfish are taken on spinners, feathers and, in perfect conditions, on float-fished fish strip. Good sport is enjoyed by locals, so the visitor is advised to make friends with somebody who will enable him to find success on this rugged, slightly dangerous, shoreline. There are a number of tackle dealers in Weymouth, several of whom can direct the visitor to a charter skipper.

11 Chesil Beach Some of the best fishing from this extremely steep beach is to be had after crossing the Fleet by boat, but that requires the visitor to bring his own boat. A deep channel runs inshore in front of the Fleet, and is to be found after a 120 yard cast, with bait. Very big cod are taken here each winter, with Christmas time providing the best sport. Live baits fished at long range score best for these fish. The trick is to cast out a double hook rig, the lower hook being about size 2, baited with worm, and hope that a pouting or whiting will swallow this hook and remain tethered close to the larger number 5/0 hook. A similar trick will take conger in the summer months, together with bull huss, spur dogfish, tope, outsize bass and similar predators. Often large mackerel shoals come close in and work along the beach. It is unwise to go down the slope to sea level in a big sea. Many anglers have been washed in while trying to beach fish. Stay up top and try to heave the fish to within gaffing distance. Turbot, rays and monkfish have also been taken here.

At the Portland Harbour end of the Fleet, bass, mullet and flounders are to be taken, this water being tidal – a drowned river estuary.

Access is from Portland, Abbotsbury, Bexington and Burton Bradstock. This beach is likely to reward perseverance from a big fish hunter as there is much yet to be learned. Local tactics, as is often the case, are geared for the safe bets – flounders, plaice, dabs, whiting, codling, and bass. Bigger predators are present, but few fishermen have bothered to systematize a suitable approach.

12 Bridport Although the town is set inland from the sea, its harbour is on the River Brit, which almost dries out at low water. Stone piers flank the entrance to the harbour, but the fishing from them is mainly for small fish. Mullet abound inside the harbour, all thick-lipped, though they are rarely fished for. The occasional bass, conger etc is taken from the piers, but otherwise small wrasse, whiting, pouting, pollack and so on make up the bulk of somewhat scanty catches.

13 Seatown East of this pleasant little spot lies Eype Mouth, where a small stream meets the sea. Early and late in the summer, night fishing produces bass which come in to feed on the many small fish that inhabit this rocky ground. At Seatown itself, the shingle moves about a lot, covering and uncovering rocks, making unfishable marks fishable and vice versa, according to winter storms. Some good bass are taken from here, under conditions similar to Eype Mouth. The area repays a thorough survey at low tide for best fishing results. Mackerel shoals sometimes come in close on thundery evenings at high tide.

14 Charmouth West Beach, St Gabriel's Beach and Charmouth Gap are all rocky, with occasional beds of sand among the boulders. Bass, with the occasional conger, come in here at night and are taken on standard baits and tackle.

15 Lyme Regis The sandy beach here, encircled by picturesque cliffs, makes a sheltered spot to fish when a west wind stirs up the sea for many miles in each direction, between Exmouth and Portland. The harbour, known locally as The Cobb, is partly tidal. Dabs, small pollack, pouting, wrasse and the occasional school bass make up most of the catches nowadays from this flat shore. The best fishing is to be had from The Spittles to the east or towards Seven Rock Point to the west where boulders, sand patches and shallow rock ledges are more attractive to bass and dogfish, which will take standard baits fished close to the bottom. Details from P. Johnson, Lyme Bay Marine, 26 Broad Street, Lyme Regis. (Tel: Lyme Regis (029 74) 2948). Contact him also about local danger points to be noted concerning boat launching.

Bait Areas

A In Poole Harbour, good ragworms can be dug with a flat-tined potato fork at Baiter's Point, Newton Point, Lilliput, Hamworthy and Goathorn. Around Weymouth, small red ragworms can be dug in the banks of the Fleet and around the Backwater, and inside Bridport harbour.

B Lugworms are quite plentiful inside Poole Harbour, especially on the harbour side opposite the Tudor Bar and Sandbanks Hotel, and on the sandy shores outside towards Bournemouth. There are some to be found close inside the Fleet and, much further west, west of Black Ven at Lyme Regis.

C Peeler crab can be picked along Whitecliffe shore and rocks at Baiter Point inside Poole Harbour. Crabs can also be picked from some suitable locations among the boulder-strewn beaches further to the west, though locals keep such information a closely-guarded secret.

D Slipper limpets can be gathered at low water on spring tides from Evening Hill, at Poole Harbour, and outside on the beaches after a good blow from the south-west through to the east.

E Prawns can be caught in drop-nets and in scoops along much of the rocky ledge-land of the Dorset coast. Clouded water and dull conditions are best, clear seas and blue skies are useless. Kipper is an excellent bait for the drop-net. The boat angler would do well to set a few prawn pots – and, indeed, some lobster pots too!

This conger took the baits of two anglers, spun fiercely at boat-side, and twisted both steel traces together!

FOR THE FAMILY

The Dorset coastline is of outstanding beauty and variety, with white cliffs, sandy beaches, and an unspoilt countryside inland. No shortage of holiday activities and entertainment at Bournemouth, Weymouth and the other resorts, coastal towns and villages.

Abbotsbury home of great herds of swans and many other wild birds for 500 years. Visit the huge tithe barn and sub-tropical gardens. May–Sept.

Maiden Castle south of Dorchester. The largest prehistoric fortress in Europe. 2 mile panoramic walk.

Brownsea Island boat from Poole. Home of the first Boy Scout camp and now has a Nature Reserve, lakes, etc.

Higher Bockhampton nr Dorchester. Thatched cottage where Thomas Hardy was born and wrote some of his novels. House by appt. Garden March–Oct.

Dorset Coastal Path 72 mile scenic footpath of great wildlife and fossil interest. Visitors should keep to cliff paths and not take risks.

Compton Acres Gardens Canford Cliffs, Poole. Famous gardens in several styles, including Japanese and Italian. April–Oct.

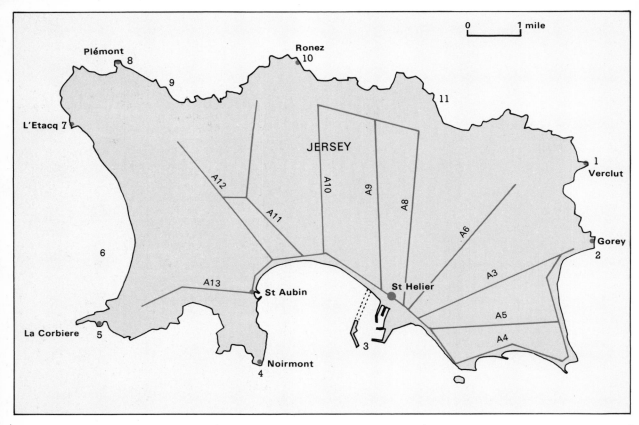

Very prolific sea fishing is to be found in the clear, unpolluted waters around this group of islands just off the coast of Normandy. The water is rich in marine life and a wide variety of species is attracted to this part of the English Channel (or should it be Atlantic Ocean? – the islands are sited at the junction between the two). Tides can be fierce, with an extensive range between high and low water. Some shallow beaches strip a long way at low tide. Perhaps this is one of the factors that draws in the fish.

From the shore, the most common species are angler fish, bass, red and black bream, coalfish, cod, conger, dab, lesser spotted dogfish, bull huss, flounder, garfish, gurnard, John Dory, ling, mackerel, golden-grey mullet, thick-lipped mullet, red mullet, plaice, pollack, pouting, rays, scad, sea-trout, starry smooth hound, sole, tope, turbot, and wrasse. Quite a variety. From boats, add spur dogfish, monkfish, extra ray species, whiting, blue and porbeagle sharks.

Interestingly, wreck boats from Plymouth set out in the small hours of

the morning to make the long haul out to these waters in February and March after pollack, coalfish and ling. They catch them by the ton – big fish, naturally. Yet it is indicative that the Guernsey boat-caught record for coalfish is a mere 5 lb. The ling and pollack records at 36 lb 14 oz and 22 lb are more respectable. Even so, fish of this calibre and better are frequently caught by the Plymouth boats. The fact is that charter boat facilities are not nearly as well developed as those at Plymouth. But then Plymouth draws from the entire British Isles for its clientele and few anglers would approve of paying the excess baggage surcharge for taking half a ton of fillets home on the plane.

If you decide to make the run to the Channel Islands in your own boat, or take it over by ferry, you should know that all boats under 30 feet and with a speed of more than 12 knots must be registered at the Harbour Office, St Helier, Jersey if they are to be used in Jersey waters. There are numerous ramps around the island and excellent facilities at St Helier, St Aubin, St

Catherines and Gorey. On Guernsey, St Peter Port is the best place and, on Alderney, head for Braye.

High water at St Helier occurs about 4 hours after London Bridge times.

Jersey
There is a 40 foot range between high and low tides around this island, resulting in very strong tides. During the peak run of a spring tide the water deepens by about two inches per minute. Jersey is tilted from north to south, with the north coast the steepest part, and some shallow southerly beaches (around La Rocque, for example) stripping for a mile or so at low water. These conditions demand that the visitor seeks local expert guidance. Mullet, pollack, black bream and bass are very common and may be encountered virtually everywhere.
1 St Catherine's Breakwater This pier extends for ¾ mile into a fierce tide race. Locals fish around low water slack as that is the only time it is possible to hold bottom. Fish from the extreme end, casting due south on to

sand. Long casting is recommended with big baits of fresh mackerel or sand-eels for large blonde and undulate rays and conger eels.

2 Gorey Harbour Fish from the wall here for black bream, pollack, mullet and mackerel. Rockworm, also known as red cat, is a favoured bait for the bream. It has to be chiselled out from cracks in the rocks, but lasts for up to three weeks in the fridge.

3 Elizabeth Castle Maroon yourself with safety at high tide and fish for bass, conger eels, mullet, black bream and pollack from the wall here.

4 Noirmont This rocky headland produces fair fishing for the usual local species.

5 La Moye–La Corbiere Rocky headlands between these two points produce black bream, bass, pollack, wrasse and large conger. There are more rocks around to La Pulente.

6 St Ouen's Bay Like an Irish surf beach, this, except that the tide strips further than usual. High water is best for the bigger bass – small ones predominate on the flooding tide in the shallow water. Best results for bass are at the rocky extremities of the bay. Use peeler crab or rockworm gathered on site (around the rocks).

7 L'Etacq It is like a lunar landscape here when the tide is out, with 30-foot-deep gullies leading out towards the low water line. Locals use hooks on poles to ferret out crabs and lobsters from the rocky pools. Seaweed is stacked up here by autumn storms and bass and mullet feed on the maggots washed out on spring tides. To the north, cliffs deny access to the shoreline.

8 Plémont It is a difficult climb, but the fishing for bass in the tide race can be excellent. Also for mackerel and pollack.

9 Grève de Lecq Fish from the jetty for bass, pollack, wrasse and mullet – and the ubiquitous black bream. Locals use 'chervy', an evil-smelling mixture of putrefying rabbit guts, fish and other horrors mixed with grain to attract the mullet – and fish most successfully. The beach nearby is deep and offers good bass, plaice (large ones run around the island in November and December), pollack and mullet.

10 Ronez Wrasse, black bream, pollack and mackerel are caught from the headland hereabouts. In winter a few cod are taken, and plaice before Christmas. Similar fishing is found from the jetty at Bonne Nuit Bay.

Action with codling in heavy surf. Channel Island tides can be strong with an extensive range, possibly the factor which draws the fish in quantity.

11 Bouley Bay Black bream, conger, wrasse, pollack and most other local species may be caught here and at Rozel Bay to the east.

For further information about Jersey fishing, contact R. G. Smith, Wheways, 16 Broad Street, St Helier (Tel: Jersey (0534) 20194).

Guernsey

Tides around Guernsey are less severe than round Jersey, with a rise and fall of 31 feet on big spring tides and just 7 feet on neap tides. Since the island is just six miles long by about four wide, it would not take long to walk right round it. Surf bass fishing is practised at Vazon, Cobo, L'Ancresse, Petit Port and Petit Bot bays. Rock marks are abundant, with Fort Doyle in the north east and Jerbourg Point in the south east offering good sport. Piers at St Peter Port and St Sampsons offer fair sport too.

There are few charter boats – only about three boats operate out from St Peter Port.

Sand-eels are abundant and may be bought cheaply. Rockworm, ragworm, crab and lugworm have to be gathered by the angler. Mackerel are abundant in summer, as also are grey mullet – a neglected fish bait that is equally as effective as mackerel.

The best season is regarded as June to early November, though locals fish throughout the year.

Details from Baker's, 43 The Pollet, St Peter Port (Tel: Guernsey (0481) 21139); G. L. F. Domaille, The Bridge, St Sampson's (Tel: Guernsey (0481) 44542); Marquand Brothers Ltd., North Quay, St Peter Port (Tel: Guernsey (0481) 20962) and Tackle and Accessories Center, 30 Bordage, St Peter Port (Tel: Guernsey (0481) 23225).

Channel Islands

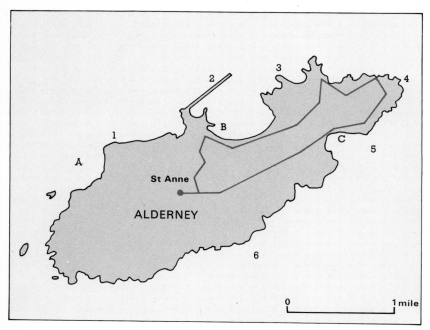

For details of fishing around Alderney, contact H. G. L. Pike, Le Jardin, Colimbot (Tel: Alderney (048 182) 3194) and The Sail Loft, Braye (Tel: Alderney (048 182) 2702).

A magnificent catch of cod.

Alderney

This tiny island offers a great deal to the shore angler. Bait is plentiful and there is no shortage of fish. Charters can be arranged through the local tackle dealers. Tides are a little less fierce here than around the islands to the south – but not much!

The island tilts from the precipitous south west to the more shallow north east, where most of the shore fishing is done. There are cliffs along most of the southerly shore between Essex Castle and Fort Clonque. Where access is possible, excellent rock fishing can be had from the headlands, but take expert advice before setting out.

1 Platte Saline Gather rockworm or peeler crab from Clonque Bay, to the west of the Fort Tourgis headland and fish Platte Saline beach for a wide spectrum of species. Locals catch everything from tope to garfish here. Mackerel and sand-eels make good baits too. Fish throughout the flood tide and the first hour of the ebb, especially when there is an onshore breeze. To the east, Crabby Bay also offers good fishing, especially at night for conger, during the summer and autumn months.

2 Braye Breakwater Mullet, pollack, mackerel and garfish are caught here – and some larger species. Permission is a tactful formality from Department of the Environment.

3 Saye Bay Excellent mixed fishing here. To the east, Chateau A L'Etoc offers good rock fishing with bottom or float-fished baits, especially for wrasse, pollack and mackerel. Nearby Arch Bay and Corblets Bay offer good shore fishing for bass, sole, flatfish and so on.

4 Cats Bay There is good fishing all round here. Marks exist for rock and for bottom fishing for a wide variety of species. Likewise Fort Houmet Herbe and the beaches to the south east. Good plaice are taken along here each autumn.

5 Ile de Raz Walk the causeway at low tide and maroon yourself for good fishing around high water. There is no danger from being cut off here.

6 Cachalière Pier Take the cliff path to beach level and fish for pollack, wrasse, mackerel, garfish, bream and so on.

Bait Areas

Rockworm, which has to be chiselled from the rocks, is abundant. Likewise peeler shore crabs in summer. Mackerel and sand-eels are easy to come by, either fresh or bought. Most bait collecting is undertaken in Clonque Bay, Braye Bay (where you can dig lugworm) and Longis Bay, where there are more lugworm.

A Rockworm, lugworm.
B Peeler crab.
C Sand-eels.

FOR THE FAMILY

The Channel Islands, with their mild climate and spectacular coast, have much to offer in good bathing, boating, walking and entertainments. Jersey and Guernsey's resorts have many annual festivals and sporting events and the smaller islands have a special charm.

Jersey Zoo Gerald Durrell's fine collection of animals and birds and a sanctuary for rare species.

Fort Regent St Helier, Jersey. Vast assembly of sport and leisure facilities in 22-acre Napoleonic fort. Pool, music, exhibitions, even giant chess.

German Occupation Museums on Jersey and Guernsey there are forts and tunnels, relics and tableaux recalling the Channel Islands in wartime.

Hauteville House Guernsey. Visit Victor Hugo's house with its fantastic interior and 'look-out'. Apr–Sept.

Regular ferry services take you from island to island to enjoy the beaches of Alderney or explore Sark, Little Sark, Herm and Jethou. Hydrofoil to France.

Museums of Island History in Jersey there are splendid tableaux at Mont Orgueil Castle and at St Helier. On Guernsey a new museum and art gallery has been opened at Candie Gardens.

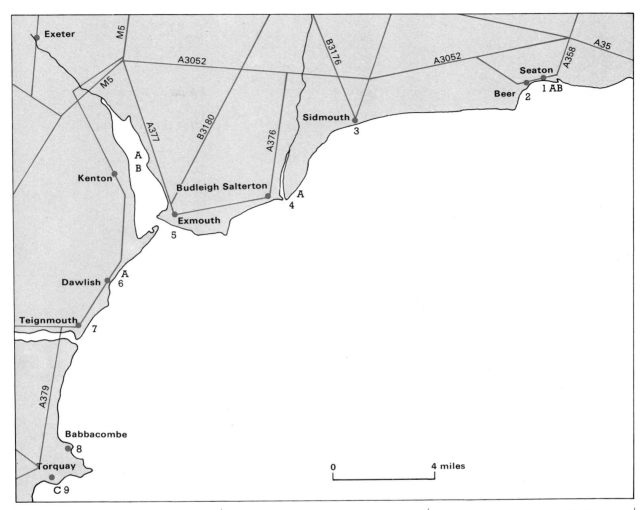

West of Lyme Regis runs a stretch of cliff that ends at the mouth of the River Axe. Beneath this cliff are shallow reef and stony bays filled with boulders that gradually give way, west of Axmouth, to beaches better suited to the building of sandcastles. Seaton is situated in a cleft in the cliffs with shallow reefs flanking each side. Around Beer Head, the next point of access is Branscombe Mouth, lying between steep and often precipitous slopes and the National Trust-owned foreshore is largely of sand and shingle, with a few outcrops of reef, the terrain becoming softer at the mouth of the River Sid at Sidmouth.

South west from here, to the mouth of the River Otter, the shoreline is largely cliff with access only at Ladram Bay. Budleigh Salterton lies on a wide pebble bay, though cliffs

rear up again, with exposed rocks at low water, towards Straight Point, similar country extending to sandy Exmouth, a town built on the east bank of the mile-wide Exe estuary. At its mouth, the sands of Dawlish Warren are interrupted by just one rocky outcrop at Langstone Point before reefs again intervene at Clerk Point, and then become sandy again towards Teignmouth.

South from here, the shoreline is protected from south westerly winds by the cliffs that mark the geological edge of Dartmoor, interspersed with little bays. The sea bed varies considerably from rock to stone to sand as far as picturesque Hope's Nose, then similar cliff-backed ground extends westwards to Torquay, with its harbour and sandy beaches – interspersed with the familiar rocky

outcrops of red sandstone. Similar rock-and-stone ground extends past Paignton and Brixham to Berry Head, and on past Dartmouth harbour entrance to Strete Head. Here begins a sandy, curving stretch of shoreline, backed in part by the A379, that boasts only two minor rocky outcrops before turning abruptly eastward to the rocky promontory of Start Point.

Cliffs and heavy inshore reef characterise the stretch of coastline west of Start – Lannacomb Bay, Prawle Point and on round to the pretty town of Salcombe on the west side of the muddy Kingsbridge estuary. If you can imagine smuggler's country, this is it, from Bolt Head round to Plymouth there are reefs, rocky ledges, steep and not-so-steep cliffs, secret coves, and long, tree fringed estuaries. The area is one of the most beautiful and

South Devon

romantic parts of Britain – and it is largely unspoilt.

Plymouth is famous for its offshore wreck fishing, with skippers going well out towards the Channel Islands in order to find wrecks that will produce the half-ton and greater catches of pollack, ling and so on that have brought this place its reputation. Off Dartmouth, the Skerries produce excellent plaice fishing in April, and also some good wreck fishing. The peak season for pollack around here is February to March, while ling are best before they spawn in March. The coalfish, nearly always very big over wrecks, are best early in the year – weather permitting.

Dartmouth also offers good fishing for shoaling bass around September, while July sees some large blonde rays taken from the Skerries and Brixham has long been famous for its wreck conger catches. Several of the harbours along here boast charter fleets: these are Exmouth, Teignmouth, Torquay, Paignton, Brixham, Dartmouth and Plymouth.

Offshore catches include blue sharks and the occasional porbeagle, tope, turbot, rays, monkfish, dogfish, red bream, the usual wreck fish, but few cod. Inshore fishing is for black and red bream, the rare gilthead bream (around Salcombe), bass, all the flatfish, whiting, wrasse, lesser spotted dogfish, bull huss, conger, thornback and small-eyed rays – and a few rarer types – mullet (thick-lipped), sea-trout in the estuaries, pollack, small coalfish, mackerel, garfish and scad. There are also many other species swimming around in these south Devon waters.

Tides are as follows: at Seaton and Sidmouth high water is 4½ hours after London Bridge, at Exmouth 4¾ hours, likewise Teignmouth, Torquay and Paignton. At Brixham it is 4½ hours, likewise Dartmouth. Salcombe is 4 hours after London Bridge high, and so too are the Yealm estuary and Plymouth.

Slipways, some of them public, are available at Exmouth (4), Lympstone, Topsham, Teignmouth, Hamworthy, Torquay, Paignton, Brixham (3), Kingswear, Greenway Ferry, Galmpton, Totnes, Dittisham, Dartmouth (3), Kingsbridge (3), Salcombe (several), Newton Ferrers, and Plymouth (several). Boats can be launched at other places, though most of them require the craft to be manhandled across sand or beach.

If this is possible to countenance, then the craft you have in mind is probably not suitable for offshore fishing – or you are very strong!

At various places along this stretch of coast there are small boat owners who are happy to hire out a dinghy and outboard for a day. Ask at local tackle shops for names and addresses. Also, this is the home of mackerel fishing trips – two hours out in the bay with a hand-line strung with feathers. As an amusement for tourists, this form of fishing is unlikely to appeal to the serious angler unless he requires a lot of fresh mackerel for bait; and even then he may have to buy them off the boatman, even though he caught them himself.

Clubs exist at many places, but are small though the membership is keen. One such is Paignton SAA, South Quay, The Harbour (Tel: Paignton (0803) 5531 18) also Brixham SAC, Castor Road, Brixham (Tel: Brixham (080 45) 3930) and South Devon SAC during opening hours at the Jolly Sailor at Newton Abbot.

1 Seaton Bass are taken from the mouth of the River Axe, the best time being between low tide and half flood, using crab, prawn, live or dead sand-eels, with fish and squid baits second best. The beach in front of Seaton produces small conger, the occasional bass, with dogfish and pouting most prolific, using standard baits. Thick-lipped mullet are taken from the Axe estuary on bread and harbour ragworm.

2 Beer Crowded by boats and holiday-makers in summer, the best places to fish are close by the rocky outcrops at each side of the bay for species similar to those at Seaton. Wrasse and some pollack can be had by casting out from the rock ledges using bait or, for the pollack, spinners, feathers and so forth.

3 Sidmouth Shingle beach flanked by high cliffs with rocky outcrops beneath them. To the west lies an area of rock and sand. At Branscombe Mouth, to the east, pouting, small conger eels, dogfish and wrasse are to be had, with more wrasse and pollack from the rock ledges. Further west, closer to Sidmouth, Weston Beach produces similar results. Night fishing is by far the best bet. At the mouth of the River Sid, similar species, together with a few bass, can be expected. Mackerel sometimes come in close enough to interest the shore caster. West of the town, the rocky

outcrop of Chit Ledge produces some small wrasse and conger, with pollack and the occasional bass. More bass can be expected when a south easterly wind builds up the surf on the sandy beach just west of here.

4 Budleigh Salterton There is good mullet fishing to be had, using float tackle baited with bread or ragworm fishing from the seaward side of the bridge (quite a way upstream) over the river Otter. You can also mullet fish higher up the river, where a rod licence is required. At the mouth of the Otter, stand on the point on the west side when the tide has covered the rocks and you will catch good bass on crab and similar baits. Wrasse and pollack can also be had here, casting close to the rocks at the river mouth.

To the right of the steps to the beach in front of the public toilets further west along the beach some good bass fishing is to be had, with night tides the best time, while dabs can be caught to the left of the steps around low water.

Further westwards, round to a couple of rocks that dry out at half tide, good bass are taken, with the occasional plaice, flounder and gurnard. The bass prefer dark tides, when conger are also taken. Black bream will appear here after a summer storm, and bull huss, too, when the water is dirty. There is very little current here after low water.

At Otter Cove and Littleham Cove, bull huss and lesser spotted dogfish can be caught. Bass, too, when the water is not dirty. Dogfish species come best to fish baits at low water or spring tides, with the occasional ray.

To the east of Straight Point, below the rifle range, the rocks dry out to provide access from half tide down round to half flood. Fish here for good wrasse, nocturnal conger, bull huss and some pollack.

5 Exmouth West of Straight Point, the beach is made up of rocky ledges with patches of sand in between. Surf conditions by day bring the bass close in at Sandy Bay, Rodney Bay and Orcombe Bay. Flounders take best, along with some plaice, during the day time when baiting with crab, mollusc or worm baits. West of the old sewer pipes at the Maer Rocks, flounders and school bass are to be had two hours each side of high water. West of here a sand-spit appears at low water of spring tides, when bass and some plaice can be taken, together with flounders. Near the old

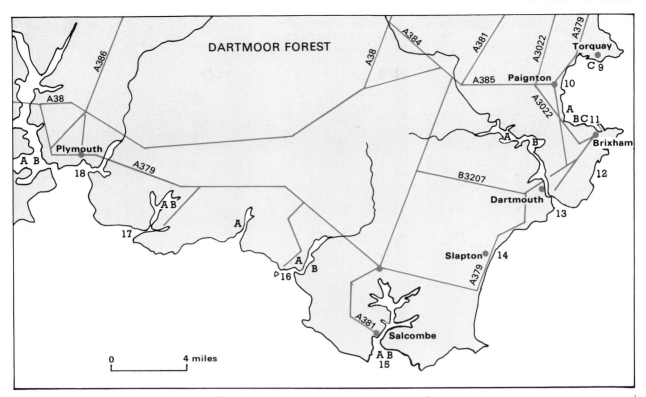

lifeboat slipway, bass are to be had around low water, by day or night. Tides become too strong at other times. Also some plaice in March further west towards the Mamhead Slipway. Up-estuary from the docks, the best fishing is mainly for flounders which are present all year round except February. The bass arrive in May and leave in October, though warm winters see some taken right through the year. More information, and fresh bait can be had from Fred Statham at Fred Statham's Tackle Box, Pierhead, Exmouth, Devon. He is open till after 9 o'clock in summer and provided us with more information than we have space for here. (Tel: Exmouth (039 52) 72129, daytime, and 75251, evening). Contact him for charter bookings out from Exmouth and for lots more information about points of access, firing times at Straight Point and so on.

6 Dawlish Warren   At the north east end, the sand-spit curves into the mouth of the River Exe and the currents are fierce. Bass, plaice and flounders are to be had from deep water close by, though currents are often too fierce to fish. Further south, the beach becomes more shallow and

a surf will bring the bass close in where they take crab, ragworm and shellfish baits, with fish baits and squid second best. In March, some fair plaice are taken here. Otherwise flounders are the best bet, together with the occasional dogfish which will take a fish bait.

7 Teignmouth   The Teign estuary is famous for its autumn and winter flounder fishing. Two-hook traces are used baited with crab, or one hook behind a flounder spoon. Here, as in many West Country estuaries, crabs are gathered for bait commercially, the locals setting 'pots' of old bits of pottery and pipe and they resent strangers reaping the rewards of their diligence. At the estuary mouth, bass and sometimes mackerel are taken both spinning and by float-fishing. Legering soft crab also accounts for good bass. Live sand-eels float-fished with the tide from the point on the east side work very well. Casting off the railway wall, a public right of way, further east catches small conger, pollack and sometimes mackerel at high water on spring tides. Mullet abound in the estuary. On the west side, The Ness offers float fishing for bass using live sand-eels, spinning

for bass and mackerel and pollack and some wrasse fishing. Bull huss are also taken, especially at night on fish baits. Boats can be hired on the beach for easier access to estuary and inshore reef marks.

8 Babbacombe   The best places to fish from are the small rocky outcrops along here. Small conger eels and bull huss, with the inevitable lesser spotted dogfish, will take fish baits, especially at night. Some plaice and dabs are taken from sandy patches on worm baits. Float fishing over the rocks produces wrasse, pollack, garfish and mackerel. The occasional ray is also taken hereabouts.

9 Torquay   Hope's Nose is one of the best known local marks, because most of the nearby beaches become crowded with holiday makers. Dabs, dogfish and wrasse are taken in winter. More wrasse, bass, mackerel, garfish, pouting, bream and conger are taken on mackerel, squid, sand-eel and peeler crab, together with some flatfish and the occasional small-eyed ray. Float fishing is popular from the sewer near here, for thick-lipped mullet on bread and harbour ragworm. Princes Pier and Haldon Pier are popular, with garfish, mackerel, mullet, pollack and small wrasse taken spinning, float fishing and legering bottom baits. Conger eels, too, at night. A toll is payable. Details available from Ted Tuckerman, 141 St Marychurch Road, Torquay (Tel: Torquay (0803) 36216).

10 Paignton The sandy beaches around here produce bass, mackerel and flatfish, with rising tides in summer and autumn the best time. Spinning, legering and feathering produce the best results. Bait with peeler crab, prawns, ragworm and squid. Local surveys show the best fishing spots. More information from David Clark, 46 Cecil Road, Paignton (Tel: Paignton (0803) 554244); also Mr Jack Butterworth at Jack's Sports, 371 Torquay Road, Preston, Paignton (Tel: Paignton (0803) 523023).

11 Brixham Berry Head, on the north side, is very deep and produces mackerel, garfish, wrasse and pollack on float tackle, also bull huss, some bream and conger eels. The south side allows easier access, with similar species. Peeler crab, fresh mackerel, squid, prawns and sand-eels produce the best results. Brixham Breakwater is famous for its big, night-time conger eels (long-liners permitting), taken on fish and squid baits. Also taken are pollack, wrasse, dogfish and mackerel. Live prawns, caught while fishing, are also good bait.

12 Sharkham The sandy beaches with rocky headlands along here produce similar results to those found further north here.

13 Dartmouth Wrasse, pollack and some bass are taken from the rocks around the mouth of this picturesque spot. Also bull huss on bottom baits and mackerel. Thornbacks come into the estuary in March, with bass following later and staying longer. Plenty of mullet and flounders along the upper reaches. Some excellent charter skippers with good boats here. See the angling press for advertisements.

14 Slapton Sands Surf conditions at Blackpool Sands, Slapton Sands, Beesands and Hallsands produce good bass when the surf-boards are not too thick on the water. Summer and autumn offer the best fishing using live sand-eels, peeler crab, ragworm, squid and razorfish. Sometimes small turbot invade the beach in calm conditions, together with mackerel. At the southerly end of this stretch, Start Point fishes well for pollack taken

spinning, feathering and float fishing with live prawns, sand-eels, mackerel strip etc. Also wrasse, the occasional small-eyed ray and bull huss. Conger eels and the occasional bass are also taken from here, and from rock marks further west, access permitting.

15 Salcombe Much of the shoreline outside the estuary is impeded by rocks. Wrasse, bass, pollack and a few other species are to be found here. Mullet abound inside the estuary, along with flounders. Use standard baits and tackle.

16 Bigbury Bay At Hope Cove there are sandy beaches and rock ledges from which a few bass can be taken, together with pollack, wrasse, mackerel and garfish. Sand-eel, live prawn, peeler crab and squid strip are all recommended. Some bream and other small bottom feeders are also to be had from here. The sandy beaches at Bigbury produce bass in surf conditions, while similar rock species as those found further east can be taken from the rocky headlands. Similar species are caught at Erme Mouth.

17 Yealm Bass, pollack and wrasse are caught at the mouth of this estuary on crab and standard baits. Local rock marks produce some bass, but mainly wrasse, pollack and bottom-feeding predators on the usual tackle and baits. Plenty of mullet and flounders up-river.

18 Plymouth Thick-lipped mullet abound in the harbour, though access is restricted in some areas. Pollack, bass and wrasse are to be found from many of the vantage points that give access to good water around the harbour. The inner harbour abounds with flounders, although it is very muddy in places. Contact one of the numerous tackle dealers around the town. Charter bookings can be arranged through the Plymouth Angling Boatman's Association (Tel: Plymouth (07852) 21722).

Bait Areas

Although peeler crabs are plentiful, few are gathered from the open rocky coastline. Locals set pots – bits of broken pipe, old tyres etc – in the estuaries for peeler shore crabs and so it is easiest to buy from a tackle dealer or watch out for 'bait for sale' notices outside longshore houses.

Prawns can be gathered from most of the rocky marks. Steep rocks and piers allow a baited drop-net to be lowered, while shallow gullies are

best fished with a scoop net. This is best when the water is clouded. Live prawns are a very effective bait for pollack, wrasse and other species.

Mackerel can be bought fresh, though it is difficult to know just how fresh it is. There is rarely any shortage of mackerel spinning and feathering to be had off rocky promontories in the summer, between May and October.
A Lugworms. Dig these with a potato fork.
B Ragworms – mainly small.
C Razorfish. Some beaches offer salting and spearing opportunities for this excellent bait on low water spring tides. Digging in Torquay harbour is restricted by local bye-laws. This also applies to several other estuaries and harbours.

Sand-eels are an excellent bait, and contact with a sand-eel seiner can be made through a local tackle shop, who will also tell you where they can be dug or scraped. Many dealers stock frozen sand-eel, itself a very effective bait and equally as good as fresh.

FOR THE FAMILY

From the South Devon coast you can explore cliffs and coves, quiet villages and the remoter stretches of the Dartmoor National Park. See historic Plymouth and the famous South Devon resorts with their maritime museums and modern attractions.
Bicton nr Sidmouth. Acres of lovely gardens, narrow-gauge railway, countryside museum, hall of transport, picnic area playground, licensed restaurant.
Dartmoor National Park Ashburton or Tavistock are good starting points for the southern area, the Dart valley, Widecombe, Buckfastleigh and Dartmoor.
Torbay and Dartmouth Railway 7-mile panoramic trip from Paignton to Kingswear.
The Dart Valley Railway from Buckfastleigh to Totnes gives superb views of the River Dart. Open early Apr & May–Oct.
Powderham Castle Kenton. Impressive castle in a deer park. Falconry. Apr–Sept.
Beer Modelrama miniature railway, pleasure park, indoor exhibition with many model railway layouts, Pullman Car restaurant and Station Buffet.
Exeter Maritime Museum boats from many countries and periods, indoors and afloat. The world's biggest collection.

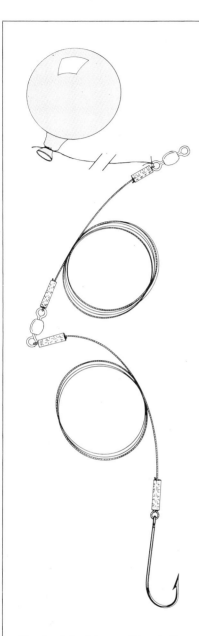

Standard shark trace set for shallow fishing with partially-inflated balloon float tied with cotton to swivel. Strong swivels and crimps make a neat job.

Fishing for mackerel at sunset.

Cornwall

Fishing the morning tide for cod from a breakwater.

The south Cornish coast boasts more fishing records than any other part of Britain. From both beach and boat the fishing can be extremely good, both for plenty of average size fish and for specimen size monsters. Exotic species, more familiar in the tropics, are taken from here; years ago a sailfish was washed ashore at the mouth of the River Yealm. More recently, the wreckfish record was broken over a hundred times in one day.

The multiple estuaries to the west of Plymouth are best explored by boat. To the south, rocky Rame Head offers good fishing but is hard to negotiate as compared with the sandy curve of Whitesand Bay. At Portwrinkle the rock begins again, running round to Looe and on to Fowey with its five-mile-long estuary.

Once round Gribbin Head the rock pattern continues to St Austell. Sheltered from the prevailing westerly winds, there are some fine sandy beaches here. The pattern of sandy beaches combined with precipitous outcrops of rock continues south of Black Head to Mevagissey, Dodman Point, Veryan Bay, Nare Head, Gerrans Bay and Zone Point to the wide estuary of the river Fal at Falmouth.

South of Rosemullion Head lies the sheltered Helford River, but there are more cliffs and secret, sandy coves around Manacle Point and another Black Head (the British shoreline is liberally sprinkled with Black Heads) and on to where England's southern-most tip, Lizard Point, juts into the Atlantic. Rocky headlands and little coves crowd one after the other on both sides of this headland, as fine a place as anywhere on earth when summer weather brings out the colours of moorland heather, rock, sea, sand and sky.

At Porthleven, with its long surf beaches facing into the prevailing winds, the white sands offer respite from the harsher surrounding rock areas. Then cliffs and coves again from this beach towards Penzance. South of Mousehole, the cliffs and coves thicken around Land's End, England's most westerly point where place names such as Tredavoe and Porthcurno recall a strong Celtic ancestry.

Virtually every worthwhile fish species is to be caught along this varied coastline. Cod and similar cold-water species are taken only offshore. Offshore wreck fishing peaks for pollack and coalfish in February and March. Shark fishing, mainly for blue shark, is carried out from several ports. More information about this can be obtained from the Shark Angling Club of Great Britain, The Quay, East Looe (Tel: Looe (050 36) 2642).

Inshore fishing is mainly for bass, pollack, rays, wrasse, conger eels, flatfish, bull huss, lesser-spotted dogfish, mackerel, mullet, tope and a variety of small species.

Charter boats are available at Falmouth, Penzance, Looe, Coverack, Mevagissey and one or two smaller ports. Several ports offer round-the-bay mackerel fishing trips, and many areas have small boats for hire.

Slipways exist at the following places, but check first on launching conditions: Calstock, St Dominic, St Germans, Millendreath, Looe (3), Polperro, Polruan (2), Fowey,

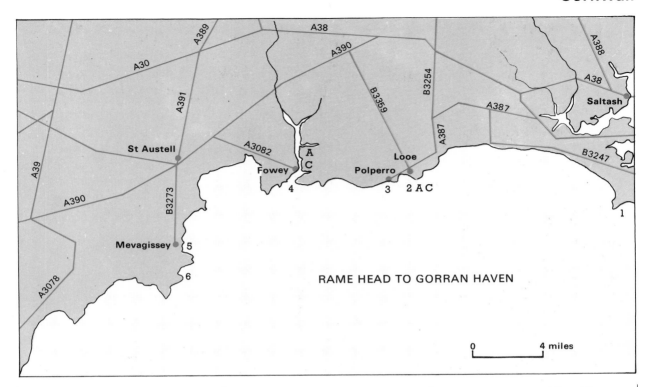

RAME HEAD TO GORRAN HAVEN

0   4 miles

Porthpean, Porthscatho, Place, Percuil, St Mawes, Feock, Mylor, Flushing, Trevissome, Falmouth, Helford, Coverack, Mullion, Porthleven, Penzance (3), and Mousehole. Some are private and require arranging in advance. Other facilities exist for smaller craft that can easily be manhandled over the beach for launching.

Tide times: Looe – 4 hours after high water at London Bridge, Falmouth 3½ hours, The Lizard 3¼ hours and Land's End 3 hours.

1 Rame Head One of the better known fishing headlands in Cornwall. .It offers excellent sport for mackerel from late April through to October, weather permitting. Rays, small turbot, conger eels, bull huss, lesser spotted dogfish, pouting and whiting all take fish baits legered on the bottom. Mackerel strip, sand-eels, herring and local squid all produce good results. Float fishing and spinning for pollack is also successful. Wrasse take lumps of hard-back crab, lugworm, prawns and mussel.

2 Looe This port is famous for its blue shark fishing, although the more serious angler may have doubts about the way this has been touristified. Excellent skippers are to be found here who approve of light-tackle shark fishing with 30–50 lb class tackle rather than the crow-bar gear offered to the novice. Bass, flounders, eels and thick-lipped mullet abound in the estuary. Rock marks offer wrasse, mackerel and pollack fishing, while sandy Whitesand Bay offers excellent surf bass fishing early and late in the year. Information from J. Bray, The Quay, Looe (Tel: Looe (050 36) 2504).

3 Polperro This picturesque harbour offers good rock fishing facilities for mackerel, wrasse and pollack; while bass, flounders and dogfish can be had from clearer ground. General fishing is with a float from rocks. More information from The Rod and Line Tackle Shop, Little Green, Polperro.

4 Fowey Excellent bass fishing in the estuary here with soft crab, starting in May, with a mid-summer pause, and continuing again from September to October. To the west, Par Beach offers good sport in surf conditions while rock fishing with peeler crab, sand-eel and prawns at Polruan yields good fish. In high summer start early (around dawn) or late (after sundown) for the best results. Rock marks offer conger eels, rays, wrasse and pollack. More

information from The Gift and Sports Shop, 10 Esplanade, Fowey (Tel: Fowey (072 683) 2207) also Fowey Sea Angling Centre, 20 Fore Street (Tel: Fowey (072 683) 3392).

5 Mevagissey This harbour – little more than a cleft in the cliffs – contains several very professional skippers with offshore wreck-fishing boats. Shark fishing is also available from here. The shore fishing is largely for rock species – some bass, pollack, mackerel, wrasse, rays, bull huss and dogfish. Excellent fishing can be had on fish baits in the harbour for thick-lipped mullet. Crinnis Beach, towards St Austell offers good fishing for bass, flounders and plaice. The rock ledges at each end of this beach are best float-fished for pollack, mackerel and garfish. Fish for two hours each side of high water on the steep-shelving beach. There is no need to cast far – but use live sand-eel if possible, otherwise freshly dead or frozen. Car parking facilities are excellent here. More information from Mevagissey Shark Angling Centre, East & West Quay, Mevagissey (Tel: Mevagissey (072 684) 3430) also The Tackle Box, 13 Market Street, Mevagissey (Tel: Mevagissey (072 684) 3513).

Cornwall

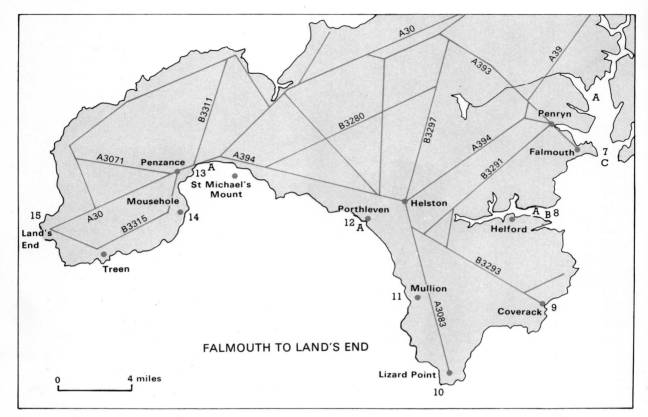

FALMOUTH TO LAND'S END

0   4 miles

6 Gorran Haven
Float-fished ragworm, dug locally, produces flatfish, small pollack and wrasse from the pier of this pretty fishing harbour at around high tide. Mackerel are also caught spinning. When a strong easterly wind blows, take live sand-eels to Big Perhaver Beach for bass and chicken turbot, the best months being August to October. Long casting is advantageous – after a long walk of a mile to get here. The rocks flanking Colona Beach, after another cliff-top walk, produce specimen wrasse, conger, scad, mackerel and bass. Beyond the rocks are called Chapel Point. Deep water is found on the Mevagissey side of the bay. Mullet feed on the shallow side during light easterly winds. Artificial lures work here for pollack, mackerel and scad. Pentean Beach offers good bass fishing in a sou'westerly wind, on night tides from August to October. Fish towards either end of the beach rather than the middle. Mackerel strip, sand-eel and lugworm produce bass, rays and flatfish around low water at Carne Beach during easterly winds. Likewise Pendower Beach. Similar species are found at Port Holland, fishing from two hours after high water down to low water. Long casting is not required, but you will find that a sou'westerly wind is essential.

Four fathoms of water is to be found on the west side of Dodman Point, looking in towards Hemmick Beach. Elsewhere it is rocky. In May, September and October large bass make their way past here. An easterly wind fills the cove with thick-lipped grey mullet. Fishing for them – and other species such as wrasse, pollack and mackerel – is on the flood tide. The bass feed best at 2 hours before low water. Spin with dead sand-eels or float fishing with live sand-eels.

Caerhays Beach on a flooding tide with a wind whipping up some surf is one of the better places in England for good sport. This very shallow shore (less than 2 fathoms deep 400 yards out at high tide), produces some of the best local summer bass fishing.

All this information came from Mevagissey Shark Angling Centre, West Quay, The Harbour, Mevagissey (Tel: Mevagissey (0726) 8434 30).

7 Falmouth
Excellent bass fishing from here and St Mawes, with rays, pollack, wrasse, mackerel, huss, mullet and conger from the rock marks. Easterly winds provide the best surf fishing and push the mullet close inshore. These shoals hang like black clouds in the clear water some way out when the wind is off the shore, while a tickle of surf on the rocks excites them. Details from A. B. Harvey & Sons Ltd, 1 Market Strand, Falmouth (Tel: Falmouth (0326) 312796) also Bill's Tackle Box, 34 Arwenack Street, Falmouth (Tel: Falmouth (0326) 315849).

8 Helford
Sheltered estuary flats offer excellent flounder fishing, with good bass fishing at the mouth of the estuary. Flanking rock marks offer good fishing for specimen wrasse, large pollack, the chance of a bass using float-fished live sand-eels, mackerel strip and artificial lures. Mackerel, scad and garfish too. Bottom fishing produces bass on sand-eel in surf in sandy coves when east winds blow. From rocks fish baits produce tope, rays, conger and dogfish, though local specialists are

reluctant to reveal the precise location of tope marks.

9 Coverack Excellent mixed offshore fishing, especially around the Manacle Rocks for large pollack on live sand-eels and prawns. Record turbot have been taken from here. Rock ledges produce small turbot when bottom fishing with strips of fish over sandy ground. Rays, huss and tope too. Also excellent wrasse and pollack fishing with a float producing the best results. Big late-season mackerel are taken from rock marks.

10 Lizard Point More excellent rock fishing. Pollack, mackerel, garfish, scad and some bass on float-fished fish strips, live sand-eels or, if the water is choppy, dead or frozen sand-eels – the chop provides movement. Fish the rough water with light paternoster tackle or a float for wrasse, baiting with crab, lugworm, mussel and, sometimes, mackerel strip. Bottom fishing from rocks over sandy ground produces rays, dogfish and occasional tope. Access is frequently tricky around here. Beware of heavy swells when rock fishing.

11 Mullion Flatfish and bass are taken from the sandy coves around here, with south westerly winds producing a useful surf. Plenty of rock marks – many relatively unexplored – produce superb pollack, wrasse and species similar to those mentioned for areas 9 and 10.

12 Porthleven Rocks at Mount's Bay produce bass, for which this area is justly famed. Do not expect a lot of large ones – here a 5 pounder is a good one, though there are good numbers. Rocks also produce pollack, mackerel, garfish, wrasse and, if you can find a sandy patch among the snagging boulders on the bottom, rays, conger and small turbot. For more information contact A. P. Gilbert, 34 Meneage Street, Helston (Tel: Helston (032 65) 2527) also Helston Sports, 6 Wendran Street, Helston (Tel: Helston (032 65) 2097).

13 Penzance No shortage of opportunities around here. Onshore winds produce the best sport with bass from sandy beaches outside the tourist season, and right through to Christmas if the weather holds. Mullet fishing from rock marks, the piers and inside the harbour is excellent. Rocks produce pollack, wrasse, mackerel, rays, small turbot and mullet and a few bass. More information from The Quay Shop, 18 Quay Street, Penzance (Tel: Penzance

(0736) 3397) also Westrens Fishing Tackle and Chandlery, The Bridge, Newlyn, Penzance (Tel: Penzance (0736) 2413).

14 Mousehole A harbour sheltered from the prevailing winds provides excellent rock and beach fishing when other marks are made impossible by bad weather. Species are typical of those to be found around this part of the world, and similar methods obtain for their capture. Offshore fishing is very good – not just over the reefs for pollack, but for bass, rays and congers among the usual species.

15 Land's End Access is the major problem for the fishing areas along this rugged stretch of coastline. Sandy coves offer premier bass fishing, but can be hit-or-miss when the fish decide to congregate in one bay – not the one you are fishing. Mullet come very close in to the rocks when there is some wind – not too much – and can be caught by very heavy groundbaiting with minced fish or mashed bread. Rock marks, where accessible, offer rewarding bass, mackerel and pollack spinning, with wrasse, rays and some tope available.

Bait Areas

Because the coastline is so rugged as a result of thousands of years of erosion, there is little rock out in the open sea under which to hunt peeler crabs. These, along with ragworm and lugworm, are to be found in any of the long, muddy estuaries. Sand-eels can be netted or raked from sand-bars at the mouths of smaller estuaries. Mackerel, the universal bait for major predatory species, are readily

available most of the summer from rock marks. Mussels are also easily gathered from rocks and pier piles.

A Ragworm and lugworm.
B Razorfish.
C Live sand-eels.

FOR THE FAMILY

Along Cornwall's legendary south coast there are countless good places to visit – famous seaside towns and villages, beaches and coves to explore, historic houses and excursions inland to Launceston, Bodmin Moor and the Tors, not forgetting Truro and Penzance.

Mount Edgcumbe Country Park Cawsand. Fine house, gardens and park with 10 miles of coastal walks. Woodlands.

Goonhilly Down Radio Station Helston. Viewing area of satellite radio station open to the public.

Cornwall Aero Park Helston. Jets, piston-engined aircraft, 'choppers', etc., and aviation exhibition.

Forest Railroad Park Dobwalls. Nr BR station at Liskeard. Miniature railway with US-style locomotives in rocky mountain scenery. Easter & May–Oct.

St Michael's Mount castle, tropical gardens and marvellous views of Land's End's dramatic coastline. Causeway at low tide or ferry from Marazion or Penzance Quay.

Cotehele House Calstock. Medieval mansion finely preserved with original furnishings, chapel, etc. Gardens, old mill, blacksmith's shop, forge, museum on the quay and sailing barge.

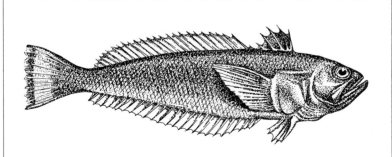

Beware the weever! Venomous spines on dorsal fin and gill covers inflict painful wounds. Not to be confused with dragonets, gobies etc.

Cornwall

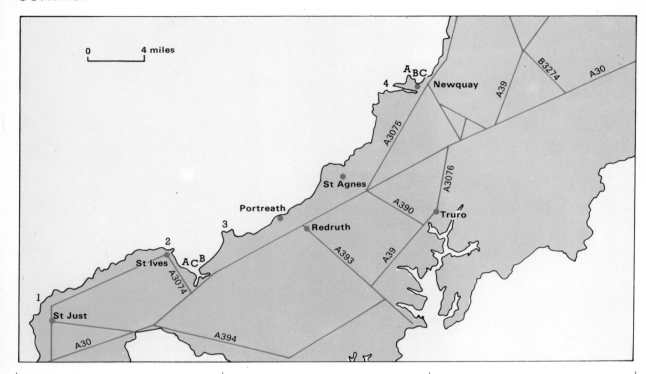

On the north side of the Land's End peninsula rocky headlands and secluded sandy coves are to be found round to St Ives, the holiday town lying on the western side of a sandy bay. Northwards lies the River Hayle in the middle of a wide surf beach. The sands at the estuary mouth offer both excellent catches of sand-eels and bass fishing. At the north east end of this sandy shore a heavy outcrop of rock at Godrevy Point makes access difficult to the excellent shore tope marks. But this is a turning point. The rocky grounds gradually become more easy to reach and more liberally interspersed with sand that has been brought by the rainfall of millenia down the River Severn from the Welsh hills. And as one travels further north east, the effect of the estuary bottleneck on the tides gradually becomes more pronounced.

Surf and clear water characterise Porthtowan, Perran Beach, Holywell Bay and the beaches at Newquay, with the pattern of rocky coves again becoming more noticeable towards Boscastle. North east from here, are the sand and rocky outcrops of Cambeak Head and Crackington Haven, famous for its offshore (but not far offshore) fishing for probeagle shark. The rock

becomes more pronounced towards Bude, interspersed by large, flat, surf beaches of clean sand that vary from small to medium at Widemouth Sand to extensive at Bude itself and northwards to Steeple Point. Much of this sandy shore is backed by steep cliffs over which hedgehogs keep falling – they are a common sight washed in along several parts here.

The sand diminishes north of Carnakey Cliff and the rocky outcrops become more frequent, leaving just narrow strips of sand between the jutting granite ribs of land. Inland, small villages characterise this wild terrain, no towns. Although the A39 (T) runs along this small peninsula, it stays well back from the shore – an average of 3 miles or so, avoiding Hartland Point and Clovelly in Devon. Much of the shoreline between Bude and Clovelly is accessible only after a sweaty scramble over rough country. Several streams drain the moors and flow through steep valleys into the sea along here. It is still largely unexplored both by tourists and by shore fishermen.

Beach fishing is largely for plaice and other flatfish, including small turbot which often commit suicide when there is no surf running on the surf beaches. The bass fishing is

excellent, both in the surf on live sand-eel, and from some rock marks by spinning either with an artificial lure or with a dead sand-eel. Tope fishing from several rock marks that fall on to sand can be very productive, with October often a premier month. Rays – blonde, small-eyed and thornback – take fish baits from some similar sandy bottomed rock marks, with late May to July the best months. The heavy rocks offer excellent wrasse, pollack and mackerel fishing, and, of course, there are dogfish – bull huss, lesser spotted and the occasional spur dogfish. Winter fishing is largely for smallish bass with the hope that some of the summer species may have lingered on. Cod fishing is negligible, although some winters see an influx of small fish with just the occasional one pushing double figures. Whiting fishing in winter is the major activity.

Offshore fishing is largely for more of the same species as are caught from the shore. Conger fishing, albeit for medium size fish, is often excellent. Tope and rays offer good sport, but you never know just what might turn up, especially further south in porbeagle shark country.

Charter boats operate out from Port Isaac, Padstow, Newquay,

Boscastle, and, if you do not worry too much about facilities, one or two of the smaller harbours. Sometimes it is possible to hire a small boat, but care must be exercised – the North Cornish coastline is not a place for the unwary or inexperienced.

Those with small boats of their own on a trailer can use public launching facilities at St Ives, Newquay, Padstow, Wadebridge, Boscastle and, if the boat is light enough, on the Stratton side of Bude bay. West of St Ives the roads are often so narrow and winding that a decent size boat cannot be taken to any of the sheltered coves with ease since there is the problem of meeting a caravan-towing car half way up a one-in-five hill with steep banks on each side of the road.

Tides are as follows, compared to London Bridge high water times. Sennen Cove plus 3 hours, Newquay plus 3½ hours, Bude plus 3 hours. The further inside the Bristol Channel one goes, the greater the difference – and the stronger the currents.

1 St Just The coastline south and west of St Ives offers interesting coves from which to catch bass, flatfish and dogfish among the clear ground, with rays from sandy areas underneath rock ledges. These rocks also offer useful pollack spinning and float fishing, together with wrasse, mackerel and, if you can find a suitable deep water headland, more than a good chance of tope.

2 St Ives Plaice, flounders and a few small turbot are all caught along the sandy beach. Bass fishing in a rolling surf either before or after the tourist season produces excellent results if the fish are in. Mullet, mackerel and pollack are all available locally. Nearby at the mouth of the Hayle estuary, spur dogfish, small turbot, small-eyed rays, plaice, occasional tope and weevers are caught. In winter the odd codling and some reasonable whiting are taken along here. More information from Bob Baird, 40 Fore Street, Hayle (Tel: Hayle (0736) 752238); Cornwall Fishing Tackle Supplies, Fernlea Terrace, St Ives (Tel: St Ives (0736) 795424) and the Fisherman's Co-Op, ᵉ Wharf, St Ives (Tel: St Ives (0736) 5424).

headlands and sheltered re typical bass country for the ler in Cornwall.

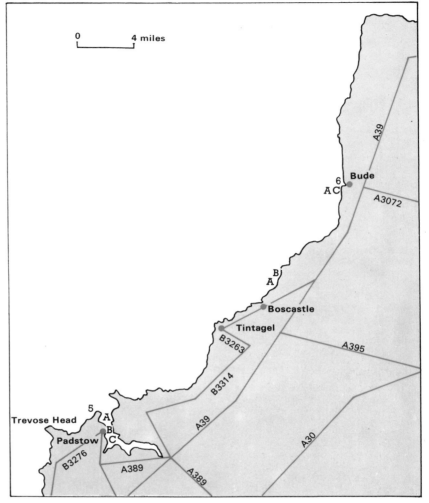

Cornwall

3 North Cliffs Also known as Godrevy Point. An excellent shore mark for tope, especially in the autumn, using frozen or fresh dead greater sand-eel or fresh mackerel strip. Long casting from the rock ledges or adjacent beaches produces good results. Also reasonable pollack, mackerel, wrasse, small turbot, plaice and occasional bass from sandy coves nearby. More information and directions on how to find the cliff path available from local tackle shops. Other information from West Cornwall Angling Centre, 25 Penpol Terrace, Hayle (Tel: Hayle (0736) 745292).

4 Newquay Excellent fishing around here — mackerel, pollack, tope and rays from the rocky headlands. The surf beaches are famous among surf riders and bass fishermen alike. Best surf bass fishing is in May/June and later, in October. The best surf bait is undoubtedly sand-eel, with crab, king ragworm, razorfish and similar standard surf baits scoring. Rock marks offer, in addition, wrasse and conger fishing, as well as some tope. More details from Central Sports, 2 Crantock Street, Newquay (Tel: Newquay (063 73) 4101).

5 Padstow Famous as a shark angling centre, this town offers good shore fishing for pollack, wrasse, mackerel, garfish, conger eels, rays and the occasional tope from nearby rock marks. Good bass from the estuary on sand-eel, red ragworm and peeler crab. Thick-lipped grey mullet in the harbour and backwaters take bread or mashed fish. Trevose Head is a famous local mark for general fishing.

6 Bude Excellent surf bass fishing, especially at the mouth of the river. Nearby rocky marks offer pollack, rays and tope together with the usual Cornish rock species. Some very good mullet fishing in the river. More information from Victor French, 19 Queen Street, Bude (Tel: Bude (0288) (2367) also North Cornwall Pet Supplies, Princes Street, Bude (Tel: Bude (0288) 2635).

Bait Areas

As can be realised from the general lack of tackle dealers in these parts, the visitor has to provide much of his own. There are not many reefy places where peeler crabs can be gathered, however, estuaries offer good facilities for this, together with digging for ragworm and lugworm, and, where there is a good sand-bar, vingling or raking will produce sand-eels – a murderous local bait. Mussels, razorfish and some other shellfish are available locally. For much of the time success comes to the angler who is prepared to scout about.

A Ragworm, lugworm.
B Soft and peeler crab.
C Sand-eel.

FOR THE FAMILY

Rugged cliffs, wide sandy beaches, waves ideal for surfing, plus lively resorts like Newquay, Padstow and Bude for entertainment, offer plenty of scope for family activities. Inland you can explore the hill country of Bodmin Moor and the Tors.

St Agnes Leisure Park model village featuring Cornwall in miniature and 'Fairyland'.

Portreath prospect for your own tin at Tolgus Tin Works and Craft centre. As a follow-up visit the Holman museum and Cornish engines museum at Redruth.

Cornwall Coastal Path miles of way-marked footpaths with magnificent scenery and seashore life.

Chysauster nr Gulval. Prehistoric British village. Remains of 8 Iron Age houses probably occupied from 1stC BC up to Roman times. Ringed by massive walls.

Tintagel Castle legendary ruins on a rocky coast associated with King Arthur.

Boscastle there is a museum of witchcraft covering the whole range of black magic and sorcery in this peaceful harbour.

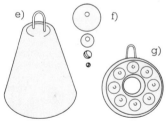

a) Fold-over, Wye and Jardine leads useful for trolling and spinning with Redgill sand-eels.

b) Basic bombs for short range beach fishing in weak currents. Also good for rock fishing.

c) Angular torpedo leads are useful for general sea fishing.

d) The Capta lead – digs into sand, casts poorly, and gives the impression there is a fish on when reeled into tide.

e) Basic large boat lead – 8–38 oz.

f) Drilled bullets and split shot are vital for cocking floats correctly.

g) Studded round grip lead casts poorly and catches the tide, so is inferior from beach and boat, ev[en] though still widely used.

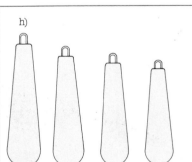

h) Torpedo sinkers cast best of all. This design is used in tournaments.

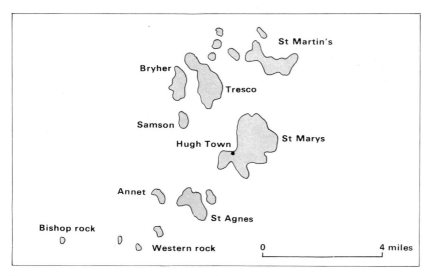

With no rivers to cloud the water, the sea around here is clear and blue. Species are largely the same as those listed for Cornish rock marks, though bass are virtually non-existent. Wrasse and pollack are common, together with rays and conger where the sea bed is not too rough and, where there is sand, plaice and immature turbot. Mackerel arrive early in the spring and linger until November, together with garfish.

Peninnis Head and Deep Point on St Mary's Island are favourite local spots. Much of the area is relatively under-explored and certainly not over-fished. Ask local netsmen and lobster potters about the nature of the sea bed hereabouts, they know it well.

Some shops stock tackle, but the visitor is wise to bring all that will be required. Offshore there is excellent fishing for blue sharks, especially in hot summers.

While visitors are encouraged to leave their cars at Penzance before taking the 40 mile ferry trip to Hugh Town, St Mary's – there is not much road and little need for a car, anyway – boats may be launched straight from the ferry into the water or from the hard foreshore.

Visitors are advised to make enquiries about tides, submerged rocks and other navigational problems. Local fishermen are very helpful. Some will charter their boats for offshore fishing. Enquire on site. Details from The Clerk of The Council, Town Hall, St Mary's (Tel: Scillonia (0720) 22537) also, St Mary's Boating Association, St Mary's.

A fair-sized bass caught from the rocks supporting a harbour wall. Mevagissey is a favoured spot for harbour fishing; the steeply-shelving beach with its rocky ledges can be fished for two hours on each side for pollack and mackerel.

FOR THE FAMILY

Apart from sea fishing the 5 inhabited islands and over 100 others offer plenty of open air enjoyment – with boat trips, coastal walks, bulb fields, beaches, tropical gardens, golf, and annual events such as the August Water Festival. For those interested in botany, birdwatching and Bronze Age tombs there is much to see.

Valhalla   fascinating collection of ship's figureheads in the subtropical Tresco Abbey gardens which are a delight in themselves.

Star Castle   St Mary's. A 16thC fortress in the form of a star, built at the time of the Spanish Armada.

Uninhabited islands   trips by boat from St Mary's to watch sea birds and enjoy the rugged scenery and remote beaches.

Isles of Scilly Museum   St Mary's. Has relics of famous ships which were wrecked on the islands.

Bryher   among the most rugged of the islands. Visit Shipman's Head for a sensational view of waves breaking over the rocky headland.

Flowers of St Mary's   700 acres of daffodils, narcissi, irises and gladioli grow here. Wild flowers in great variety on many of the islands.

North Devon

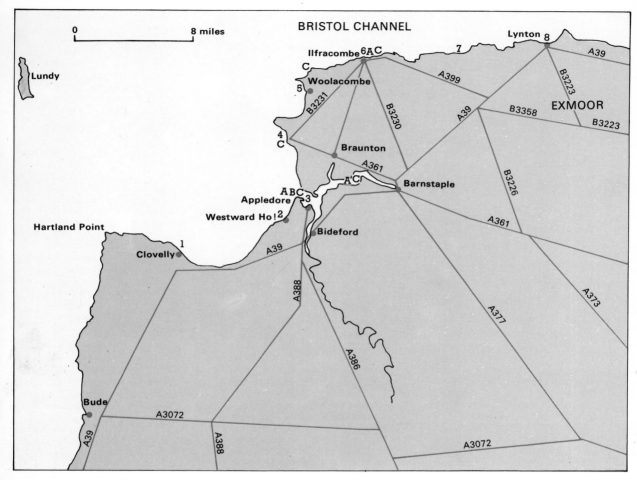

Clovelly, with its famous steep street, is not very remarkable as a fishing area. To the west, heavy afforestation round this sheltered bay has turned the moorland green, sloping from the heights of Exmoor to the sea. Boulders, some stony sand and rocky outcrops abound, the rest tending towards rock, especially as one travels eastwards to Westward Ho! and where cliffs run behind the beach.

The combined estuaries of the Taw and the Torridge come down to the sea at Appledore. Baggy Point breaks up an extensive area of sand that stretches northwards to Woolacombe from Westward Ho! Eastward from Morte Point, cliffs again proliferate, interrupted by Ilfracombe and the occasional small bay. There is more stony sand at Combe Martin and eastwards towards Lynmouth Bay sheltered among massive outcrops from Exmoor.

There is a singular lack of charter boat facilities here, though the inquisitive visitor might find a boatman to take him out at Barnstaple, Appledore, Bideford, Combe Martin, Ilfracombe or a boat for hire at one of the small harbours. The man who trails his own craft will find reasonable launching facilities at Appledore, Braunton and Lynmouth. Elsewhere boats have to be manhandled over the beach. Note, however, that the waters off North Devon demand expert seamanship.

Tide times difference from London Bridge high water can be calculated by adding about 4 hours to that time. Locally the mean port is Avonmouth (Bristol), and high water is minus $1\frac{1}{2}$ hours at Clovelly, minus $1\frac{1}{4}$ hours at Bideford and Woolacombe, minus 1 hour at Ilfracombe and Lynmouth.

1 Clovelly   Some conger, bass and small pollack are taken from the harbour wall and adjoining rock marks. It is exceptionally easy to get snagged on the sea bed hereabouts, but sandy patches should produce the occasional small-eyed ray. Huss come to fish baits cast out on night tides.

2 Westward Ho!   Sand-eels fished in the surf at the mouth of the estuary or into the sandy ground near rocks at the southern end of this beach will catch bass, with the best part of the season in June and September. Wrasse and pollack are taken from nearby rock marks which are not very deep. Some bass, too, on artificial lures and float-fished sand-eel.

3 Appledore   Bass are the main attraction round here. Fish from the estuary shore (either side), from jetties, at Braunton Pill, and in the surf on Saunton Sands. Sand-eel is the best bait, with king ragworm a useful alternative. Peeler crab gathered in the estuary also works. When the water is clear, artificial lures can be used with success from most of the vantage points. Further inside the estuaries, flounders on harbour ragworms provide good sport, especially early in the year. Where deeper water is found, small-eyed and occasional thornback rays take sand eel-bait. Fish two hours each side of high water. More information from B & K Angling Supplies, 14 The Quay, Appledore, Bideford (Tel: Bideford (02372) 4613).

4 Baggy Point Braunton Sands offer good surf bass fishing. The sand here shelves very gently, so it is wise to put a bit of power behind your casts, fishing close to the rocks at Baggy Point. Bass, dogfish and the occasional conger and ray are taken from flat Saunton Reef and, where access is possible, from the rocks around the headland. Note that this deep-fissured rock can prove treacherous to the unwary, so ensure that if there is a gully between you and dry land that you are clear of the area before the flood tide cuts you off.

5 Woolacombe Night fishing on a flooding tide with a good westerly wind behind it will often produce good catches of bass, especially in June and September. Sand-eel, ragworm, crab and lugworm produce results, although other surf baits like razorfish would also work, but are not available locally. One of the better places is close to the rocks that form the northern side of Baggy Head. Some rays are also taken here. Morte Point, at the other end, produces reasonable rays and smallish conger around the high tide. Occasional tope have been landed here, using fish baits, by anglers fishing the north east side. More information about this area from K. E. Morgan, Rod 'n Reel, 48 Bear Street, Barnstaple (Tel: Barnstaple (0271) 5191).

6 Ilfracombe Fishing from the pier, which is open all day, produces pollack, garfish, pouting and flatfish by day, with conger eels, bass, dogfish and rays coming closer at night. Mackerel, squid, sand-eel, ragworm and lugworm are the popular baits, and the best time is when a westerly wind is blowing. During the peak summer months, try early and late in the day for the plentiful thick-lipped mullet. In winter, bull huss, spur dogfish and cod take over from the bass, with crab, worm and fish baits scoring well. The pier

toll and car parking are very cheap. The north side is rocky-bottomed, the south sandy. Similar species are taken from several rocky ledges and small beaches around the town. More information from The Sports Centre, 139 High Street, Ilfracombe (Tel: Ilfracombe (0271) 64546).

7 Combe Martin To the west of this picturesque bay lies Watermouth Cove where the British shore-caught record coalfish was caught – a freak, as are so many records, of course, but the area has that feel about it that ancient cartographers must have experienced when they wrote 'here be monsters' on their maps. There are several useful fishing stations along here, so to walk about is likely to pay dividends. Not only are species like those at Ilfracombe taken, but the occasional tope, too. At Combe Martin itself, the beach is not over-productive, although a few bass are taken, together with small species from nearby rocks. Besides, the place becomes packed out with holiday makers during the summer season. More information and ideas from Clem's Tackle Shop, 5 The Quay, Ilfracombe (Tel: Ilfracombe (0271) 63460).

8 Lynton Beaches to the west, at Heddon's Mouth, produce good conger, dogfish, rays and some bass. At Lee Bay, a rolling surf produces bass over the low water period using the baits outlined earlier. The sea bed is rougher at Woody Bay and back towards Lynmouth. Pollack, pouting, small conger eels and some flatfish are taken, along with a few bass. To the east, impressive Foreland Point is virtually inaccessible from the shore. Fishing tackle shops at Lynmouth also sell lingerie and souvenirs, so do not expect first class specialist information!

Bait Areas

Mackerel are available from most rock marks, and prawns can be drop-netted from many of the rocks and piers. Mussels are also used locally, and these may be gathered at Instow, Morte Point, Ilfracombe and various other places. Bait digging is not allowed in Ilfracombe Harbour from April to September – but it is not very good anyway.

A Ragworms and lugworms
B Sand-eels
C Peeler crab

FOR THE FAMILY

Devon's north coast has fine cliff scenery and sands, the historic seafaring towns of Bideford and Barnstaple, access inland to the beauties of Exmoor, the seaside attractions of Ilfracombe and picturesque spots like Lynton, Lynmouth and Clovelly.
Valley of the Rocks west of Lynton towards Woody Bay. Wonderful walking country on part of the North Devon coast footpath.
Exmoor National Park has unlimited prospects for family picnics and exploration, walking or pony trekking.
Lundy Island a day return from Ilfracombe takes you to this peaceful island of granite cliffs, seals and seabirds.
Hartland Point Lighthouse you can visit the lighthouse on its rocky headland and Clovelly nearby.
Braunton Burrows National Nature Reserve. Two nature trails along dunes and on the seashore.
Arlington Court nr Barnstaple. Fine Regency house with gardens and park. Collections, displays, horse-drawn carriages, rides, Shetland ponies.

Above: The cast-off shell. These crabs are a favourite bass bait.
Below: A soft-velvet swimming crab.

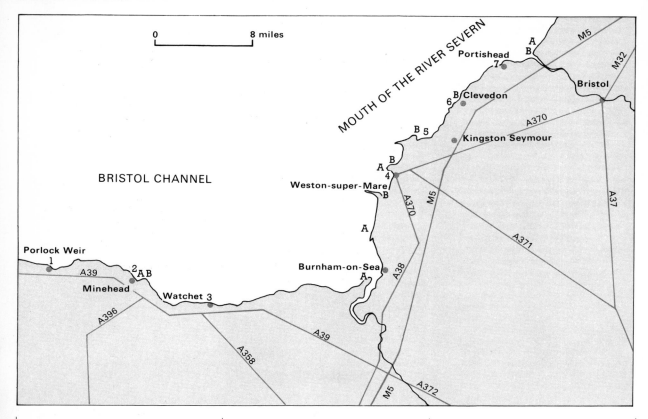

At Porlock Weir there is a good sandy beach extending round to the headland at Hurtstone Point where the land falls steeply to the sea. There is sand and rock below the headland, with more sand at the popular holiday resort of Minehead and the shallow flats of Blue Anchor Bay. Rocky outcrops are rare, the northern rim of Exmoor lying further inland. There are areas of shallow reef around Watchet, and shallow areas of flat rock and sand are frequent towards Burnham-on-Sea, an area characterised by several miles of sand and mud flats that dry out at low water and over which the Bristol Channel tide floods at an amazing pace. Not even the National Trust's headland, Brean Down, south of Weston-Super-Mare does much to break up this area of flats and shallow gullies. Another National Trust headland, Middle Hope, has shallow reef at its base, but almost unbroken sands stretch round to Clevedon, with mud and rubble becoming more common at Portishead and on up to the Severn Bridge. Although this latter area produces good fish for

canny locals, such shallow grounds, fast tides and an increasingly muddy and despoiled shoreline are unlikely to appeal to many visiting anglers.

Boats may be chartered to fish the productive Bristol Channel at Minehead, from which a dozen or so craft operate, Weston-Super-Mare offers several boats and one or two other places along this coast – if you are not too anxious about facilities. The fisherman with his own boat on a trailer will find reasonable launching facilities at Minehead, Watchet, Combwich (at The Harbour Garage, launching into the River Parrett), Burnham-on-Sea, Weston-Super-Mare (several places), Clevedon and Bristol. The shoreline is very shallow in many places, and the tides fast. This coupled with a wind – even a force 4 – against the tide and very tricky seas will build up within minutes. This is an area where it is highly unwise to take chances.

Tidal variance from London Bridge is around 5 hours after high tide there. At Minehead, high water is some 40 minutes earlier than at the mean port, Avonmouth, with this time decreasing

the closer one goes towards that port.

Weston Sea Angling Club has a club house at Knightstone Harbour.

1 Porlock Weir Spring tides produce the best results in this area, even though it is not noted for tremendous fishing. The usual local species are caught, but not in great numbers. There is better fishing along Bossington Beach towards Hurtstone Point where the tide race forms. Occasional tope have been taken here on fish baits, together with dogfish, rays and a few bass.

2 Minehead Thick-lipped grey mullet, bass, small conger eels, rays and dogfish are taken from the harbour wall. Some good bass and sole are taken from the sandy shore hereabouts, though the average run of bass is little larger than school bass size. Better fish come close when there is a reasonable surf running. More details from Minehead Sports, 55 The Avenue, Minehead (Tel: Minehead (0643) 3423).

3 Watchet There are some reasonable bass from beaches hereabouts, with better fish coming from shallow reefs inshore and mullet from the harbour wall at Watchet, together with some winter cod. Nearby, at Blue Anchor Bay, reasonable catches of cod are taken under favourable winter conditions by long casters. Summer fishing is for bass, which bite better close to the rocks, and flatfish. Dogfish, pouting and whiting also grace these beaches. At St Audries Bay, better bass, conger eels and some rays are taken, too. Similar fishing continues round to Hinkley Point, with high water at night producing the best results. Strangers should consider a daylight visit at low tide an essential preparation for a night session. With so much shallow ground at Burnham-on-Sea, the best fishing is for bass – mainly school bass – in the estuary of the River Parrett, and for flounders, the ubiquitous silver eels and, for the specialist, thick-lipped grey mullet. Details from Exmoor Guns & Fishing, 3 The Parade, Minehead (Tel: Minehead (0643) 2736).

4 Weston-super-Mare Species in summer are conger, bass, thornback rays, pouting and flounders. Winter fishing produces whiting and some reasonable cod fishing. Brean Down and Berrow Sands used to be well liked by locals, who now prefer, it seems, to fish rocky promontories. Brean Down offers good conger fishing, but the sea bed is very rough so plenty of spare sinkers are required. The harbour wall at Knightstone gets crowded in summer and offers only small fish. The Old Pier offers reasonable sport, but is closed after 4.30 in winter when guard dogs patrol. At Kew Stoke, the beach is reached via a toll road between Sand Bay and Weston. The paths are well worn and hard to miss. Winter fishing produces whiting and cod. Summer fishing, when the area becomes rather crowded, is mainly for silver eels, flounders, sole and some conger eels. Sand Point itself is less good in winter than it is in summer for mullet, bass and conger eels. The rough bottom means likely snagging, but is worth the effort. Fishing from the rocks at low tide produces bass on standard baits. Ideal weather conditions should be hot, still and almost thundery. More details from 79's Tackle, Soundwell Road, ... (Tel: Bristol (0272) 567371); ...water Guns Ltd, 22 St Marys Rocky Bridgewater (Tel: Bridgewater coves a.23441); Guncraftsman Ltd, sea-ang ird Street, Weston-Super-

Mare (Tel: Weston-Super-Mare (0934) 33111) and Weston Model Aero and Angling Supplies, 1 Oxford Street, Weston-Super-Mare (Tel: Weston-Super-Mare (0934) 21031).

5 Kingston Seymour Fishing from the sea wall at high tide produces bass in summer on locally-dug king ragworms. Also flounders and some conger, though these are likely to be rather small. Although the area fishes at any state of tide, the extensive mud around the low tide period can fox the visitor. Also, grapnel leads are required when the ebb tide is fast retreating back down the Bristol Channel. These tides, which disturb so much silt as they pour back and forth, make the water invariably dirty, thus precluding spinning along here – and few mackerel make their way up here anyway. The tides make float fishing hard, too, for the tackle is hard to control.

6 Clevedon Ladye Bay is one of the most consistent areas around here. At low tide, fishing is carried out from exposed sand-bars, while at high water it is possible – and safer – to fish from the ledges. Thornback rays, conger eels, silver eels, pouting, bass and flounders are taken from here during the summer months, with cod, codling and whiting making up the winter catches. The best state of tide is generally around the slack water period at each end, ie over low tide or high tide. The currents are very fast in between. Some people are even of the opinion that it is unfishable over a spring tide.

7 Portishead Redcliffe Bay fishes well in summer for bass, conger, pouting and silver eels. Grey mullet are frequently taken in the nets along here, but are not catchable with a rod because the tides are too fierce to allow a sensible groundbaiting campaign to be launched. In winter, cod and whiting are caught, and in a good year the codling will be around for a good while into the New Year. Best bait is locally-dug ragworm or blow lugworm which is plentiful around here. At Battery Point, which is reached via the promenade at Portishead, fishing at high tide produces whiting and occasional codling in autumn, also the occasional flounder. Tides around here are very fast indeed. More details on this area can be had from several of the 20 or so fishing tackle shops in the Bristol area, although most are freshwater orientated.

Bait Areas
There may not be spectacular fishing around here, but the bait beds are notable. In the dirty water of the Bristol Channel, smelly baits work best, but they must be fresh. The ragworm is found among shingle or under the larger rocks. Lugworm is best dug by trenching. Some crab may be found in June under areas of rubble, but is otherwise scarce.
A Lugworm
B Ragworm

FOR THE FAMILY
A varied coast with many places of interest – coastal towns and villages along Bridgwater Bay, Exmoor and the Quantocks, Glastonbury, Cheddar Gorge and Wookey Hole Caves (with Madame Tussauds Storerooms and Nature Trail). A great area for riding and walking.
W. Somerset Railway 20 miles of pleasurable preserved steam line – Minehead to Bishop's Lydeard. Apr–Sept. Somerset & Dorset Railway Museum at Washford.
Fleet Air Arm Museum Yeovilton. A mecca for aircraft fans. Naval Air Service history and a Concorde museum.
Butlins at Minehead open to day visitors. The entrance fee gives access to all the funfair and sporting facilities.
Dunkery Beacon an enjoyable climb to the highest point in Exmoor for a fine view across the Bristol Channel to Wales.
Cricket St Thomas between Chard and Crewkerne. Interesting zoo and wildlife park with 'wildlife valley', tropical aviary.
Dunster picturesque village sheltering under the castle with terraced gardens. Castle open May–Sept. Picnic site nearby.

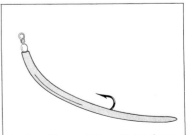

Basic rubber eel. Sometimes these produce as effectively as modern, more seductive designs.

Avon, Gwent and Glamorgan

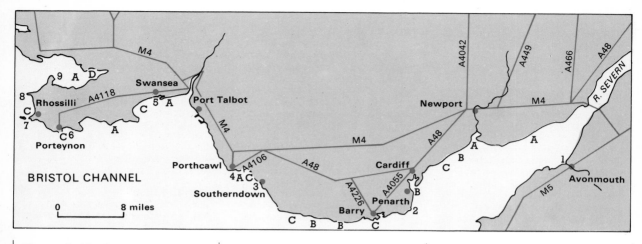

Estuary dockland at Avonmouth is barely worth visiting. Both sides of the Bristol Channel hereabouts have a foreshore of sand, mud and stony rubble. The water is shallow and fast moving, making shore fishing less than easy. This type of ground continues to Cardiff. East of Penarth the beaches are more interesting, though mainly rocky as at Ranny Bay. There is sand again at St Mary's Bay but it is rocky again from Sully Island round to Barry. This type of mixed foreshore continues round to Porthcawl where a sand/mud foreshore runs round to Mumbles Head, itself pretty stony. From here the mixed ground continues to sandy Oxwich Bay, then becomes increasingly rocky towards the Worm's Head, itself a magnificent, though esoteric, promontory. The magnificent sandy storm beach at Rhosili Bay leads into the sandy, shoaly Loughor Estuary.

Shore fishing for bass, thick-lipped mullet, diverse species of ray, plaice, flounders, dabs, conger eels, silver eels, plenty of dogfish, some tope and smooth hounds, mackerel, pollack, small coalfish and some garfish occupies the summer months. Quite a few late bass, big cod, codling, small pollack and whiting are taken in winter. The further out from the Severn Estuary one travels, the better the fishing.

Offshore there is more of the same, especially tope, thornback, blonde and small-eyed rays, bass, very good winter cod, smooth hounds, monkfish, blue and porbeagle sharks.

There is an excellent club house at the Mumbles Motor Boat and Fishing Club, 642 Mumbles Road, Southend,

Swansea (Tel: Swansea (0792) 69646) and at The Sportsman's Club, The Esplanade, Porthcawl (Tel: Porthcawl (065 671) 3975).

Weather information can be obtained from Swansea (0792) 8011 or Cardiff (0222) 8091. The Meteorological Office at Rhoose airport (Tel: Barry (0446) 710343) and at Gloucester (Tel: Gloucester (0452) 855566) and the Mumbles Coastguard (Tel: Swansea (0792) 66534) can all be approached for a more accurate weather prognosis.

Charter boats can be had from Swansea, Barry Docks, Penarth, Port Talbot and Porthcawl. Contact the individual skippers, some of whom advertise in the angling press.

Slipways for the offshore angler with his own boat may be found at Oxwich Bay (small craft only), Aberavon, Caswell Bay, The Mumbles (several), Port Talbot, Barry, Cardiff, Penarth, Porthcawl and St Donats. Check first for suitability to the size of craft you intend to bring, and for any pre-conditions or special regulations.

High water at Barry is about 5 hours, and at Porthcawl 4½ hours, after London Bridge times.

1 Avonmouth to Newport
The locals use skill and guile to extract fish from this sea area, but unless the visitor is in search of a real challenge he would be better advised to travel further west. At Newport he will find plenty of help from Dave Richards at 73 Church Street (Tel: Newport (0633) 54910). This shop is the local exchange of expert information. At Redwick, some good codling catches are made from October onwards, this area being the starting point of the peculiar Welsh achievement of

attracting the bulk of the winter cod shoals to the north side of the Bristol Channel. The foreshore at Cardiff is owned by the Port Authority who allow angling only when organised into a competition. No parking is allowed along the beach road, necessitating a long walk. However, good bass fishing can be had – and cod in winter – by casting out into the deep-water channel hereabouts during low spring tides.

2 Penarth–Barry
A very rich area for fishing west of Penarth Pier to Lavenock Point (Ranny Pool) for conger, bass, mullet, flounders, silver eels and thornback rays in summer, whiting, codling and large cod in winter and through to spring. In summer, canny locals float fish near the sewer outfall around low water, catching bass and mullet on bread, harbour ragworm, prawns and frozen cod! Beware of rising tides and crumbling cliffs. The sewer also yields winter conger and cod, though few locals had tried it until the author suggested it on a recent trip.

There are plenty more top rock marks at dangerous Sully Island, Bendrick Rock, Nell's Point, Friar's Point and Cold Knap Point, former home of the British shore-caught record cod. Locals give advice freely if you ask politely. Bull's Nose, Lime Kilns also good areas, and the Lleys at Aberthaw, famous for its thick-lipped mullet records – and for small bass in the outfall. More information from Graham Bowls, 46 Norwood Crescent, Little Coldbrook, Barry (Tel: Barry (0446) 742637).

Further west, the promontories around to Ogmore produce better than most beaches. Long casting is sometimes required on the open beaches. More details from Angling Supplies, 172 Penarth Road, Cardiff (Tel: Cardiff (0222) 20723); C. Thomas 109 High Street, Barry (Tel: Barry (0446) 746598); Clanfields, 24 Winston Square, Colcot, Barry (Tel: Barry (0446) 741707).

3 Southerndown   Thornback and small-eyed rays start in mid-May and go through to July, smooth hounds a few weeks later when the crabs come in – when the bass also start – both spending most of the summer here. Night tides produce best results. Crab scores well for the bass and smooth hounds, squid for the rays. Good bass are also caught at St Donat's Castle. There are plenty of whiting and some codling here in winter. Long casting from open beaches is the most effective, except for the bass.

4 Porthcawl   Good fishing for bass from rocks south east of the town from low water up to half tide. Also Newton Point and Ogmore ledges. Sker Rocks, north east of the town, produce eels, some bass and rays and dogfish. Codling and mainly whiting are caught here on winter nights, all on the early flood tide. More details from G. S. Jackson, 14 Well Street, Porthcawl (Tel: Porthcawl (065 671) 2511).

5 Swansea Bay   Not very good fishing from the shore along here owing to extensive wormy shallows. The piers at Swansea are restricted where access is on Docks Board property. Licenses are available, but the quality of the fishing rarely justifies the effort or the cost. Plenty of good sheltered boat fishing offshore, however, for the small boat angler. Details from Selwyn Jenkins Sports, 45 Station Road, Port Talbot (Tel: Port Talbot (0639) 882787); Capstan House, Beach Street, Swansea (Tel: Swansea (0792) 54756) and Derek Jones, South Dock Bridge, Swansea (Tel: Swansea (0792) 466096).

6 Porteynon   Gower rock bass fishing – and from open beaches in surf – is at its best from June to October from Mumbles Pier, Oxwich Point and Overton. Fish soft crab – plenty of which are available on site – in gullies early on, live mackerel around July. First of the flood and top tide produce the best results. Details from Swansea tackle shops.

7 Rhosili (Rhossilli)   Ledges to the south of the Causeway at Worm's Head (shaped like a submerged dragon) good for peeler-hunting bass in June

and September; they shoal up off Helwick Shoals and Nash Sands in high summer. Pollack, mackerel, wrasse, dogfish, conger eels, some tope, rays on the outer part of Worm Head.

It is an arduous walk to Kitchen Corner of Worm's Head for tope in July/September. Check tides first and do not travel alone. North of Worm's Head lies an excellent surf beach with best results early in the year before the fish move out after sprats. Also excellent thornback and small-eyed rays on frozen sand-eel here.

8 Burry Holms   A tidal island where crab and fish baits score well for bass and occasional rays. Loads of dogfish at times. Boat anglers fishing hereabouts should beware of strong ebb tides pouring from the Loughor Estuary.

9 Broughton Bay   Go through the caravan site and walk across open sands to where the channel narrows. Fish one hour to low water and two hours up for rays, dogfish and some flounders. Tope used to run through here when the main estuary channel came close in, but the river has cut a deeper one further out, in which they run, and where boat anglers catch loads of them.

Bait Areas

No shortage of bait in this area. Plenty of tackle shops and food shops stock squid, which, when fresh, is very useful. There are masses of peeler crab locally, with edible and velvet swimming crabs outfishing shore crabs for much of the time. Lugworm is available, also ragworm, though this requires some work. Clams and razorfish are found on lugworm beds.

A   Lugworm
B   Ragworm
C   Crab
D   Shellfish

FOR THE FAMILY
Much to see and do on both sides of the Bristol Channel – with access to Bristol and Bath, Chepstow, Newport, Cardiff, Barry, Porthcawl and Swansea, to sandy beaches, the Quantocks and Mendip Hills, the Forest of Dean and the Brecon Beacons National Park

Claverton Manor   Bath. Overlooking the Avon Valley. American museum. Rooms and USA exhibits from 17th-19thC. Gardens. Much to see in Bath itself – from Roman to Regency architecture.

SS Great Britain   Gt Western Dock, Bristol. Brunel's great Atlantic steamship. See the restoration in progress. Visit the Industrial Museum.

Tropical Bird Gardens   Rode nr Trowbridge. Hundreds of exotic birds in lovely natural surroundings. Gardens, lake.

Dan-yr-Og Show Caves   Abercrave. Fantastic tour of vast caves of weird shape and colours. Nearby dinosaur park with reconstructed monsters.

Cardiff Castle   Welsh National Museum, Welsh Folk Museum and among the capital city's many attractions for a day out.

Rhosili Nature Trail   Gower Coast. Cliff walk, interesting seabirds, limestone flora – from Gower Countryside Centre.

Off-shore sand banks offer large shoals of bass in high summer.

Dyfed

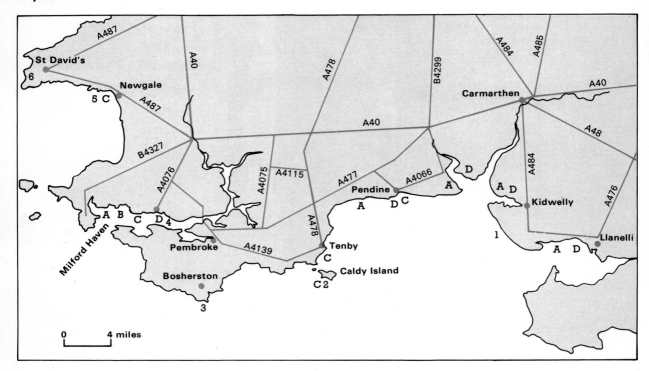

The sandy sweep of Carmarthen Bay opens with Cefn Sidan (the silken sands), but rocky outcrops break up the sands between Amroth and Tenby. From here round to St David's the sandy beaches are limited to small bays at Lydstep Haven, Freshwater East, Barafundle Bay, Broad Haven and the beaches each side of Rickets Head, south of Newgale where there are some interesting rock platforms. Unlike the gentler rock marks further south, many of these are steep, sometimes precipitous, giving on to deep water close inshore. This part of Wales offers much to the serious shore fisherman who wishes to escape from summer holiday crowds and few places are better for this than Caldy Island.

Charter boats are to be found at Burry Port, Llanelli, Pembroke Dock, Saundersfoot, Tenby, Burton, Milford Haven and Dale. Contact the individual skippers via tackle shops or through advertisements in the angling press. Slipways exist at Burry Port, Saundersfoot, Tenby, Pembroke Dock (several), Hobbs Point, Lawrenny. Llangwm, Neyland, Milford Haven, Dale, and St David's Other sites are available for those with small craft that can be manhandled across the beach, but these are not

advised for serious offshore fishing. High tide is generally 4½ hours after London Bridge times.

Weather information can be gathered from telephone numbers listed in the previous section, also from the coastguard at St Ann's Head (Tel: Dale (064 65) 218), and Aberporth RAE Meteorological Station (Tel: Aberporth (0239) 810117).

Gunnery, rocket and bomb firing ranges extend out to sea between Burry Port and Pendine, Caldy Island and Freshwater West. Take care when planning an offshore trip. Sadly, the noise of these hostilities severely disturbs the ambience of this lovely coastline.

1 Cefn Sidan and the Storm Beaches
This is blue water Wales. There is limited winter fishing, but the summer night-time surfs can be excellent for bass – trammel nets permitting – from May to November with a mid-summer lull. Surf beaches where ragworm, lugworm, crab, sand-eel, razorfish and clams take bass and good flounders are to be found all along Cefn Sidan and at Pendine Sands, Marros Sands (with its murderously steep path), Amroth, Saundersfoot, South Beach (Tenby), Freshwater East, the southern end of Freshwater West on the Castle Martin Peninsula; then

Broad Haven Bay and Frainslake Sands. The first 3 hours of the flood produce the best results at Cefn Sidan – one of the few beaches where white ragworm can be dug. Advice from Barry Llewellyn Sports, Cowell Precinct, Llanelli (Tel: Llanelli (055 42) 3720); also John James, 65 Robinson Street, Llanelli (Tel: Llanelli (055 42) 3981).

2 Caldy Island One of the more beautiful places on Earth from which to fish for bass on a fine day. The magnificent site may account for the monastery's position there. Summer bass are caught in the tidal sound between St Margaret's Island and Caldy Island on crab which is abundant locally (you can fill a two-gallon bucket with prime peelers – all edibles – in June), by spinning and by fly fishing. Sea-trout also hunt around this lonely shore. Advance permission to fish is required from the Father Prior. Access is by ferry from Tenby with a good walk over the cliffs with gulls' nests around your feet. Or launch your own boat, in fine weather, at Tenby for landing close to the Sound.

On the mainland, Giltar Point, south of Tenby, is an excellent spot for crabbing and bass fishing and the place to escape from crowds.

3 Barafundle Bay Dogfish, rays, monkfish and good tope from the rock ledge on the south side of this bay during the summer months. Mackerel spinning is excellent at high water and provides the very best bait. The tope also come in at high water. Similar fishing is to be had at St Govan's Head and on round to Frainslake. Local expert knowledge is essential. Contact Fisherman's Friend, Willing House, Main Street, Pembroke (Tel: Pembroke (064 63) 2893); Morris Bros, 37 Main Street, Pembroke (Tel: Pembroke (064 63) 5767) and Frank Donovan, 61 Bush Street, Pembroke Dock (Tel: Pembroke (064 63) 2756).

4 Pembroke Dock and Milford Haven Fishing in this industrial landscape is less productive than it was before the docks and oil refineries sullied the waters. There is much better fishing elsewhere. However, the mullet fishing inside this sheltered water can be very good.

5 Newgale The shallow surf beach here is good on the ebb tide in summer for bass and flounders, with winter whiting and a few codling. Night tides around low water produce the best results. Some nice bass are taken from the rock ledges at Nolton Haven to the south. Sheltered St Bride's Bay provides good inshore dinghy fishing for tope, skate, pollack, gurnard, and mackerel. Dangerous currents run outside the bay, so get local advice. Tackle and information from County Sports, 3 Old Bridge, Haverfordwest (Tel: Haverfordwest (0437) 3740) also T. Newing & Sons, 13 Hamilton Terrace, Milford Haven (Tel: Milford Haven (06462) 3180).

6 St David's Mackerel, pollack, wrasse and conger are taken from rocks around high water using standard rock fishing techniques. Some bass are taken on evening and night-time flood tides in early and late summer at Whitesand Bay. Bait with razorfish, lugworm, sand-eels. By day surf-boarders interfere. Best rock marks are between Porth Clais and St David's Head and similarly on to Abermawr. Beware of very strong currents around the headlands. Advice from Chapman's Fishing and Shooting, 25 Nun Street, St David's (Tel: St David's (043788) 301) also R. O. Evans, 10 High Street, St David's (Tel: St David's (043788) 339)

Bait Areas
Plenty of bait can be had from here. Rock marks produce plenty of mackerel. Herring and squid is freely available frozen from tackle shops. However, local fish markets provide the freshest fish baits and, as a general rule, are always worth investigating.

A Lugworm
B Ragworm
C Crab
D Shellfish

Sadly, some of the best bait collecting grounds at Milford Haven require a boat for access, such as Kilpaison, because of dock installations and oil refineries.

Top: Night tides in Welsh estuaries produce many flounders like this. Below: A big pollack is hooked while the boat drifts over a wreck.

FOR THE FAMILY
Castles, sandy beaches, and a spectacular coastal footpath are the main features of this beautiful coast, with Carmarthen, Pembroke, and Tenby as its main centres. Walking, sailing, riding, birdwatching, coastal trips and all kinds of seaside activity with visits to islands included.

Pembroke and Manorbier Castles contrasting examples of finely preserved 12th–14thC castles, the former towering massively above the town, the latter compact (and still lived in) guarding an inlet of the sea. Both open May–Sept.

Bosherston Lily Ponds lakeside paths beside acres of waterlilies leading to a sandy shore (and sea fishing).

Pendine Sands 6 miles of firm sands once used for speed records. A chance for the children to explore rockpools.

From Tenby interesting in itself, take the boat to Caldy Island with its monastery and fine cliff walks.

Graham Sutherland Gallery Picton Castle on the River Cleddau nr Haverfordwest. Fine collection of the artist's work in recently built gallery in lovely castle grounds.

Manor House Leisure Park St Florence, nr Tenby. In 12 acres of wooded grounds there are animals, birds, reptiles and aquarium – plus adventure playground, picnic area, pets corner, bar and cafe.

Dyfed

The area is generally quite rocky, with deep water close in to the shore, interspersed with small sandy bays: Abereiddy Bay, Aber Mawr, Fishguard, Newport, Poppit Sands at Cardigan, Penbryn Sands, Llangranog, and New Quay. Around Aberaeron the beaches are a mixture of rock and stones, such ground continuing northwards to Aberystwyth, which has a few pleasant sandy coves. Beyond Borth lies the broad sweep of sand which runs northwards for many miles to the Dovey estuary and beyond.

The fishing here is mixed. Tope, rays, dogfish and conger eels can be taken from some rock marks, along with mackerel and garfish and pollack. The open beaches provide good fishing for bass, usually when there is good surf running, and flounders. Some dogfish and the occasional ray – even tope – are caught from these beaches when there is not much wind to drive the waves. Offshore lies some of the best mixed fishing in England for tope, rays, bull huss, turbot, conger, monkfish and sharks.

Charter boats may be found at Fishguard, Newport, Goodwick, Cardigan, St Dogmaels, New Quay, Gwbert-on-Sea, Aberystwyth and Aberdovey. The Endeavour group of boats operating out from Aberystwyth are well known to readers of the angling press.

Slipways exist at Fishguard (several) Newport (four on the town side of the Nevern estuary), Aberaeron, Cardigan, New Quay, Borth, Aberystwyth and Aberdovey.

Check the weather first before launching, either from numbers listed in the Avon section or in the telephone book, or from the Fishguard coastguard (Tel: Fishguard (0348) 3449). High tide is 6 hours after London Bridge at Aberystwyth, and 5½ hours earlier at Fishguard.

A local mine of information is at the Aberystwyth Sea Angling and Yacht Club, The Harbour, Aberystwyth (Tel: Aberystwyth (0970) 612158).

1 Abereiddy Bay Sandy ground close to steep rock is typical here, allowing the angler to explore for the best pollack, mackerel, wrasse, tope and ray marks. Spin, float fish or leger in this stretch of blue coastal water. You will find some bass, but they prefer less steep rocks. Strumble Head Lighthouse is within casting distance of very deep water. Watch out for extra large swells while fishing the rock ledges.

2 Fishguard Some rays, conger eels and bull huss are caught from the port breakwater – but small pollack, pouting, plaice, dabs and flounders are more common. Good mackerel, pollack, conger, ray and tope fishing is to be had from the promontories from Fishguard Bay round Dinas Head to Newport Bay. Very hot calm summer spells bring the odd porbeagle shark within casting range here. There are more bass in the Nevern estuary than at Fishguard and they often take spinners – sometimes fly tackle. Plenty of thick-lipped mullet are taken on bread and harbour ragworm in the harbours and from some rock marks. Try also local sewer outfalls. More information from Beynon's Fishing Tackle, Temple House, Newport (Tel:

Newport (0239) 820265) also Fishguard Yacht and Boat Co, Main Street, Goodwick, Fishguard (Tel: Fishguard (0348) 873377.

3 Cardigan There is good mackerel and pollack spinning in summer in the sound opposite Cardigan Island and from other rock ledges around to Ceibwr Bay to the west and Traeth-y-Mwnt to the east. Watch out for heavy swells. Excellent bass – and a chance of a sea-trout – are taken in the mouth of the River Teifi, legering inside or outside the estuary mouth. Plenty more bass are to be found close to rocky outcrops at Traeth Penbryn and Tresaith beaches. Headlands here fall – a reasonable cast away – to clean sand. Excellent rock ledges at Llangranog provide good fishing with fish baits for tope, pollack, dogfish, thornback and small-eyed rays, conger and gurnard. Wrasse, dabs, pouting, whiting and rockling take smaller baits of worm or mollusc.

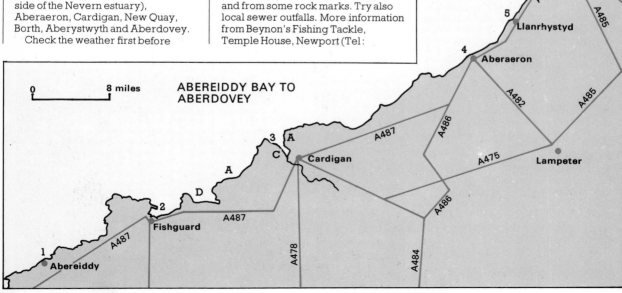

ABEREIDDY BAY TO ABERDOVEY

0 — 8 miles

Tackle and details from M & A Williams, 10a Pendre, Cardigan (Tel: Cardigan (0239) 2038) also Teifi Sports, 4 Black Lion Mews, Cardigan (Tel: Cardigan (0239) 3679).

4 Aberaeron (Aberayron)   A small harbour that holds good mullet. The sea bed is fiercely rocky in this area, and at New Quay Headland. Summer and autumn spinning and float fishing for mackerel, wrasse and pollack (using crab, lugworm or mussel for the wrasse). Unless you can obtain precise local knowledge, bottom fishing for conger eels and bull huss is too costly in terms of lost tackle and snagged fish to justify the effort. The promontory of Carreg Ina has good crab fishing for bass in summer.

5 Llanrhystyd   Very stony beaches, these, and a heavy surf will be continuously dragging tackle on to rocks. Either the rocks or the river mouths here give up the odd good bass from time to time, but the fishing is not consistent.

6 Aberystwyth   A university town with a renowned faculty of marine biology is hardly likely to be set in an ecological Sahara. There is a great deal of good fishing here, both on and offshore. Excellent bass fishing can be had from rock ledges, along with a few dogfish and, late in the year, whiting. Even though much of the shoreline is inaccessible, there is some spinning and float fishing for mackerel and pollack. More varied is the offshore potential. Details from Endeavour DSAC, Schooners

A record catch of plaice.

Landing, St David's Wharf, Pen Yr Anchor, Aberystwyth (Tel: Aberystwyth (0970) 612818). Tackle and bait from J. E. Rosser, 3 Queen Street, Aberystwyth (Tel: Aberystwyth (0970) 7451).

7 Aberdovey   Flatfish are taken in and around this estuary on worms and shellfish. Flounders come down to the sea to spawn in February. Some bass are taken in the channels and during surf conditions close to the river mouth, along with the occasional ray. The best time to fish is on the third tide after a good blow. Tackle and information from W. D. Evans & Son, London House, Seaview Terrace, Aberdovey (Tel: Aberdovey (065 472) 353), or from Charles Bartlett, 52 Sandilands Road, Aberdovey (Tel: Aberdovey (0654) 710869).

Bait Areas
Not the best of bait collecting grounds around here, although sheltered ground inside estuaries produces the best results.
A   Lugworm
C   Crab
D   Shellfish

FOR THE FAMILY
From the rocky coast of St David's to the Dovey estuary, west Dyfed has many good places to visit – Aberystwyth, Cardigan and Fishguard, the Preseli mountains, and Devil's Bridge.
Cenarth Falls   inland from Cardigan, where you may watch salmon leaping and Welsh coracles nearby at Cilgerran.
Vale of Rheidol Railway   one of Wales's finest 'Little Trains'. A spectacular 11-mile run from Aberystwyth to Devil's Bridge. Easter–Oct. 300 ft waterfalls.
Strumble Head   nr Fishguard. A visit to the lighthouse by bridge from the cliffs. Look for seals and seabirds from this exciting section of the Pembroke Coastal Way which stretches over 160 miles from Newport to Amroth.
St David's   the Cathedral and the Bishop's Palace on a coastal promontory. Well worth a visit. Take the boat to Ramsey Island from St Justinian.
Centre for Alternative Technology Machynlleth. Ideas of the future, solar energy, new technology in a forest setting. Visitors welcome.

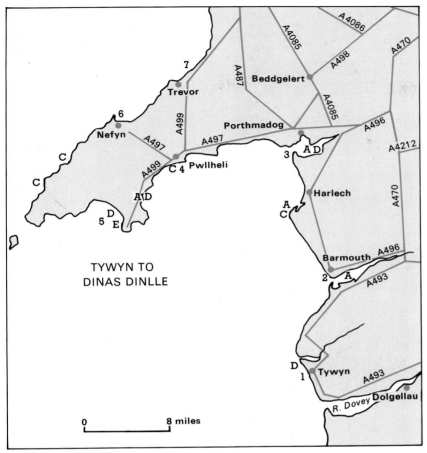

TYWYN TO
DINAS DINLLE

0   8 miles

on Anglesey (Tel : Valley (0407) 2288).

High Tide is earlier than at London Bridge by 6 hours at Pwllheli, 4 hours at Caernarvon.

1 Tywyn (Towyn) This is an area of surf beaches with some good bass early and late in the year. School bass are more common with the occasional decent fish among them. Plenty of flounders grace these beaches and, when the weather is settled, dogfish. Similar fishing is at the mouth of the River Dysynni, when a good surf is running. Just to the north of the river mouth lies a causeway of rocks. Bass and sea-trout sometimes shoal up around here, waiting to run the river. Upstream is a tidal lagoon from which some good flounders are taken. More details from The Sports Shop, 6 College Green, Tywyn (Tel : Tywyn (0654) 710722).

2 Barmouth There is some fair bass fishing from the estuary and viaduct on crab and sand-eel bait or artificial lures, and plenty of flatfish in the bay. Also stacks of thick-lipped mullet around here. Summer fishing can become complicated when the vast strand that stretches northwards to Mochras becomes populated with fine-weather tourists. But when a southerly wind rolls in a steady surf, better fishing is available. Out in the bay are tope, pollack, rays, bream, flatfish, dogfish, mackerel, gurnard and whiting, especially towards the north west. Fishing is restricted in the area of the harbour. More details are available from W. H. G. Owen, 1 High Street, Barmouth (Tel : Barmouth (0341) 280591) also Allsports and Hobbies, Beach Road, Barmouth (Tel : Barmouth (0341) 280240).

3 Tremadog Bay, East and South Sides There are bass, flounders and mullet on the east side on a flooding tide and more in the lugworm-filled lagoon at Mochras. The island on the south side is private property – a camp site. In the estuary at Traeth Bach some tope run with the tide and can be caught after a very strenuous walk to Harlech Point. Otherwise flounders, plaice and very good bass (at times) are caught in the estuary. Warm, overcast weather, rising pressure and flooding tides combine to produce the best catches, especially at evening light. Offshore there is good fishing for tope, dogfish, rays, pollack, gurnard, plaice and so on in summer, very little in winter. Tackle and details from R. T. Pritchard and Son, Sheffield House, Criccieth

North of Aberdovey lie miles and miles of sandy beaches, barely interrupted by the occasional outcrop of rock, right on up to Tremadog Bay on the southern side of the Lleyn Peninsula. The Lleyn beaches vary widely, from open surf strands like those at Pwllheli, Abersoch and Porth Neigwl (Hell's Mouth) to the precipitous cliffs at Trwyn Cilan and Braich y Pwll. Sand becomes less frequent on the north side of the Lleyn – there is a small beach at Porth Oer (Whistling Sands), another at Porth Golmon.

The fish species around here are largely similar to those further south. With such shallow beaches, deep water species are less evident – tope, for example, are rarely caught from the shore here. In these more northern latitudes, there are more codling to be caught in winter, along with large

Fruits of the storm, a good catch of cod and bass.

shoals of small coalfish which invade the beaches in autumn. Dogfish are a staple for many local fishermen. Offshore the picture is as bright as ever, with plenty of fish, both large and small, to justify the Welsh claim that they have some of the most varied offshore fishing in the British Isles.

If you want a charter boat, you will have to scan the angling press for advertisements or contact tackle dealers locally to get a boat out from Barmouth, Trevor, Nefyn, Abersoch, Caernarvon, Pwllheli. Slipway facilities can be found at Barmouth, Porthmadog (Portmadoc), Abersoch, Criccieth, Pwllheli, and Llanbedrog. Check out the suitability of the slip for the size of craft you intend to use – a few of these slips involve some shoving over the beach.

Weather information can be had from the Barmouth Coastguard (Tel : Barmouth (0341) 500), from weather and coastguard numbers listed in the telephone book, or from RAF Valley

(Tel: Criccieth (076 671) 2116);
Angling and Gun Centre, 11 High
Street, Porthmadog (Tel: Porthmadog
(0766) 2464) also Pugh's Tackle Shop,
94 High Street, Porthmadog (Tel:
Porthmadog (0766) 2392).

4 Tremadog Bay, North Side   The
unrelieved sandy shore at Criccieth
does have a pier from which you can
float fish on summer's evenings with
crab or small fish for bass. Otherwise
it is flounders, plaice, dabs and other
small species – with the odd big bass
just to spice things up. Better fishing
is to be had from Pwllheli Marina,
Gimblet Rock, Llanbedrog and
Abersoch. Bait collected from fertile
Abersoch scores well on the north
side of the Lleyn Peninsula.

5 Lleyn Beaches   Flounders, plaice,
rays and dogfish are taken from
Trwyn Cilan rock ledges, bass from
Porth Ceiriad. The best baits are king
ragworm, sand-eel, soft crab and
razorfish. Codling, small coalfish and
dabs are taken here in winter. At
Porth Neigwl (Hell's Mouth), the beach
is more gentle than the name suggests,
and the best fishing is after a good
blow. The most productive area is
close to the rocks at the southerly end
on the early flood tide. Species found
here are bass, flounders and dogfish.
There is good fishing too around Porth
Cadlan to the west but less good at
Aberdaron where trammel nets
cause problems. Early and late
fishing – at each end of the tourist
season – produces the best results.
At Porth Oer, the beach lies at the
bottom of a steep track, good bass are
taken from the rocks at the southern
end, along with immature coalfish in
autumn, whiting and codling. Small
bass are plentiful along this surf beach
which becomes unfishable at its
northern end during rough weather.
Plenty of rock marks produce
mackerel, small coalfish and
reasonable pollack. Most marks are
hard to get at and give on to a sea-bed
with many snags. No shortage of
wrasse in this type of country.
There is the possibility of a shore tope
at Porth Oer or Porth Golmon, though
the surf bass fishing is more consistent
– if the small species allow the bait to
stay out there long enough. Good bass
at Porth Tywyn and Porth Ysgadan
from the rocks and into the surf after a
good southerly blow. Wrasse,
mackerel and pollack are taken from
projecting rock headlands where
bottom fishing produces some rays
and dogfish. Details from Brian Jones

at Abersoch Craft & Angling Centre,
Abersoch (Tel: Abersoch (075 881)
2646).

6 Nefyn and Trevor   Bass, flounders,
dogfish and dabs on night or early
morning tides are caught using
ragworm, lugworm, razorfish, squid
and fresh mackerel. All this plus
winter cod, whiting and flounders at
Trevor. The best time to fish is early
flood tide at night after a blow onshore.
Sand-eel is a very effective bait here.
At Porth y Nant a steep climb takes you
away from tourist crowds to the
possibility of good mackerel fishing
from rock ledges.

7 Dinas Dinlle   From Trevor north
to the Menai Straits lies one long sandy
strip that produces school bass, rays
and dogfish in summer, whiting, small
coalfish, codling and dabs on dark
tides in winter. The water is invariably
shallow and could produce tope if
tackled correctly, and with abundant
patience, especially at Belan Point on
the Menai Straits. Tides at the point are
fierce even on neap tides and
could prove unfishable on spring
tides. Holidaymakers are often heavily
in evidence so fish early or late, or
above the spot where the road turns
inland north of Dinas. Autumn months
produce good mixed fishing when
some good bass are taken. Bait with
mussel, crab, razorfish, king ragworm
or sand-eel.

Bait Areas
At Abersoch, when the author was last
there, razorfish were being carried
off the beach by the sackful for the
Chinese to eat. Whether this bait area
can tolerate this sort of pressure is
doubtful. So, as ever, it is best to make
a special effort to hunt these superb
baits at low water on big spring tides.
In the Menai Straits giant king
ragworm are found up to three feet
long. One should last a good while!
Crab is sparse around here, though it
can be found in good quantities in the
Menai Straits.
A   Lugworm
C   Crab
D   Shellfish
E   Sand-eels
At Porthmadog there are restrictions
about taking mussels and digging in
the mussel beds.

*A satisfying moment for any sea
angler. The larger bass weighs
$10\frac{1}{4}$lb. Both fish fell to peeler crab bait.*

FOR THE FAMILY
From the peaceful Dovey estuary
north to Anglesey is some of the finest
mountain and coastal scenery in
Britain. No large towns – but rivers,
waterfalls, mountain and forest
walks, beaches, cliff tops, quiet
market towns and many interesting
places to visit in the Snowdonia
National Park.

Panorama Walk and **Precipice Walk**
both near the beautiful Mawddach
estuary, the first at Barmouth the
second among many fine forest and
hilltop walks around Dolgellau.

Harlech Castle   on its rocky perch
with superb views. Nearby Shell
Island is a fascinating spot for shells
and seabirds.

Llechwedd Slate Caverns   Blaenau
Ffestiniog. Mountain Tourist Centre.
Underground ride through
reconstructed 19thC quarry.
Museums, exhibits, panoramic walk,
grotto.

Portmeirion   enjoy a day out in this
Italian architectural fantasy village.
The famous fruit, flower and butterfly-
decorated china is made here. Hotel,
shops, crafts and cafe.

Talyllyn Railway   through lovely
scenery inland from **Tywyn** (museum).

Ffestiniog Railway   a 13-mile scenic
trip from Porthmadog.

Craftsmen at work   at Beddgelert
you can visit one of many craft
potteries and at Dinas Mawddwy
woollen mill you can buy hand woven
clothes or tapestries.

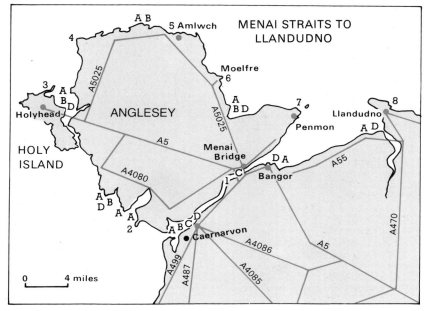

Details from Howards Fishing Tackle, 72 Pool Street, Caernarvon (Tel: Caernarvon (0286) 2671); Ronald Edwards, 6 Dean Street, Bangor (Tel: Bangor (0248) 2811); D. Huxley Jones, 1 South Penrallt, Caernarvon (Tel: Caernarvon (0286) 3186) and Tackle & Guns, Devon House, Water Street, Menai Bridge (Tel: Menai Bridge (0248) 714508).

2 Llanddwyn Island Some bass along with codling, whiting, rays, small pollack and coalfish, flounders, plaice and dabs are taken from the clear ground between rocky promontories. Plenty of dogfish too, which are often first to find the bait. In autumn, after a sou'westerly blow, neighbouring sandy beaches produce good bass. Similar species are found at Malltraeth and Aberffraw beaches. Lugworm, ragworm, crab and fish strips produce results, and sometimes spinning or fly fishing pays off for shoaling school bass, mackerel, small pollack and immature coalfish.

3 Holyhead Sandy and stony beaches at Porth Penrhyn and Penthos produce bass, dabs and flounders on ragworm, crab and lugworm. Lots of thick-lipped mullet are found in sheltered areas around Holy Island. Deep water close in to the harbour piers produces bass, rays, conger, dogfish, flatfish and the occasional tope. This is a good mark for winter codling and whiting. Between North Stack and Penrhyn Mawr are several good rock platforms from which to leger bait or spin for bass, float fish for wrasse, pollack and small coalfish. Similar mixed fishing exists at Trearddur Bay and Rhoscolyn Bay and round to Rhosneigr. For more details contact R. P. Owen, Stanley House, Old Market Square, Holyhead, (Tel: Holyhead (0407) 2458); R. V. Thomas, County Sports, County Buildings, Stanley Street, Holyhead (Tel: Holyhead (0407) 2059) also J's Fishing Parlour, 16 Newry Street, Holyhead (Tel: Holyhead (0407) 4171).

4 Carmel Head On the south side, at Church Bay, legered or float-fished crab will catch bass among the rocks while fish baits pushed out onto the sand pick up rays and dogfish. Worm baits catch plaice, dabs and flounders. To the east at Cemlyn Bay the strand fishes well for surf bass after a nor'westerly blow, especially as the tide ebbs out from the lagoon – a nature reserve. Rock ledges towards Carmel Head produce pollack and coalfish on artificial lures.

The beaches around the Isle of Anglesey are among the most varied in Britain. Walk round a headland from a small sandy bay and you are likely to find an identical bay – but full of boulders. The Menai Straits produce good fish even though – or because – the tides are very fierce through here. The windward side of Anglesey is said to be the most productive area. Between the island and the mainland, shallow Colwyn Bay is well sheltered from the prevailing winds, making it a useful spot for the fisherman with his own boat on a trailer.

Charter boats operate out from Conwy, Deganwy, Beaumaris, Caernarvon, Menai Bridge and Cemaes Bay and Amlwch. Slipways are fairly abundant – but do check on local sea conditions before launching and ensure that your boat is fast enough to make headway into the fierce currents hereabouts. Launch from Conwy, Llandudno, Llanfairfechan, Penmaenmawr, Bryn-Siencyn, Moel-y-Don, Port Dinorwic, Menai Bridge, Beaumaris, Bangor, Amlwch Port, Benllech, Bull Bay, Cemaes Bay, Moelfre or Traeth Bychan. As usual, check on suitability of facilities to the size of your boat and find out if any local restrictions apply.

Weather information can be obtained from the GPO recorded forecast or from the coastguard at Holyhead (Tel: Holyhead (0407) 2051) or RAE Valley near Holyhead (Tel: Valley (0407) 2288). High tide is earlier than at London Bridge by 4 hours at Caernarvon, 3½ hours at Holyhead and 3 hours at Menai Bridge.

Shore fishing around here produces bass in fair numbers, some tope, a few rays, pollack, coalfish, dogfish, wrasse, conger and flatfish in summer, with the winter fishing being largely for codling, whiting, small coalfish and dabs.

1 Menai Straits There is good summer bass fishing on crab, ragworm and mussel at several points inside this Strait. Different marks fish better at specific states of tide. Some tope run into the Strait with the fierce tides (up to 5 knots on spring tides), but they have thinned over the years. Make sure that you do not become so intent on your fishing that you fail to observe a channel filling up with the tide behind you, cutting off escape. Fish the main channels for tope and bass and the creeks and lagoons for flounders and thick-lipped mullet. In some places bass spinning pays off especially for shoaling school bass. Big bass, small wrasse and pollack can be had from the more rocky marks while plaice may turn up wherever the bottom is relatively sandy. Winter months see cod, codling and whiting inside the Strait. Bait with lugworm, mussel, crab etc. The codling linger late in the spring.

5 Amlwch To the west, at Cemaes Bay, the fishing is not too hot, with small species predominant. There is more of interest at Amlwch, a small harbour – but with a restricted area near the underwater pipeline opposite East Mouse Island. Dabs, whiting, codling and dogfish come into the shallow areas, while deeper ground produces conger eels, plaice, wrasse, pollack and coalfish on mackerel, herring, squid, crab, lugworm, ragworm and mussel. Best spots are Trwyn Tew, The Tables, Graig-Ddw, the Breakwater, Llam Carw, Porth Newydd and rocky Point Lynas. This area suffers a hangover from winter and spring fishing does not really get under way until around May. More information from Peter Williams, Amlwch Port Boat Club, 11 Craig y Don, Amlwch Port (Tel: Amlwch (0407) 83169); M. T. Houghton, 1 Mona Street, Amlwch (Tel: Amlwch (0407) 830267) also Anglesey Boat Centre, Beach Road, Cemaes Bay (Tel: Amlwch (0407) 89510).

6 Moelfre Bass, conger eels and a few tope can be caught here in summer on the usual baits. Dabs, whiting and codling come close in on evening tides between September and April, with the better codling fishing starting after Easter. Otherwise, mackerel, pouting, dogfish and pollack are available to the visitor. Nearby sandy beaches are too flat and shallow to entice major predators to within casting range. Stony rocks at Benllech produce similar results as Moelfre.

7 Penmon Fishing for mackerel from this headland at high water with spinners of feathers frequently produces fast and furious sport. At low water slack and on the early flood tide the bass come through and are taken on crab and ragworm. The best time for them is very early and very late in the day. There is bottom fishing for bass and small species from beaches towards Beaumaris.

8 Llandudno Beaches in front of Llanfairfechan, towards Penmaen beach, produce bass on the flooding tide, especially during rough weather, as well as plaice, flounders and dabs. Fishing at the mouth of the Conwy produces large bass at times, starting in June, going through to October. Fish early and late in the day outside hours of peak estuarial traffic. The open sands produce dabs and plenty of dogfish. Details from

Anglers Den, 12 Madoc Street, Llandudno (Tel: Llandudno (0492) 79931).

Bait Areas
Stacks of bait around here, even though it may require some work to obtain the best. The sands are liberally stocked with lugworm, and where rocks lie on sand or grit, big king ragworm up to three feet long can be found. Crabs abound in the Menai Straits.
- **A** Lugworm
- **B** Ragworm
- **C** Crab
- **D** Shellfish

FOR THE FAMILY
Three great castles to visit – Conwy, Caernarvon and Beaumaris and the resorts of North Wales with all their holiday activities. Inland you have the valleys, mountains, waterfalls and lakes of the Snowdonia National Park.

Plas Newydd Isle of Anglesey. Splendid gothic mansion on the Menai Strait within view of the mountains of Snowdonia. Paintings, military museum, gardens, teas. Apr.–Nov.

Museum of Childhood Menai Bridge. This fine collection includes dolls and their houses, toys, games, music boxes going back 150 years. Easter–Oct.

Cabin Lift Gt Ormes Head, Llandudno. One of many attractions is to ride high over the north shore to the 680 ft summit. Descend by the famous tramway.

South Stack Lighthouse see seals and sea birds from the rugged cliffs of Holyhead and visit the lighthouse.

Snowdon from Llanberis you can reach the top (3560 ft) by gently sloping track or the famous cable railway. Do not try other routes unless experienced.

Bodnant Gardens Tal-y-Cafn. One of the finest in Britain. Terraces overlook the River Conwy, waterfall, wild garden, rare and exotic plants. March–Oct.

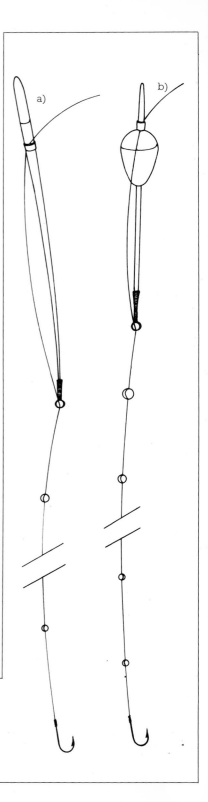

a) *Quill float for mullet fishing in sheltered waters.*

b) *More buoyant float for mackerel, garfish and mullet fishing in choppy conditions.*

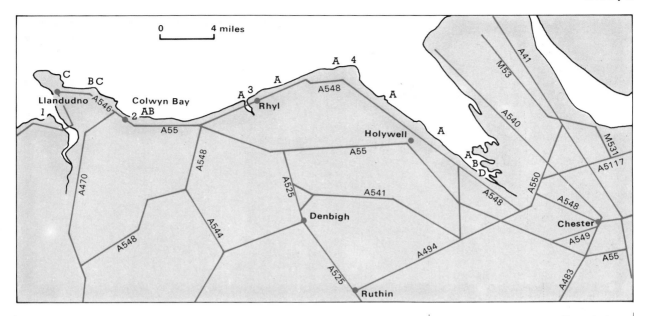

Sheltered from the prevailing winds, this area is one long sandy beach with occasional small rocky areas as at Great Orme's Head, Little Orme's Head, and at various points around Colwyn Bay, and at Rhos-on-Sea. This area is so popular with summer holiday makers that the only peaceful times to fish are early and late in the day. The general beach fishing is hardly spectacular, but fishing from certain areas with specific fish-attracting features can be very rewarding. Main summer species are bass – with a good chance of an outsize specimen – mackerel, pollack, flounders, plaice, the universal dogfish and the occasional ray, with more dogfish, whiting and codling in winter. Offshore sport also includes gurnard (red and tub), better rays and tope.

Tope run the Welsh Channel, but strong tides and shifting channels around the mouth of the Dee Estuary make shore fishing dangerous for the visitor. From a boat, up-tide legering scores well over shallow ground. When fishing the mouth of the Dee remember that there will be powerful out-going currents, together with overfalls on the ebb tide. A great deal of local know-how is required to fish efficiently and safely. Charter boats are available from Conwy, Mostyn and Rhyl. Slipways can be found at Barkby Beach at Prestatyn, Rhyl, Rhos-on-Sea, Colwyn Bay (several). Beach launching is possible at

Large catches of ray like this one are taken each summer by boats out of Amlwch.

Clwyd

Llanddulas and Abergele. High tide at Llandudno is 3 hours before London Bridge times.

Weather information may be obtained from the coastguard at Rhyl (Tel: Rhyl (0745) 53284), though this station is not always manned, and from RAF Valley's meteorological office on Anglesey (Tel: Valley (0407) 2288).

1 Llandudno, North Shore Fish over the last two hours of the ebb tide and the first two hours of the flood for good bass, when some very big ones are taken, between July and September on crab or king ragworm. Other shore species are also about at this time. Night tides produce the best results during the tourist season. Nearby Penrhyn Bay is a noted bass area with very rocky ground. Fish over low ebb and high water with crab and ragworm when the sea is not too rough. Do not cast too far here – the fish are close to the rocks. Bass are to be found around high water at Rhos Point, especially during a northerly blow, as this beach is shingle and sand. Spinning produces results if the water is clear early or late around high water.

2 Colwyn Bay The gullies among the sand produce fish on all states of tide, but mainly dabs, whiting and flounders, all the way through to Old Colwyn from Rhos Point. The Pier here can be fished, mainly for small species and on the ebb tide, only during the day unless there is a disco on a Friday or Saturday night. Below the quarries at Tan-y-Lan, which requires a fair walk along the beach from Old Colwyn, the bass fishing from the rocks under calm sea conditions at low water can be

excellent. This is also a fair winter mark when a bit more distance on those casts will produce good catches of codling. The Colwyn Bay Victoria SAC has its own headquarters and social club, closed on Mondays and Tuesdays, opening other days at 8 pm. More details from Keith Roberts, 45 Princes Drive, Colwyn Bay, (Tel: Colwyn Bay (0492) 30873); Geoff Blazier, Angler's Den, 12 Madoc Street, Llandudno (Tel: Llandudno (0492) 79931) also Stan Ronald at Tackle Box, 50 Sea View Road, Colwyn Bay (Tel: Colwyn Bay (0492) 31104).

3 Rhyl Extensive sandy beaches hereabouts are often deeply gullied and it is these that often produce well for bass, flounders, dabs and eels. Fishing into the surf at low water can be very good for bass, even during daylight, while other species bite best under cover of darkness. On some occasions, and especially during the winter months, it pays to put some power into those casts. Offshore lies excellent summer fishing for rays and tope. Extra details from The Anglers Den, 29 Queen Street, Rhyl (Tel: Rhyl (0745) 54765).

4 Point of Air The sandy mouth of the Dee estuary produces good fish for those with the expert knowledge to venture out on the sand-flats without ending up drowned; so the visitor is advised to join up with somebody who knows this area, or obtain guidance from local tackle shops like William Roberts, 131 High Street, Rhyl (Tel: Rhyl (0745) 53031).

Bait Areas

The area is virtually one large lugworm bed interspersed by ragworm beds and crabbing grounds.

Plenty of excellent bait.

A Lugworm
B Ragworm
C Crab
D Shellfish

A breakwater is shortly to be built, at Rhos Point, jutting 450 yards out to sea. This will produce better fishing, if fishing is allowed here, and good crabbing ground.

FOR THE FAMILY

Plenty of seaside entertainment along the North Wales coast, with Colwyn Bay and Rhyl the main centres and five smaller resorts. Easy access to Snowdonia's mountains, lakes and forests and opportunities for canoeing, sailing, walking and riding.

Rhyl's Marine Lake Leisure Park offers many attractions, especially for children. The Royal Floral Hall, with aquarium and aviary, is worth a visit.

Ruthin in the Vale of Clwyd. Medieval banquets held nightly in Ruthin Castle. Many interesting buildings and local crafts shops.

Welsh Mountain Zoo Colwyn Bay. Birds, animals, reptiles, treetops safari restaurant, children's zoo, in botanical gardens and mountain setting.

Dyserth Falls South of Rhyl. Spectacular 60 ft waterfall. 17thC manor house and Iron Age fort nearby.

Llangollen Canal Museum and cruises, Valle Crucis Abbey and Plas Newydd house and museum.

Grange Cavern Military Museum Holywell. North Wales' largest collection of vehicles and militaria in an unusual underground setting. Picnic area, etc.

United Kingdom casting champion Paul Kerry demonstrates the pendulum cast: 1. The sinker is swung away from the angler. 2. and 3. It is pulled back high above the head. 4. and 5. The angler uses his arms, shoulders and trunk to pull the rod around his body into full compression. 6. This movement peaks at the moment the reel is released.

Merseyside and Lancashire

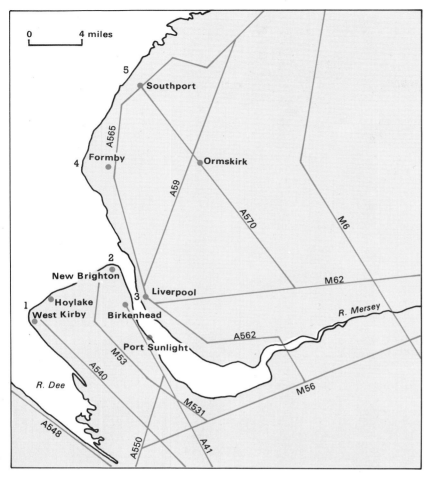

Vast areas of sand, mud and shingle form the shoreline from the mouth of the River Dee round to Liverpool Bay. This heavily built-up and industrialised area produces fish, but it is improbable that the holiday angler would linger here over-long. Much of the waterfront of the River Mersey is taken up with dockland and similar harbour installations. The flat coastal plain north of Liverpool, round Formby to Southport, echoes the almost featureless shoreline of sand and mud along here. The tide goes out a very long way. The estuary of the River Ribble forms a vast firth flanked by wetlands beloved of wildfowl, but not by the shore angler. There is little here to concentrate the fish and although these sands are rich in marine life they are largely too shallow to entice inshore much in the way of predatory fish species.

Tides here are about 2½ hours earlier than those at London Bridge. There are charter boats working out from Preston, Liverpool and Birkenhead, otherwise such craft are thin on the shoreline. Those with their own boat on a trailer may launch at Heswall, West Kirby, Hoylake (several slips), and Wallasey.

Although there is some good fishing for tope, rays, conger eel, cod, whiting, flatfish and so on in summer and also cod and whiting in winter, most of it is offshore. Because the tide goes out so far, local sea anglers set lay lines in distant gullies and retrieve them on the next low tide – an exciting, even if slightly primitive, way of catching fish. Whiting, codling, dabs, flounders, eels and rockling are caught in this way. Locals do not like an easterly wind.

1 Hoylake and West Kirby In addition to the usual local species some mullet are taken in summer. The best state of the tide for general fishing is from low water and upwards. Sand-eel produces bass in summer, and long casting is sometimes essential to contact the fish. At Hoylake the best marks are Dove Point and The Bank. At West Kirby the shore beyond the yacht club or the marine lake are preferred. At low tide it is possible to fish off the marine lake wall into the sea. This lake also becomes populated by summer mullet.

Plenty of fish at this spot! Mark an 'X' on the side of the boat!

2 New Brighton (Harrison Drive) All the local species are taken here, together with some bass and mackerel in summer, fishing two hours before and after high water. Long casting is advised, and baits of sand-eel and crab are suggested. The best marks are about a mile west of the open-air baths on the promenade, and of the rocks round the Fort Perch Rock. But it is slippery and beware of the rising tide.

3 Liverpool Night fishing is preferred round here for the better fish. The best fishing is at slack water on either side of the tide. Currents are very strong. Preferred baits are lugworm, ragworm, and sprats fished on paternoster tackle hard on the somewhat snag-ridden sea-bed. The longer the cast, the better. Preferred marks are the rocks at Seaforth radar station, anywhere along the sea wall, and various harbour installations. More information can be had from G. Dodd, Fishers Tackle, 109 Wavetree Road, Liverpool, also M.P.R. Duffy, Liverpool's Angling Centre, 429 Smithdown Road, Liverpool (Tel: Liverpool (051) 733 2591), or any of the forty or so tackle dealers that supply this area.

4 Formby A long walk out towards the sea from Formby Point should take you to the Mersey Channel in which dabs are to be taken with lugworm. Hardly seems worth the effort. If your taste is for one to two mile treks out into the muddy brown yonder, take a compass in case fog, darkness or a sprained ankle mean a change of plans.

5 Southport It would be nice to imagine that the fishing is any easier up here, but it is not. It is just as much hard work. Details from Howard Sports Ltd, 8–10 Hoghton Street, Southport (Tel: Southport (0704) 34111).

Bait Areas
Although they are often a good way out from the shore line, this area is one huge line of lugworm beds. Trench through where the casts are thickest, remembering to fill in as you go. At Ainsdale a one to two mile trek is recommended from the high water mark in pursuit of good bait.

Ditch-caught flounders taste dreadful but testify to the adventurousness of the species!

FOR THE FAMILY

Within easy distance of this coast are the entertainments, houses, museums, concerts, etc in and around Manchester, Liverpool and Chester. The Dee estuary to the south and the Lancashire coast to the north offer varied seaside attractions and sporting activities.

Chester Zoo one of the finest anywhere. See it from canal waterbus. Many rare species. In Chester see the cathedral, medieval walls, Roman remains, etc.

Jodrell Bank Withington Green. A Space Age trip to see radio telescope, exhibition area, planetarium, etc.

Lady Lever Art Gallery Port Sunlight. Superb collection of paintings, china, furniture, etc to delight art lovers.

Little Moreton Hall Congleton. Visit a perfectly preserved example of a 16thC black and white moated house.

Pilkington Museum of Glass history of glass-making from Egyptian times with fine examples from many countries.

Tatton Park Knutsford. Fine mansion, gardens, park and mile-long Tatton Mere. Works of art, furnishings, old vehicles, varied gardens, 1000 acre parl. Walking, picnicking, sailing, etc.

This dogged angler is fishing for winter dabs and codling.
Use lugworm, ragworm, crab, mussel as bait. Weather
information for an area can be obtained from the GPO
recorded forecast or from the coastguard.

Merseyside and Lancashire

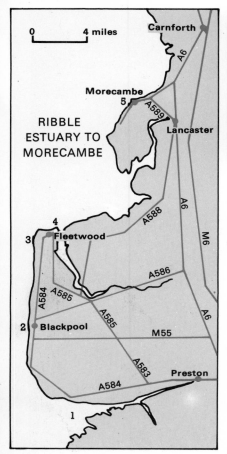

0   4 miles

RIBBLE
ESTUARY TO
MORECAMBE

A fine specimen of garfish.

From the Ribble estuary the sands continue unbroken to Blackpool and Fleetwood and on to the vast sand and mud flats that characterise the estuary of the River Lune. Shore fishing can be tough here, and mainly for small species and flatfish that love such sandy grounds, though the offshore fishing is excellent for tope, rays and big cod. These inshore sands, being stable and not easily turned over by heavy seas, support a huge population of life forms.

The Wyre estuary is a haven for flounders – but built up on its west bank and very marshy on the east bank. The littoral land is so flat around here that it climbs to no more than 16 yards above sea level some four to five miles inland, so the coastal plain tends to be marshy, which is more favoured by the wildfowler than by shore anglers. Such flat shores make the setting of long lines a better bet than rod-and-reel fishing. At Heysham there is some fishing from

the harbour installations while to the north the undulating sands and muddy creeks of Morecambe Bay stretch to the horizon. Here the local commercial fishermen use tractors to harvest the shrimps and cockles far out on the flats, with trammel nets set miles out on the sands. The visitor would be classed as insane to set out across these grounds without a guide. Quicksands and rushing tides claim several lives each year.

Offshore fishing is mainly for sand hunters – conger eels, cod, whiting, plaice, skate, tope, dogfish, bass, occasional angler fish and so on. Inshore the fishing is largely for eels, plaice, flounders, dabs, the occasional conger eel, a few bass, codling and whiting.

Charter boats operate out from Fleetwood and Morecambe. The Blackpool and Fylde boat fishing club owns a tractor for towing boats out of the water. Slipways and shore launching facilities exist at Lytham St Annes, Blackpool, Skippool, Stanah, Knott-End-on-Sea, Fleetwood (several), Glasson Dock near Lancaster (private facilities requiring prior agreement), and Morecambe.

Tide times are about 2½ hours before London Bridge.

1 Ribble Estuary Fish here if you must with lugworm for the flounders and silver eels. Soft mud and dangerous gullies make it hazardous for the slim rewards. In winter very little is caught from here. More information about Ribble fishing from Riding Brothers, 135a Church Street, Preston (Tel: Preston (0772) 23954) also R. Millington, 32 Steeley Lane, Chorley (Tel: Chorley (025 72) 72392).

2 Blackpool Both the south and central piers at Blackpool are private, but the north pier is open to the public for angling. Here plaice, dabs, flounders, silver eels, occasional

bass, mackerel, and infant tope are caught in summer. Cod, whiting, dabs and the odd plaice are taken in winter. Black lugworm and peeler crab score best, with night tides from October to March yielding most fish. A flooding tide with a westerly wind putting a chop on the sea provide best sport. Long casting is useful on these two marks. Details from Brian Ogden, 254 Church Street, Blackpool (Tel: Blackpool (0253) 21087).

3 Rossall Fish the flooding tide with an onshore wind, casting your baits as far out to sea as possible. Lugworm, ragworm, sand-eel, fish strip and squid all work here for flounders and other flatfish, eels and the winter fish. Fish behind the school, from the sewer pipe towards Fleetwood, or the fifth and sixth beaches between the groynes on the right of the launching slipway where there is a deepish channel a fair cast offshore. Details from Fred's Angling Centre, 35 Beach Road, Cleveleys (Tel: Cleveleys (0253) 860616) also Edmondsons, 15 Chapel Brow, Leyland (Tel: Leyland (077 44) 21318) or any of the many other tackle dealers in this area.

4 Fleetwood Locals choose to fish either into the Wyre estuary for flounders, dabs, plaice and eels or for the bass, cod and codling that are also taken from Rossall Point round to the sea cadet base. Flooding tides with westerly winds score best, using baits that are standard for local species. More details from C. E. Howarth, 128 Watson Road, Blackpool (Tel: Blackpool (0253) 44016). Also, from among the several tackle shops in the area, Langhorne's, 80 Poulton Road, Fleetwood (Tel: Fleetwood (039 17) 2653).

5 Morecambe Plaice, flounders, eels, bass, mullet are to be caught on lugworm, ragworm and peeler crab

A record blue shark from Welsh waters.

during daylight hours between May and September. September to February produces codling, whiting, flounders, and dabs on lugworm, ragworm and fish strip. The bottom of the ebb tide is not worth fishing. Long casting is essential from open beaches. However the pier and the sewer pipe are considered to be the best marks. A large deep pool forms to the left of the pipe as the tide runs out and fishes well for dabs, plaice and flounders. As with many areas around here, watch out for the incoming tide cutting you off, which is why the sewer fishes best for two hours to low water and two hours up. Other marks can be located after a visit to Charlton & Bagnall, 15 Yorkshire Street, Morecambe (Tel : Morecambe (0524) 410282).

Bait Areas
This coastline is one large bait bed – mainly for good red lugworm, very few black lugworm and some ragworm. Peeler crabs can be found where there is enough shelter for them. In Morecambe Bay digging is prohibited without a permit from the Town Hall. This is indicated.by longshore notices.

FOR THE FAMILY
More entertainment per square mile at Blackpool and Morecambe than any other part of the coast. But also easy access to the unspoilt countryside of the Lakes, the Pennines, and Bowland. You can visit many historic towns, nature reserves and museums.
Marineland Morecambe. Sea lions, seals, dolphins, etc displaying their amazing skills. Shows Apr.–Sept. The estuary is a mecca for ornithologists.
Leighton Hall Carnforth. Stately home in Lakeland setting. Nature trail. Free-flying eagles on display in good weather. May–Sept.

Steamtown Carnforth. A major collection of steam locomotives. See the Flying Scotsman and many famous engines.
Martin Mere Wildfowl Trust nr Ormskirk. Wildfowl gardens – over 1500 birds, 300-acre refuge with 7 hides. Visitor centre and coffee shop.
Blackpool Tower for the view, and the zoo and the world's largest entertainments complex alongside.
Hornsea Pottery Leisure Park Lancaster. Grounds where rare breeds are preserved, gardens, children's amusements, tours of pottery.

Cumbria

At Arnside there is some excellent flounder fishing in the estuary of the River Kent. The county boundary places everything west of here in Cumbria. In terms of fishing quality, the sands of Morecambe Bay are not worth the cost of hiring a guide. While the A5087 picks its way over low coastal hills to the west of Morecambe Bay, there are few features to concentrate the fish and the visitor may as well push on south towards Barrow-in-Furness, where Rampside, Roa Island and Foulney Island look interesting. There is plenty of flat sand on both sides of the Isle of Walney, the long, narrow spit that shelters Barrow-in-Furness from the open sea. Similar flatlands continue north to Askam in Furness and into the mouth of the Duddon Estuary, which breaks up a stretch of shallow, sandy coast that would otherwise run in one straight line from Walney to St Bees Head. The estuary of the Esk at Ravenglass is more modest than the mouth of the Duddon.

The shoreline and marshes for two and a half miles on each side of Drigg Point at the mouth of the Esk, are designated a Ministry of Defence Danger Area. For an easy survey of much of this shoreline, take a train from Barrow-in-Furness through Whitehaven, Workington and north to Maryport

St Bees Head is divided into a north and a south head with a half-mile sandy/stony beach in between, set among the cliffs and the rocky outcrops at their feet. These outcrops and sand alternate from Whitehaven north to Workington where the coastline again becomes extensively shallow and sandy around Maryport and on to that vast complex of low-lying coastal plain and shallow, muddy estuaries, the Solway Firth. Here there is another Morecambe Bay and River Esk. Much of this area of marshland requires expert guidance.

Boats may be chartered from Workington, Whitehaven, Barrow-in-Furness (Roa Island), Haverigg, Maryport and Ravenglass. Chartering facilities are, sadly, quite inadequate here because the offshore fishing potential is excellent. Only a handful of boats covers these grounds. Those with their own boats on trailers can launch them from Roa Island, the Isle

Kitted out and ready to go, this traditional craft anticipates its crew of keen, early-morning anglers.

of Walney (opposite the Ferry Inn with a second ramp at Garnse Bay), Arnside (beware tidal bore), Ravenglass, Seascale, Whitehaven, Harrington, Workington and Maryport. Check facilities, preconditions and so on first. Tides are about 2½ hours earlier than at London Bridge. Offshore, this area has recently acquired a sound reputation for big winter cod. Each year some large fish are taken from Whitehaven. General local species include plaice, cod, tope, thornback rays, dabs, mackerel, pouting, occasional conger and small pollack.

1 Arnside Famous for its winter flounders, this part of the River Kent also produces dabs, plaice and the occasional sea-trout or bass. The place is fishable in any weather because it is so sheltered. However, a heavy tidal bore – warning given by a hooter 20 and 10 minutes before it is due – makes fishing impossible two hours before high tide. Fish from low water up in the two main channels, casting into these with a baited spoon rig. The best place is from the railway bridge round to the coastguard station. A rod licence is required for the sea-trout.

Details from V. Carlson, 64 Kirkland, Kendal (Tel: Kendal (0539) 24867).

2 Greenodd From Humphrey Head flounders, eels, school bass and the odd tope are caught, but fishing is unpredictable as the position of the channel alters. Best baits are harbour ragworm (called creepers around

here), lugworm, peeler crab and, for thick-lipped mullet, bread. May through to January fishes well, but autumn into winter provides the best sport. At Greenodd, there is no need to cast far from the road lay-by to catch the resident flounders on lugworm. Spring tides, however, produce the best results.

3 Barrow-in-Furness Bass, flounders, codling and plaice come, at low water or high water, to the long to medium caster fishing by day or night at Foulney Island. But watch out for dangerous gullies and fast tides – it really is an island at high tide. Thorney Nook and Black Tower produce bass to the specialist, plaice, dabs, flounders and codling around the high tide period on lugworm, ragworm and crab. Roa Island and the Walney Channel produce the same species, but at any state of tide. On winter nights, from November to February, good catches of codling are made here. Calm weather at Roan Head sees good catches of flounders, plaice, bass and eels from half flood to high tide and the same time back. More information from Angling & Hiking Centre, 1 Astra Buildings, Abbey Road, Barrow-in-Furness (Tel: Barrow-in-Furness (0229) 29661); Hannays of Barrow, 50 Crelin Street, Barrow-in-Furness (Tel: Barrow-in-Furness (0229) 22571) and Harvey Jackson, Market Place, Ulverston (Tel: Ulverston (0229) 52247).

4 Silecroft Flounders, plaice, bass and winter codling are taken here

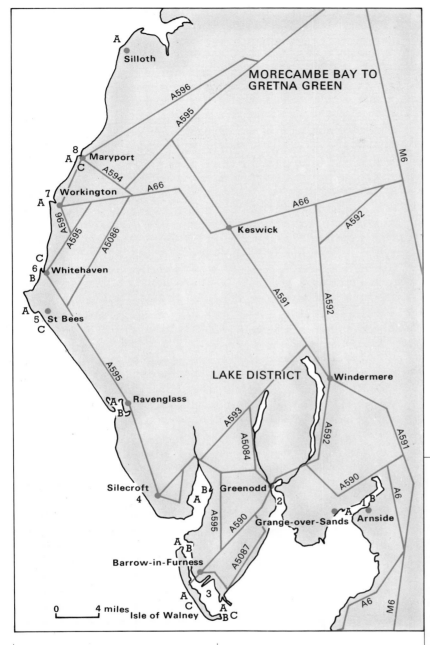

MORECAMBE BAY TO
GRETNA GREEN

LAKE DISTRICT

0   4 miles

Taylor, 20/21 King Street, Whitehaven
(Tel: Whitehaven (0946) 2252).

6 Whitehaven   The usual local
species – and the occasional giant cod
– are taken from the quay, the rocks at
Parton (and St Bees) and along local
beaches, like Wellington. Mackerel
arrive late here, with July to early
September the main season. The high
water period produces most fish.
Find out more from Mark Taylor (see
St Bees).

7 Workington   Local beaches are
not as productive as those at
Harrington to the south or at Siddick
to the north for the usual local species.
More details from Mark Taylor at
Whitehaven (see St Bees), or at the
Workington premises: 2–4 Murray
Road, Workington (Tel: Workington
(0900) 3280).

8 Maryport   Some pretty fair fishing
around here for the usual local
species. The shore south of the
harbour is rocky and yields good cod,
conger eels and some bass.
More details from Reg Thompson,
127 Crosby Street, Maryport
(Tel: Maryport (090 081) 2310).

Bait Areas
No shortage of good lugworm around
here, with quite reasonable ragworm
beds – even though they are a bit
small – and fair crabbing.
A   Lugworm
B   Ragworm
C   Crab

FOR THE FAMILY
All the pleasures of exploring the
Lake District, the Solway coast and
the Furness area in the south. Cumbria
has superb scenery, historic
buildings, towns and villages.
Ravenglass to Eskdale Railway   from
the coast to the heart of the Fells by
narrow gauge railway. Nearby
Ravenglass Dunes Reserve for
birdwatchers.
Brockhole National Park Centre   at
Windermere, for displays and
lectures on the Lake District and
gardens with shore and woodland
nature trail.
Castlerigg   nr Keswick. Largest of
Cumbria's stone circles set in
magnificent mountain scenery.
Hadrian's Wall   walk the western
stretches of the Roman wall which runs
close to Carlisle and see some of its
major forts.

from half flood, over the top of the
tide, back to half ebb tide. Spring tides
are more productive than neaps, and
even so long casting is vital for
maximum catches.
Details from A. Parker, 23 Market
Street, Ulverston (Tel: Ulverston
(0229) 52061).

5 St Bees   Although there is
reasonable general shore fishing

along this coat, St Bees Head offers
more variety. Conger eels, some
skate, bass, mullet, mackerel, cod –
and the more usual flatfish – are
caught around here over the top of the
flood tide and the early part of the ebb,
with night fishing more productive.
Shore tope fishing is practicable off
the headlands – if you have the
patience. More details from Mark

Isle of Man

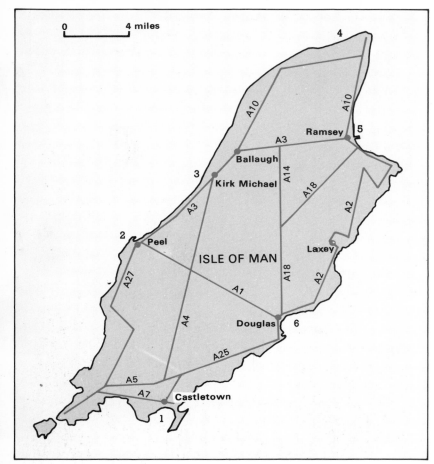

An island that is some 31 miles long by a dozen wide does not take too long to explore. In addition, the locals cannot go driving off long distances to fish some remote spot and neglect their own patch, as is so often the case nowadays on mainland Britain. And there is not too much fresh water fishing to distract their attention from the sea fishing.

Add to this a fair stock of fish and it soon becomes obvious that the Isle of Man is one of the better bets for a fishing holiday. If a sou'westerly gale hurls abuse at the southerly edge of the island, Ramsey is comfortably fishable, and in a biting easterly, Peel offers reasonable fishing conditions.

For about 8 miles south of low-lying Point of Ayre the shore is sandy – extensively so at Ramsey – backed by shingle. The Maughold Brooghs to the south east form the steep northern shore of a promontory that falls to rocks running out to Maughold Head.

South west from here there are a couple of sandy coves, then extensive rocks – with stony bays at Port Cornan and Dhoon Bay, running to the sands at Laxey Bay. To the south, Clay Head is a rocky area with low reef running round to the stony beach at Port Groundle, with more rocks to Douglas Bay. Here the beach is sandy, with outcrops of flat rock.

Low rock and reef extends from Douglas Head, with just a few tiny coves among it, to Dreswick Point. On each side of this point lie beaches of stony sand.

Castletown Bay is flanked by extensive areas of low rock running along its outer reaches, with sand inside. Likewise Bay Ny Carrickey, which has low rocks among the sands along its northern shore. Little bays proliferate towards Spanish Head, with headlands in between.

Northwards to Port Erin the rocks are quite steep – again with a few little sandy coves. Bradda Head is extensively rocky and steep. Apart from a few little bays of stony sand, this pattern of rock continues northwards to Peel.

North east from here the rocks become more evenly interspersed by sand and the coastline less steep. The rocks peter out completely about a mile and a half south of Kirk Michael. From this point a beach of sand and shingle runs to Jurby Head then curves north of east to Point of Ayre, a distance of 16 miles.

From the Point of Ayre to the Calf of Man there is a good network of roads to take the angler about his business. While catches are not measured in half tons or more, as they are at the wreck fishing capitals of Great Britain, there is fair fishing both offshore and from beaches, rocks, piers and breakwaters.

Charter boats operate out from Port Erin, Peel, Ramsey, Douglas and Castletown. Trailed boats may be brought over on the ferries from Liverpool and, during the summer months only, from Fleetwood, Ardrossan, Belfast and Dublin. For information on fares etc, contact the Isle of Man Steam Packet Co Ltd, Imperial Buildings, Douglas, Isle of Man (Tel: Douglas (0624) 3824).

Launching sites for heavier craft are to be found at Douglas, Derbyhaven, Castletown, Port St Mary, Port Erin, Peel, Ramsey and Laxey. At most of these sites there are two or three suitable ramps.

There are several clubs on the Island. The addresses of the current secretaries can be obtained from tackle dealers.

Offshore fishing is for cod, the size is somewhat low, but this deficit is made up by numbers of rays, conger eels, pollack, coalfish, bull huss, dogfish, spur dogfish, tope, all the flatfish, gurnard and skate.

The shore fishing is largely for bass, pollack, wrasse, mackerel, garfish, small coalfish (billet size), plaice, flounders, dabs, small turbot, dogfish, conger eels, and mullet.

Years ago large skate were frequently taken by boats off this island. Numbers have reduced in recent years, but there is still the chance of one turning up. Porbeagle sharks pass by this island, though it appears that nobody has bothered to try for them.

Tide times are virtually identical to those given in the daily papers for

Dover, or subtract 2¾ hours from London Bridge times.

1 Castletown Beach fishing is mainly for flatfish and other lesser species. Codling are caught here in winter. Rock marks here and further west provide excellent spinning in summer for mackerel and pollack, with wrasse to be had on bottom bait. Conger fishing is available from the rocks, too, from here to Port Erin. Details from Sporting Sams, Church Road, Port Erin (Tel: Port Erin (0624) 832181).

2 Peel The breakwater here offers fine fishing for plaice, gurnard, large (by shore standards) coalfish, pollack, mackerel and mullet. The local method of catching mullet is with fish – the school children are experts at catching them. In winter, whiting, codling and dabs are caught here. Haddock are also taken at times on shellfish and worm baits. Bass, while not abundant on the island, seem to prefer the western side and are taken from the beaches between Peel and Point of Ayre.

Float-fishing or spinning off St Patrick's Isle produces pollack, coalfish, mackerel and, when suitable bait is used under the float, wrasse. Ragworm is the premier bait for the pollack when float fishing.

3 Kirk Michael Beaches from here to the north fish well for bass when a surf is running, and for flounders, especially after a storm.

4 Point of Ayre Excellent fishing from here, at times, for spur dogfish, especially during the early summer months, and for bull huss. Both species roam close inshore at night.

5 Ramsey Rock and breakwater marks between the town and Laxey are excellent for codling to about 5 lb which invade this coastline when the weather turns chilly in autumn and, some years, linger through to June. With them, early in the summer, are wrasse, pollack, small coalfish, and mackerel, though this species is more prevalent after June. The tackle dealer in Ramsey will provide further information: J. Mead, 9 Parliament Street, Ramsey (Tel: Ramsey (0624) 813092).

6 Douglas The breakwater is currently being extended and is closed for building works. When access is again allowed, some fine fishing will be available for codling, coalfish, flatfish, gurnard, dogfish, and conger eels. Victoria Pier offers good fishing, but the continuous use by ferries disturbs the better fish. Winter fishing, when the tourist trade is light, sees best results here. From the many rock marks along the eastern side of the island there is some fine rock fishing for codling. More details from Nods for Rods, 11 Castle Street, Douglas (Tel: Douglas (0624) 21562) also R. C. Turner, 12 Villiers Buildings, Douglas (Tel: Douglas (0624) 5950).

Between Douglas and Port Erin lie several deep-water rock marks from which ling averaging 4–6 lb may be taken. Anglers who are more familiar with boat-caught ling may be surprised at their colouration – they are reddish maroon – like summer rock cod.

Bait Areas
Lugworm, ragworm, crab and fresh mackerel can be obtained from a few sites around this island.

Use a lead clip for beach fishing in order to protect the line from being abraded by sand and shingle – it makes casting safer.

Choose your weapons!

FOR THE FAMILY
No shortage of places to see and things to do on this historic island – with its sandy beaches, coast and country walks, mountains and glens, castles and museums. There are festivals, carnivals, entertainments and, of course, the international motorcycle races, car racing and cycle racing.

Manx Electric Railway enjoy superb scenery and climb from Laxey, with its unique Victorian waterwheel, to Snaefell, the island's highest point.

Douglas the capital with its magnificent bay and famous horse trams, has every kind of holiday attraction – entertainments, sport, pony trekking, etc.

Manx museums at Douglas, the museum traces the island's history. Castletown also has a fine maritime museum. Other museums of folk and rural life, and at Port Erin visit the Marine Biological Station.

The Wildlife Park Ballaugh. A good day out in a botanical park containing animals, birds, reptiles, etc. May–Sept.

Castle Rushen and Rushen Abbey, Castletown. Fine medieval castle and the burial place of Viking kings.

Dumfries and Galloway

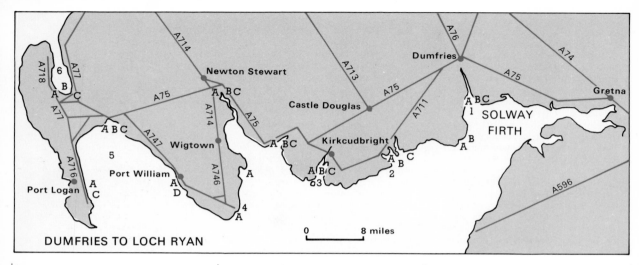

DUMFRIES TO LOCH RYAN

The north side of the Solway Firth characterises lowland Scotland at its flattest. Flounders, dabs, whiting and some codling can be taken from Annan westwards to the mouth of the River Nith and onwards past Southerness Point to the western end of the Mersehead Sands. This is shallow country, with best shore results being produced on lay lines left overnight far out on the sands.

From Port o' Warren Bay the coastline becomes more featureful with a couple of useful marks to be found south of Rockcliffe. Rough Firth and Auchencairn Bay are both shallow and sandy – more attractive to the sightseer than to the visiting angler.

Scottish fishing proper begins at Balcary Point, home of large shore cod. From here round to Kircudbright Bay there is a fine mixture of rocky outcrops and sandy bays, even though the area south of the A711 between Dundrennan and Buckland Burn is designated a Ministry of Defence Danger Area.

From Little Ross Island north westwards to the Islands of Fleet, a mixture of rock ledges and sandy bays will entertain the speculative fisherman. Inside Wigtown Bay sandy beaches abound, though the east side is more accessible than the hopelessly shallow west side. Southwards to Burrow Head are cliff-girt rock ledges and a sprinkling of sandy, stony bays. The going gets easier with sand and boulders interspersed along the north-east shore of Luce Bay. There is a wide sweep of clean sand (with a Danger Area behind it) between Glenluce and Sandhead Bay. Luce

Sands form Scotland's best-known bass surf beach. This sand is broken up by occasional rocky outcrops, stones and generally rough ground as one travels southwards to the Mull of Galloway.

North again, the shore is almost entirely a wall of cliffs to Portpatrick, but there are several little bays, many of which are worth exploring. Similar beautiful and lightly-fished coastline extends northwards around The Rhins to the mouth of Loch Ryan. Many a visiting angler has fished for weeks around Galloway without seeing another fisherman. The water off here is blue and warmed by the North Atlantic Drift in both summer and winter, which is why it is such productive ground. Unfortunately, much of the western side is inaccessible by road, so the precipitous cliffs and rock buttresses that form this magnificent and spectacular scenery are rarely glimpsed by the tourist.

Loch Ryan, some ten miles long by three miles wide, offers excellent shelter to the mariner. There is a lot of flat sand at Stranraer, but on the eastern side stony sand soon gives way to rock.

Inshore fish species include cod, coalfish, pollack, mackerel, tope, dogfish (lesser spotted, bull huss and spur dogfish), rays, wrasse, flatfish, conger eels and some bass. There is great variety, if you know where to look. Offshore the fishing is similar, but with more whiting and haddock.

Charter boats operate out from Kippford or Scaur, Kirkcudbright, Garlieston, Isle of Whithorn, Port

William, Drummore, Port Logan, Portpatrick, and Stranraer. In all cases it is important to contact individual skippers.

Trailed boats can be launched at several sites. The ones listed involve a minimum of manhandling, so boats that can be carried under one arm may be launched at several other sites. Annan, Dumfries, Kircudbright, Garlieston, Isle of Whithorn, Stair Haven, Drummore, Portpatrick and Wig Bay. High tides occur about 2¼ hours before London Bridge time around here. Do not take risks – the water is deep, with strong tides offshore and dangerous rocks. Seek expert local information before casting off.

1 Dumfries East of the Nith estuary and south to Southerness Point, the main fishing is for flatfish, the shallow Solway grounds offering excellent feeding for major predators offshore, with little of interest close in. At Powilli Mount Bay, flatfish – mainly flounders and some plaice – may be taken all through the year, at any state of tide. Summer months find shoaling bass in here on the flooding tide. Details from Gordon M. N. Pattie & Son, 109 Queensbury Street, Dumfries (Tel: Dumfries (0387) 2891) also D. McMillan, 6 Friars Venell, Dumfries (Tel: Dumfries (0387) 2075).

2 Balcary Point This is Scotland's answer to Kent's Dungeness. Each winter it produces a good crop of very large cod between October and February, flatfish and similar at any state of tide. Long casting is not essential, but a wind from the south or the west improves the fishing. Nearby

Airds Point, known as 'the flat rock' also produces good cod, flatfish, thornback rays, spur dogfish, conger with the usual techniques and standard baits. A little further west, at Rascarrel Bay, similar species are found. North, across the Urr estuary at Castle Point, cod are taken in winter, flatfish all year on the flooding tide and over the top of the tide. The Scottish record shore-caught cod was taken from here and the Scottish shore-caught record bass was hooked from the next mark, Almorness Point to the west of the Urr estuary. Codling, flatfish, pack spur dogfish and bass are taken here, the last two in summer only. Incidentally, the Scottish boat-caught record bass was taken just half a mile off here. More details from Tom Little, 1 Glenshalloch Road, Dalbeattie and M. McCowan & Son, 43 High Street, Dalbeattie (Tel : Dalbeattie (0556) 610270).

3 Kirkcudbright Bay To the east, just beyond Abbey Head at Abbey Burnfoot, there is good fishing for thornback rays, dogfish, conger eels at any state of tide during the summer, with codling the mainstay in winter. Torrs Point, on the eastern side of Kirkcudbright Bay, offers similar fishing. This mark is reached via the A711, turning off at Mutehill to Tarrs Farm. More information from the sources suggested in the previous section.

4 Isle of Whithorn This picturesque port is one of the few places where there exists a reasonable supply of charter boats and expertise. The offshore fishing is excellent, with the usual staple species, plus porbeagle shark, skate and so forth, especially in the tide race round Burrow Head. Rock marks around Burrow Head, Isle of Whithorn, Portyerrock and Monreith offer the species mentioned earlier, plus the chance of tope. Do not go without company when there is a swell running, and always take a rope so that when you have to get down to sea level to land a fish, you are connected to a rock pinnacle higher up and cannot be washed out to sea. More details from a man locally described as 'the oracle', John McWilliam, Harbourmaster, Isle of Whithorn (Tel : Whithorn (098 85) 246).

5 Luce Bay This area is one of the most prolific parts of a generally outstanding coastline. Luce Sands offer excellent surf fishing for bass when there is a mild wind blowing in from the southwest, while rock marks to each side offer excellent rock fishing in abundance. The best idea is to take local advice ; in this sparsely populated area everybody knows everybody else and locals are happy to impart information to strangers because the local marks are not as heavily fished as is, say, the case in the south of England. Ask in the pubs, you are bound to meet somebody who knows something !

Port William, with the bass beach at Monreith Bay, is a good place to try. Or Drummore, with its sheltered sandy lee beaches to the north, rock ledge marks to the south. The countryside proclaims excellent rock tope fishing, and skipper Stephen Woods of Craigmiller Guest House, Main Street, Drummore (Tel : Drummore (077 684) 372) has had them in plenty to 70 lb from his boat. Excellent fishing is found from Drummore to Port Logan, but dinghy anglers beware, very strong tides surge around the Mull of Galloway. More information from Ernest McGuire, Burnside Cottage, Isle of Whithorn (Tel : Whithorn (098 85) 468).

6 Loch Ryan This sheltered bay has produced several Scottish records over the years both from the shore and from boats. On the Atlantic side, from Port Logan northwards, where access is possible, there is some excellent rock fishing to be found, and much of it virgin territory. More details from The Sports Shop, 90 George Street, Stranraer (Tel : Stranraer (0776) 2705).

Bait Areas
Plenty of bait around here. The shallow, muddy grounds inside harbours and estuaries offer excellent ragworm and lugworm digging. Rocky areas where the stones are broken and loose are excellent for finding peeler crab. In other places, where rocks face the Atlantic and are therefore very stable, peeler crabs can sometimes be found in rock crevices. A steel hook is required to pull them out.

Gaper clams are often found among the lugworm beds. Many rock marks yield mackerel, while fishing harbours are a good source of mackerel or herring. Mussels are useful baits and are universally available.
A Lugworm
B Ragworm
C Crab
D Sand-eels

FOR THE FAMILY
Old harbour towns and fine sandy beaches, forests, hills and rich farmland, typify the Border country. Plenty of open air activity for the family, bathing, boating, walks, etc., and castles, abbeys, historic houses to visit. Entertainments at Stranraer and other holiday centres.

Galloway Forest Park nr Newton Stewart. 250 sq miles of magnificent scenery to enjoy. Hills, forest, lochs, trails. Visit Galloway Deer Museum and live trout exhibit.

Drumlanrig Castle nr Carronbridge. Fine 17thC mansion with rare furniture and works of art. Adventure, woodland, play and picnic areas. Easter to end Aug.

Burns Heritage Trail through beautiful countryside to places associated with Scotland's greatest poet, including the Globe, Dumfries, Burns's favourite inn.

Grey Mare's Tail a 200-foot waterfall, and the Devil's Beeftub, a huge natural hollow. Two splendid sights in Annendale.

Logan Fish Pond Port Logan. Hand-feed the tame cod in this deep tidal pool – and enjoy the exotic surroundings of Logan Botanic Gardens. Apr.–Sept.

Threave Castle Douglas. Acres of wild flowers, rock and water gardens. Visitor Centre Apr.–Oct. National Trust for Scotland. Treave Wildfowl Refuge for birdwatchers.

A dogfish's treatment of tope bait will earn the angler's unrelenting dislike.

Strathclyde

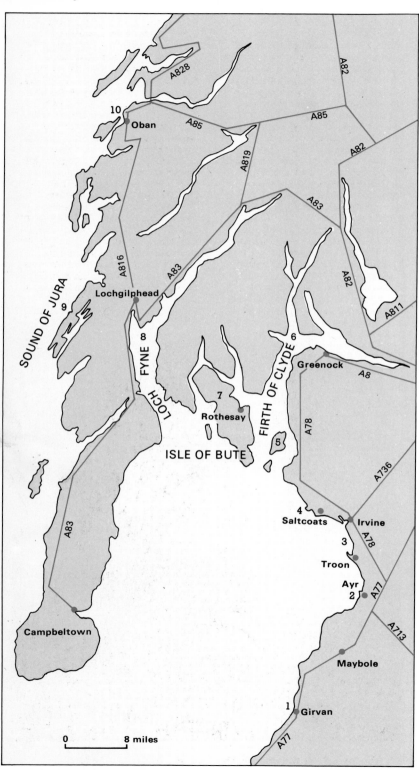

North of Finnarts Bay the foreshore is accessible at only a few places, being mountain-backed, steep and rocky. Ballantrae Bay is a mixture of stony sand, backed by the A77(T). This road follows the shoreline – a mixture of stony sand, boulders and rocky outcrops – for twelve miles to Girvan, with its shallow, sandy beach. The beaches from here north to Culzean Bay are shallow sand with rock outcrops and plenty of easy access points.

Continuing northwards, the foreshore becomes increasingly rocky for four miles. Five miles south of Ayr, shallow sand and rocky headlands give way to continuous sands on each side of the estuary. Only Troon's rock-girt harbour breaks up this huge stretch of shallow sand that continues north to Saltcoats and Ardrossan.

Except for its sandy innermost reaches, the entire Firth of Clyde is comprised of boulders, flat rock and a rubble foreshore occasionally interspersed with a sandy bay or two – and some rather fine promenades to remind the visitor that the Clyde was once a flourishing area of trade, with the architectural opulence to match. Almost the entire shoreline is served by good roads, thus allowing easy inspection. Similar shoreline is found round the Island of Bute and again on both sides of Loch Fyne. However, the western side of the Kilfinan Peninsular is broken up by secret bays, cliffs and rocky islets. This type of ground continues all the way to Ardlamont Point, which is accessible by road, even though access points are sparse.

South of Tarbert, the eastern side of Loch Fyne is accessible only by boat, the mountains tumbling steeply into the sea. The west side of Kilbrannan Sound is comprised largely of flat rock with one or two sandy bays in between. Reasonable access to any part of the foreshore along the Mull of Kintyre is via the A83 which runs down the west side of the peninsula, or the B842 which runs down the east side, leaving an eight-mile-wide strip of Highland moorland wilderness in between.

South of Carradale the shoreline becomes more mellow, with rocky outcrops interspersed with beaches of stony sand. This pattern continues south past Campbeltown Loch to Southend. The south western tip of the Mull of Kintyre sees the mountains of Currach Mor diving steeply into the sea, with sole access at the Mull lighthouse.

North again, there is some fishing to be had from the rocks to the west of Machrihanish, but to the north access is limited to dune-backed Machrihanish Bay, the best place being the car park where the A83 branches inland. Northwards from here the picture is of stony and sandy beaches with occasional rocky outcrops, becoming more shallow and sandy towards Rhunahaorine Point opposite Gigha Island. Rocky outcrops – even cliffs at Ranachan Point – break up the sands which continue up into West Loch Tarbert. Northwards from Ardpatrick Point heavy outcrops of rock and precipitous cliffs defy access to the foreshore except via a handful of picturesque little coves reached by narrow tracks off the B8024. But the coastline mellows towards Loch Caolisport, becoming very sandy at the inner end of the loch. The north side of the loch is comprised largely of rocky outcrops and rubble with restricted access.

Two miles north of precipitous Point of Knap the coastline ameliorates towards Loch Sween. North Knapdale is a ragged jumble of small lochs with stony, sandy shores and steep moorland and afforested hills that restrict access to all but the very fit, a description that is equally valid for the eastern shore of the sound of Jura where wide stretches of flat rock are interspersed with sandy coves and rubbly bays.

There is plenty of flat sand inside Loch Crinan, but access to the shoreline on the west side of Loch Craignish is via a three mile hike over heavy moorland, much of which is forested. The B8002 allows easy access to the sandy bank of the loch. Extensive bogs and moorland defy access to most of the attractive western side of the Craignish Peninsular with its rock-girt sandy bays from which one can view a mass of offshore islets between the mainland and the islands of Jura, Scarba, Luing, and Shuna.

South of Loch Melfort the A816(T) provides access to a rubbly foreshore with rocky outcrops. There is some sand around the loch, but it is very shallow, getting deeper towards Seil Sound. The shoreline of Seil is also rubbly with rocky outcrops, most of it unexplored. Similar conditions are to be found northwards to Oban. Northwards again, similar rubbly foreshore continues with sandy outcrops, the coastline mellowing around sandy Ardmucknish Bay and Loch Creran, the A85(T) following the coastal contours for many miles before branching inland to Glencoe. Much of this wild coastline is virgin territory for the shore angler, offering ample – and memorable – rewards to those with initiative.

Charter boats operate out from Girvan, Ayr, Troon, Irvine, Saltcoats, Inveraray, Tarbert, Rothesay, Millport, Largs, Gourock, Dunoon, Ardentinny, Clynder, Helensburgh, Gareloch. Here the term 'charter boats' has been used somewhat loosely. While the larger centres offer several excellent boats, fully equipped for offshore fishing, others belong to fishermen who would be happy to take you along for a pound or two. Obtain more details when you are on the spot.

Those with their own boats on trailers may launch craft of reasonable size from the following places. Obviously it is essential to check on tidal, ownership and other conditions before launching. Other sites may be used by people with small craft than can be manhandled. Bigger boats should get afloat at: Girvan, Ayr, Troon (several places) Irvine, Saltcoats Harbour, Fairlie, Largs (several places), Gourock, Inverkip, Dumbarton, Helensburgh, Rhu, Clynder, Roseneath, Port Bannatyne (several), Rothesay, Otter Ferry (Loch Fyne), Ardrishaig (Fyne), Tarbert, Campbeltown, Crinan, Kilmelford, Cuan Ferry, Oban (several), Lochaline, Drimmin (Sound of Mull), Salen, and, if you are into launching something weighing a few tons and require assistance from cranes, Greenock and Port Glasgow.

Tide times vary from London Bridge in complicated fashion, as is to

Big bass like this are occasionally taken from Luce Bay.

be expected from such a complex piece of coastline. Anglers are advised to obtain local tide tables (available from tackle and sailing shops and in local newspapers – or from tourist information beaureaux or town halls). As a rough guide, high water at Ayr is 2 hours before London Bridge, Ardrossan is 1¾ hours, Greenock is 1½ hours. However, Oban high water comes 4¼ hours after London, and at Gareloch it is 5¼ hours after London.

Fish species include mackerel, dogfish, rays, whiting, cod, haddock, conger, coalfish, pollack, plaice, flounders, dabs and other flatfish (some unusual ones, too), garfish, pouting, thick-lipped mullet, tope, and quite a few other varieties.

This is a coastline of sheltered anchorages and safe fishing grounds. Many of the locals immediately think of boat fishing rather than shore fishing when the subject of sea angling arises. When seeking information, make sure that you make clear which you are interested in.

One of the most popular offshore fishing methods around here is to feather from a boat – maybe using baited feathers – for the codling. The peak season for this is October to December, a time when the sea lochs fish poorly. They produce best – for cod and codling – from January to June.

1 Girvan If the hake is a species that you have yet to hook, this is one place where they are taken. Shore fishing from the pier, rock fishing at Horse Rock, and umpteen other rocky headlands along here. Exploration is assisted by the closeness to the shoreline of the road, especially south of Girvan, which is rated to be very good, perhaps just because it is so easy to reach. For more details consult with Thomas Gibson, 55 Dalrymple Street, Girvan (Tel: Girvan (0465) 3328) also John H. Murray at 3 Dalrymple Street, Girvan (Tel: Girvan (0465) 2039).

2 Ayr Good fishing for the usual local species from Newton Shore to the north of the harbour, from the harbour itself, and from several rock marks around Heads of Ayr. Flooding tides are reckoned to produce the best results. Flatfish – as ever – bite better by day, with codling coming closer in the darkness. Details from Gamesports, 60 Sandgate, Ayr (Tel: Ayr (0292) 63822).

3 Troon and Irvine Fair catches are made here of cod, codling, coalfish, pollack, conger, flatfish, rays and whiting. Barassie is a good mark over the low tide and the early flood, while Troon pier is said by some to be as good as anywhere. Irvine shore fishes well at night during gentle, mild westerlies for two hours before and after low water. The sea bed is very shallow here, so high-velocity casting is advised, though the dabs and flounders that predominate often come in close. Nearby Stevenson Point, reached from Stevenston Shore, fishes well around low water for cod, whiting, coalfish and dabs. Casts over 80 yards put the tackle beyond rocks onto clean ground. Lugworm and ragworm are considered the best baits hereabouts. Details from J. G. McNab, 27 Wilson Avenue, Irvine (Tel: Irvine (0294) 76886); or go into James Kirk's shop at 25 Kyle Street, Ayr (Tel: Ayr (0292) 63390) also Currie Sports, 32 High Street, Irvine (Tel: Irvine (0294) 78603). Help is also available from Irvine Water Sports Club, 126 Montgomery Street, Irvine (Tel: Irvine (0294) 74981). This club offers wide facilities to members.

4 Saltcoats and Ardrossan Three piers to chose from here – two at Ardrossan harbour, one at Saltcoats. Coalfish, conger, rays, cod, pollack and mackerel are all taken from here. This area is recommended as a good family fishing area as results are forthcoming without dragging mum and babe-in-arms for a four mile hike over rock transversed by gullies full of slurry. Flooding tides produce the best results along here, with night fishing better than by day. Details from Bud McClymont, 41 Corrie Crescent, Saltcoats (Tel: Saltcoats (0294) 61830).

5 Great Cumbrae Island The great thing about fishing from islands is that they are so easy to explore, especially when pocket-sized like this one. Cod and codling are caught all year round. Flounders and dabs are best from September to January. Ling take herring bait all year through. Mackerel come to this shoreline from July to October. Dogfish – and spur dogfish – fish best from July to October, also conger eels. Haddock, coalfish and whiting are not so plentiful. Fishing is similar at Largs on the mainland. Keppel pier is private, so do not fish there. A couple of boats may be available for charter at Millport. Find out more from F. V. G. Mapes & Son, 3 Guildford Street, Millport (Tel: Millport (047 553) 444).

6 Firth of Clyde Fishing the extensive shoreline of the Firth of Clyde enables the shore angler to combine the pleasures of sea fishing with the comfort that coarse fishermen normally enjoy. These sheltered waters hold good fish and productive grounds are rarely far from suitable car parking. Interestingly, much is known about the waters of the Clyde because it is well populated, but similar grounds to the north, as far as Cape Wrath, have yet to be opened up or publicised like those of the Clyde. Sadly, trammel netting and rapacious trawling have caused catches around here to decline.

Because of the area's popularity, much experience has been gathered by local experts who can pin-point the precise locations of fish as they move about with the weather, tides and seasons. The following is therefore no more than a sketch. In order to fish efficiently, seek out complete details from any of the addresses at the end of this section.

Wemyss Bay. This rocky area gives on to deep water where long casting scores. Cod and flounders bite on winter nights, with codling, conger and other summer species feeding best at night, too. Spinning in daytime produces codling, pollack and mackerel. The power station at Inverkip produces excellent thick-lipped mullet, with some also in the nearby marina – where shoals of baby pouting and tiny pollack are to be found. Indeed, the Clyde is excellent mullet country. Best results are had in winter when the fish group around warm water outfalls. In summer they disperse along the shoreline. Sea-trout fishing is practised here on the flooding tide. **Inverkip** is one good stance.

A long cast at high tide, a shorter one at low is good advice for the **Cloch Lighthouse** area. Deep water close in produces cod, conger and dogfish. The ground is rough, so a long-range sinker-release device may be advisable. Night fishing produces better sport.

Up **Greenock** way cod, rays, flatfish and whiting – plus some small coalfish and a few other species – can be taken from a variety of rock, beach and promenade situations. Across the water at Ardmore Point, a juicy bait cast into the deep water there will catch big fish on a nocturnal flood tide, with daytime fishing equally as good at times. Fish from low water for the plaice, mackerel and cod, the cod being best after September.

At the mouth of **Gare Loch** the Rhu Narrows are a famous pair of beaches. The west side had direct access from the road. The cod fishing is excellent here from Christmas through to June. The bottom is somewhat snaggy. Inside the loch are Naval dockyards, and access is prohibited in several places. Best fishing is at the Narrows, where 50 lb bags of cod and pollack are not uncommon.

The mouth of **Loch Goil** offers excellent summer conger fishing, especially from a boat using mackerel strip on a still summer night. From time to time restrictions are placed on this area when the Navy carries out experimental work. (Not, sadly, on how to train fish to avoid trammel nets!)

South of **Roseneath**, the fish bite better when the tide turns, at either end of its cycle, when fish, squid and other big baits will score with the big predators, worm baits with the smaller ones. At the mouth of **Loch Long**, depths of 50 fathoms or more make shore casting into very deep water as rewarding as boat fishing, without the need for sea-sick pills. Along all Clyde marks, an east wind is a valid reason to hang up the rods and go sightseeing.

At **Dunoon**, if you have no boat, yet want one to fish over the fished-out Gantocks mark, suitable craft can be hired from local boatmen or from the railway pier at Gourock. Despite heavy commercial attention, a few huge cod manage to pick their way through the labyrinth of fish traps only to be caught on large pirks and keep alive the sputtering flame of the Gantocks reputation. Fish the flooding tide in daylight between November and February. The pier at Dunoon can only be fished at night with a club's block booking from the pier master.

7 Isle of Bute Rothesay is sheltered from the prevailing winds, while easterlies render the Inchmarnock side highly desirable. Plenty of good rock marks around here, especially into the deep water off Garroch Head.

For further details contact: Jim Morrison, The Anchorage Boating Centre, Ardentinny, Loch Long (Tel: Ardentinny (036 981) 228). Neil Lindsay, 6 Balgray Avenue, Shortlees, Kilmarnock (Tel: Kilmarnock (0563) 36229); McCririck & Sons, 38 John Finnie Street, Kilmarnock (Tel: Kilmarnock (0563) 25577); John Macbeath, Polluk Castle Estate, Newton Mearns, (Tel: Glasgow (041) 639 5836) and Modern Charters, Victoria Place, Shore Road, Clynder (Tel: Clynder (043 683) 312) or any of the tackle dealers hereabouts.

8 Loch Fyne Famous for its kippers with a flavour as deep as the loch's hundred fathoms plus, Loch Fyne is also the longest in Scotland. Set in wild, rugged and beautiful country-side, it is the marine answer to Loch Ness a good two hours drive away, and its fishing has yet to be fully evaluated from the shore. Sightings of monsters should be reported immediately – except during university rag weeks. Tarbert is a useful port of call for anglers seeking quality cod, mackerel, coalfish, and other local species from the shore. Also sea-trout – to the skilled. For the angler seeking a fascinating holiday afloat, camping in a sheltered cove each night, the Kilbrannan sound, Firth of Clyde and Loch Long have immense potential. Details from local fishermen, especially the charter skippers at Tarbert and the fishermen at Campbeltown.

9 Sound of Jura Largely unexplored from the shore, but sure to offer similar species as those found in the Clyde. Remember that the sea off here once supported a thriving industry converting basking sharks' livers into oil. The air smells sweeter now, but the immense richness in the water remains.

10 Oban Fishing is best from the outer edges of Kerrera Island when the weather allows. The usual species are found around here, with plenty of haddock but no bass. More details from The Tackle Shop, 6 Aird Place, Oban (Tel: Oban (0631) 3933).

Bait Areas

There is stacks of bait around here. Ancient diggers who have grown accustomed to cunning Dungeness lugworm have been known to dig big black lugworms here with their bare hands! Lugworm, ragworm and, in summer, peeler crab can be found all around the sheltered coastline hereabouts. Mussels cling in bunches to piles and rocks, while razorfish, gaper clams and cockles are also found out on the sands. Seasonal landings of fresh herrings and sprats, together with heavy concentrations of inshore mackerel all make this area one of the least problematic with bait – provided you do not mind gathering it yourself. Tackle shops are infrequent. Bait is sold from some private houses. Ask around for the best grounds or dealers. Sand-eels may also be raked or scraped from some sandbanks and netted in certain areas. Again, ask for local advice.

FOR THE FAMILY

Seaside resorts, ferries to the islands, many tours inland to places of historic interest and scenic beauty, not forgetting Glasgow's museums, art galleries, music and theatres – just some of the attractions for the family on the Strathclyde coast.

Culzean Castle nr Maybole. Combine a visit to a fine Adam mansion with exploring Scotland's first of many country parks. Ponds, aviary, guided walks, Ranger service, etc.

Blantyre David Livingstone Centre. Birthplace of the explorer. African pavilion, exhibition, picnic area, displays, gardens.

Clyde Muirshiel Regional Park a series of splendid parks, different in character over 30,000 acres. Walking, sailing, nature study, trails, picnic areas, canoeing, etc.

Burns Heritage Trail a planned tour of places associated with the poet's life and work, through delightful countryside.

Cameron Loch Lomond north from Balloch. Free-roaming animals in a wildlife park, with leisure area, lochside picnics and fascinating displays. Apr.–Oct.

Mull take the ferry from Oban or Lochaline to this peaceful island, and perhaps a further trip to Iona or Staffa (Fingal's Cave).

Cruachan Power Station and Dam Argyll. Vast hydro-electric power station carved out of the mountain amid superb Highland scenery. Visitor centre and tours.

Artificial small fry lure.

Islands of Scotland

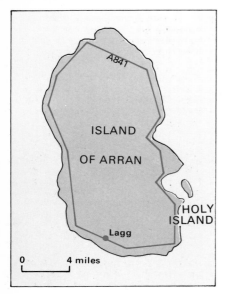

Mackerel, plentiful in this region, make a good basis for 'rubby-dubby', chopped up fish oil, bran and dry sand.

Bute

The shoreline of Bute consists largely of sand – stony in places – with patches of rubble. Short stretches of low rock are to be found, mainly to the south, with plenty of sand and shingle bays in among them. Fishing is very similar to that found off the west coast of Scotland. Garroch Head is a noted local mark for deep water.

Charter boats operate out from Rothesay. Contact Keith Todd, 3 Alma Terrace, Rothesay (Tel: Rothesay (0700) 3716).

Arran

The Island of Arran is an ideal anglers' island. Not only is there a good road running along virtually the entire coastline (except for the areas around Clauchlands Point and Cock of Arran), but there are about four square miles of sheltered dinghy-fishing water inside Holy Island at Lamlash Bay.

From Cock of Arran, travelling south east, the shoreline is of sand and rubble with occasional outcrops of rock to Brodick Bay. South from here the shoreline is rocky, becoming steep towards Clauchlands Point, with sand and rubble at Lamlash Bay. There is more rock to Kingscross Point, with sand, rubble and low rock at Whiting Bay and on to the Sound of Pladda. Long fingers of rock stretch out along the southern shore with sand and rubble in between them, with the rock fingers disappearing north west of Sliddery.

There are patches of low rock among the stones and sands of Drumadoon Bay with rock more extensive north of Drumadoon Point. From here the entire western shore of Arran is a mixture of alternating sand, rubble and flat rock running northwards to sandy Loch Ranza and then on to Cock of Arran.

Lamlash Bay is recognised as one of Britain's premier haddock grounds, with plenty of codling there too.

Prolific information is available from the Arran Sea Angling Centre, Shore Station, The Beach, Brodick (Tel: Brodick (0770) 2192), also from N. C. McLean, Torlin Villa, Kilmory.

Boats are arranged by H. A. Johnston, Atholl House, Lamlash (Tel: Brodick (0770) 6344).

Islands of Scotland

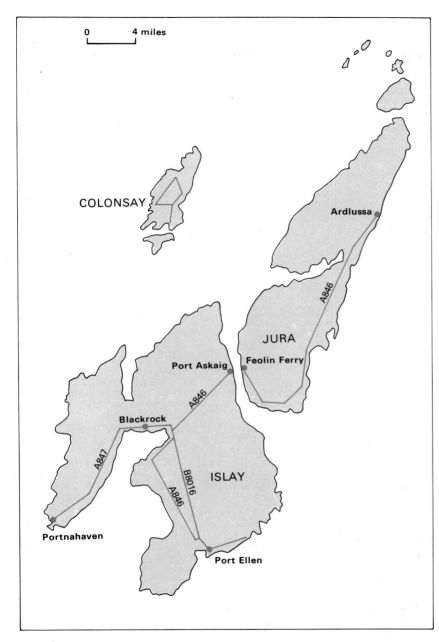

south west shore.

Sand is plentiful inside Loch Tarbert. There is no access by road to the coastline north of the loch to our starting point. The shoreline, again backed by raised beaches dating back to before the last ice age, is of mingled rock and sand for about half the way as far north as Corpach Bay. But the sand gradually decreases to just the odd little patch among the flat rocks that protrude around the indented coastline northwards. There are more raised beaches, of interest to the geologist, with a proliferation of bays backed by heavy moorland in the region towards the Gulf of Corryvreckan.

Shore fishing here is in its infancy, if you will accept such an over-statement of the facts. There is every likelihood that no shore angler has set boot upon the inaccessible northern part of this thinly populated Scottish island.

Little is known about the fishing off here – apart from the fact that it is unlikely to differ markedly from that from mainland Scotland and along the Outer Hebrides. Once you are here, you are on your own, though crofters and fishermen will be willing to provide information.

Islay

For about a mile south of Rubha A'Mhàil the shoreline is largely of flat rock, but this soon turns sandy, with occasional outcrops of flat rock. Stony sand becomes more prevalent towards McArthur's Head, which is surrounded by rocky outcrops, and on to Maol Ardtalla. South from here the rocks again become more prevalent, with small sandy bays set among reefy promontories. The coastline disintegrates into a series of islets along the south western shore, with sandy bays set here and there among more general rock. It should be noted that there is no access by road between Port Askaig for many miles to Claggain Bay.

East of Port Ellen the coastline of the Mull of Oa, the tip of the Oa peninsula, is a very steep rocky headland with a mixture of sand and rock along its three sides. Northwards again, and Laggan Bay is a wide sweep of sand, with Laggan Point at the northerly end falling to the sea amid outcrops of low rock. Inside Loch Indaal, with the A847 running close to much of the shoreline, the beach is almost entirely of sand. There is a little pier

Jura

The population of Jura is scarcely large enough to hold an argument. South east from the Gulf of Corryvreckan, the shoreline is steep and rocky as far as the hamlet at Lussa Bay, the most northerly point of access. Apart from the occasional tiny bay, the shoreline south of here is also predominantly very rocky and steep. Just to the north of Leargybreck

is a lagoon called Lowlandman's Bay, presumably because it is such a fine sheltered anchorage. There is a large sandy bay in front of this village, sheltered by the Small Isles, with rock and sand alternating to the tree covered south east corner. Inside the Sound of Islay, the shoreline consists mainly of sand, with occasional outcrops of rock, with more rock than sand along the raised beaches of the

Bute, Arran, Jura and Islay 79

near the distillery at Bruichladdich.

South east of here the shoreline is largely of low rock with boulders, rubble and sand in among it, extending out to Rhinns Point at the end of the Rhinns of Islay. There is a scrap of an island off this headland, populated by one lighthouse, called Orsay. There is a sheltered harbour just inside called Portnahaven which has a wee pier.

Extensive areas of flat rock make up the eastern shore. There are some pretty bays set along this coastal strip – Lossit Bay, Kilchiaran Bay, Machir Bay, and Saligo Bay.

North of this bay the shoreline becomes quite heavily indented, especially where Cnoc Uamh nam Fear falls craggily to the sea. To the west of this hill sandy Sanaigmore Bay lies amid rocky outcrops, such low rock, in some parts backed by near cliffs, becoming more extensive towards Ardnave Point – and around Nave Island – and into the mouth of Loch Gruinart.

The Loch is extensively sandy inside, most of it drying out at low tide. There are one or two boulders here and there. The main channel flows closest to shore on the western side, opposite Killinallen Point. The landward end is very marshy.

There is a dune-backed sandy beach to the north east of the Loch, but from Gorantaoid Point to the northern tip of the island, rocks prevail. Extensive flat rock juts out, such outcrops being heaviest among the famous raised beaches between Rubha Bholsa and Rubha A'Mhàil.

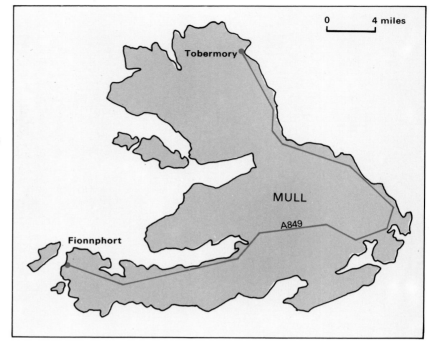

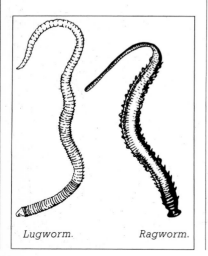

Lugworm.   *Ragworm.*

For details about the fishing here, see the comments on the Isle of Jura.

Mull and Coll

South of Duart Point, along the western shores of the Firth of Lorn, solitary coves break up the inaccessible heather-clad slopes that fall steeply to the rocky foreshore. But Lochs Don, Spelve and Buie are girt with beaches of sand, stone and rubble. The western shore of Loch Buie is of craggy, inaccessible rocks backed by mountains. But there is sand at Carsaig Bay, with areas of low rock to each side. Towards rocky Malcolm's Point and beyond the shoreline is of sand and rubble, though access is very steep and inaccessible by road. It then becomes increasingly rocky towards the heavily indented coves around Uisken. Sandy coves and rocks alternate along this section of the Ross of Mull, with sand becoming more prevalent than rock towards the lovely island of Iona. The pattern of alternating rock, rubble and sand continues eastwards into Loch na Lathaich and into Loch Scridain, with headlands all the way. Naturally, there is quite a lot of sand around the innermost reaches, especially at Loch Beg and Kilfinichen Bay. Between Scridain and Loch na Keal, the coast is called The Wilderness – and it is.

Even the shoreline is a mixture of rubble, sand and flat rock, the hills behind fall very steeply to sea – raised beaches again – with flat lands around Gribun, an area opposite Inch Kenneth island. Sand and rubble – with patches of rock – run around the coastline of Loch na Keal, with much sand inside it. The pattern of sand, rubble and flat rock continues around Ulva Island and Loch Tuath, becoming more rocky towards Treshnish Point – some two to three miles from the road.

Flat rock and sand run into Calgary Bay, with just the occasional patch of sand among extensive flat rock towards precipitous Caliach Point. North east from here the coastline becomes heavily indented, to the old village of Croig, around the steep headland of Quinish Point, into Loch Mingary and out to Sorne Point. There is sand among the rubble inside these lochs, with extensive areas of flat rock around the headlands. Cliffs, rock, steep headlands and just the odd small rubbly bay are to be found eastwards to Ardmore Point. Tobermory is flanked by sand and rubble shores. These extend from Bloody Bay, with its circus of cliffs behind, south east to the Aros estuary, but with low rock outcrops appearing some three miles to the north of the river mouth. Then there is more sand to the east, with a bit of rubble and the occasional rocky outcrop, running round Fishniss Bay, Scallastle Bay, Craignure Bay and Duart Bay lying inside the flatlands of Duart Point and almost linking with the sand flats inside Loch Don.

The Islands of Coll and Tiree are made up of rocky headlands and wide sandy bays regularly interspersed around the shores of each island. North east Coll is very rocky, and many of the sand strands on both islands are backed by sand dunes. As is to be expected, the shore and boat fishing is very similar to that found along the Scottish mainland coastal strip. Virtually all of it is relatively unexplored, especially on Tiree. Details of fishing on Coll may be obtained from Alastair P. Oliphant, Isle of Coll Hotel, Arinagour, Isle of Coll (Tel: Coll (087 93) 334).

Details of fishing around the coast of Mull may be had from A. Brown & Son, 21 Main Street, Tobermory, Isle of Mull (Tel: Tobermory (0688) 2020) and Tackle and Books, Main Street, Tobermory, Isle of Mull (Tel: Tobermory (0688) 2336).

For charter boats, contact B. Swinbanks, 8 Main Street, Tobermory, Isle of Mull (Tel: Tobermory (0688) 2458).

Above: *Fishing for flounder in a wild estuary.*

Below left: *A common skate caught off the Orkney Islands.*

Below: *A prize catch from the waters of Loch Stell.*

Islands of Scotland

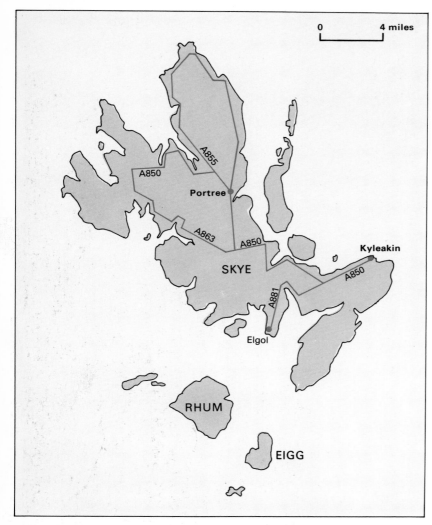

indented and heavily rocky. There are a few bays among the rocks going into Loch Eishort which, like Loch Slapin, is extensively sandy, with rubble and flat rock scattered among the sands. This type of shoreline is to be found around Loch Scavaig and Soay Sound.

The shoreline of Loch Brittle is mostly rock with sand deep inside. Rocks and a little sand are to be found round to Loch Eynort – again with sand at its throat. The coastline is very steep and inaccessible to Talisker Bay – where there is plenty of sand, then rock, sand and rubble alternate round the coast into Loch Harport and Loch Bracadale.

From Idrigill Point north west to Moonen Bay massive cliffs and natural arches defend the shoreline from invasion by anglers. Likewise the north coast round to Loch Pooltiel, and again to Dunvegan Head.

Sand and low rock abound on each side of Loch Dunvegan and into Loch Bay and round the Vaternish Peninsula, though cliffs deny access to most of this wild shoreline.

Sand, rubble and rock alternate around the shores of Loch Snizort with sand predominant inside the deeper bays like Loch Greshornish, Loch Snizort Beag and Uig Bay. This type of coastline – alternating sand, rubble and low rock – is to be found northwards to Rubha Hunish at the northerly tip of Skye, and all along the south east shore, except for the pure sand of Staffin Bay. However, for some twelve miles north of Portree the coast is too steep and craggy to allow easy access except at sandy Bearreraig Bay. Likewise the headland that shelters sandy Tianavaig Bay.

Southwards, the coastline is more gentle – rock, rubble and sand – with sand especially inside Loch Sligachan round to Loch Ainort into Loch Cairidh, with extensive flats at Caolas Scalpay, and general sand to Broadford Bay. Here there is extensive flat rock among the sands stretching eastwards to Kyleakin.

Here again the shore fishing – and boat angling – is largely unexplored. Species and angling methods remain very similar to those found off the west coast of Scotland. No precise information is available other than that the fishing here is excellent. Contact local boatmen and crofters for intelligence. Also find details at Skye Marine & Leisure Centre, Willow Bank, Broadford (Tel: Broadford (047 12) 271).

Rhum, Eigg, Muck, Canna, and Sanday
Catch the ferry from Mallaig to Kinloch on the Isle of Rhum. From here you will have to walk to the numerous bays and rock marks around this island – there are virtually no roads. Likewise the islands of Eigg, Muck, Canna and Sanday.

If creature comforts are uppermost in your mind, stick to the mainland or Skye – the fishing is just as good. However, for the adventurer with a good tent, there is fine fishing to be had off these islands, and no danger of overcrowding. Seek information from crofters and professional fishermen, but beware, Gaelic is a living language, and the English spoken on these islands includes a fair number of Gaelic words. It may take patience and a good ear to catch the patterns of speech used on these wild and unspoilt islands.

Skye
To the south of Kyleakin, the shores of Loch na Beiste consist mainly of sand with mountains falling steeply to the shore, this pattern continuing to Kylerhea where patches of rock and rubble are to be found. South west from Kylerhea Glen to Loch na Dal the coastline is steep, rocky and inaccessible by road. Generally, the shoreline is of rock, steeper in some places than in others, with little bays of sand and rubble, this pattern to be found south west to Ardavasar. The shoreline from here to the Point of Sleat and north to Inver Dalavil is

As with all the islands off the west coast of Scotland, bait beds are abundant, rich and scarcely touched. Lugworm, shellfish and crab are all abundant hereabouts.

Charter boats operate out from several harbours. Contact Skeabost House Hotel, Skeabost Bridge (Tel: Skeabost Bridge (047 032) 202); and Broadford Boat Hire, Rockbank (Tel: Broadford (047 12) 279).

FOR THE FAMILY

These uncrowded, friendly islands have plenty of good bathing beaches, hills and moorlands for walks and pony-trekking, and opportunities for sport. Islay, for example, can offer such variety as birdwatching, and visiting archaeological sites.

Duart Castle Mull. Much to see in this Maclean stronghold – banqueting rooms and special Spanish galleon exhibit.

Iona birthplace of Christianity in Scotland. You can visit the restored cathedral and other historic sites and enjoy the island itself.

Arran Nature Centre Broderick. An exhibition devoted to the rich natural history of Arran. Crafts shop, bookshop, etc.

Mountain of Gold Jura. Magnificent climb and view to the Isle of Man from this peak in the centre of the island.

Broderick Castle Arran. Among delightful formal gardens and woodlands, the castle contains fine paintings, etc.

Museum of Islay Life Port Charlotte, Islay. See the historic records of the island and ancient stone carvings.

Port Askaig Islay. Enjoy a visit to this small harbour in a wooded setting with its lifeboat station and 18thC hotel including part of a 16thC inn.

A lonely vigil as an angler waits on an outcrop of rocks for a bite.

Highlands

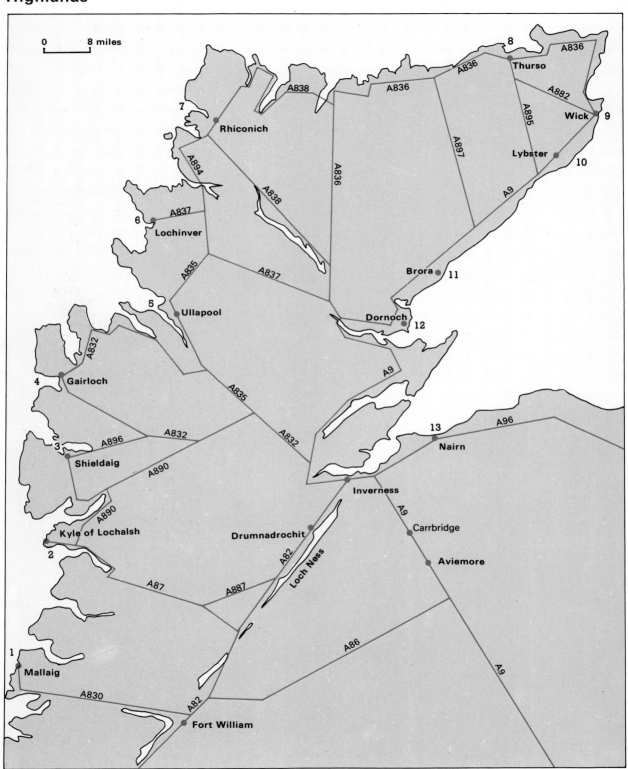

The eastern and landward edges of Loch Linnhe are a mixture of sand, stone and rubble as far inland as Fort William, the loch itself penetrating deep into the Western Highlands, which is why much of the western shore, at Kingairloch, is inaccessible. On both sides of the Sound of Mull, flat rocky outcrops are interspersed with stony, sandy bays and banks of rubble. Tides sometimes run in hard, confused patterns, so be wary.

Similar foreshore extends northwards, becoming more precipitous past the Killundine estuary towards Auliston Point, itself accessible only after a hike across heavy moorland. The shores of Loch Sunart are more accessible. The pattern of rock, stones and sand extends westwards to Kilchoan.

Rocks, cliffs and sandy bays form the shoreline of Loch Sunart, along which main roads run. However, much of the coastline of the Ardnamurchan peninsula is inaccessible by road. Most of it is comprised of granite cliffs falling away to deep water. Take a compass for when the mists clamp down on the moors.

Kentra Bay and Loch Moidart are both very sandy, though the seaward coastline is again very precipitous. The same applies to Lochs Ailort, Nan Uamh, and Nan Ceall. Much of this shoreline has never been explored by beach fishermen. Some of the lochs are too shallow to interest the bigger species of fish, while the precipitous areas deny access to the shoreline of the Arisaig and North Morar peninsulas.

At Mallaig, reached by the A830T, there is some fishing to be had around the harbour, although the shoreline of Loch Nevis, a two-mile-wide cleft in the mountains, requires a strong will – or a boat – to reach it.

The southern shore of the Knoydart peninsula, rugged though it is, has some sand with flat, rocky outcrops and rubble. There is a wide shingle and sand beach at Inverguseran, while the southern shore of Loch Hourn has never been fished from the shore. The rubbly foreshore is accessible in several places, though not by road.

Vehicular access is possible at several places along the northern shore of Loch Hourn, with a sandy bay at Arnisdale and others between heavy outcrops of rock towards the Sandaig Islands. Further north up the Sound of Sleat, there is a fine wide

beach of sand and shingle at Glenelg, with more bays – and rocky outcrops and rubble banks on each side of Loch Alsh, fronting the Island of Skye.

From Kyle of Lochalsh the railway hugs the coast, which is steep, with occasional stony coves and a rocky foreshore right round to Loch Carron. The north side of this loch, towards Loch Kishorn, has a shoreline of sandy bays and rocky coves with fairly straightforward access, unlike the north eastern side of Kishorn.

North of sheltered Toscaig the more mellow foreshore of rocky coves gives way to the sands of Applecross Bay, and a road follows the coast round to the mouth of Loch Torridon, running a few hundred yards inland from the rocky shoreline.

Sand, rock and rubble characterise the shore of Loch Sheldaig and upper Loch Torridon, with little chance of access between Alligin Shuas and Lower Diabaig. From Lower Diabaig north to Redpoint, cliffs, coves and rocky foreshore are accessible only via a rough track that crosses tumbling streams every half mile or so.

Cliffs, sandy bays and rocky outcrops form the picture northwards to Port Henderson, the sands becoming more frequent around the softer shores of Loch Gairloch and westwards to Big Sand at the mouth of the River Sand. There then follow a few miles of cliff-backed rocks. Access is possible among the cliffs via the beds of the rocky burns that tumble down. Similar grounds can be found eastwards into Loch Ewe, but access is tough going.

Loch Ewe itself is characterised by sand, mainly, with a few rocky outcrops. But north of Mellon Charles, cliffs and bays alternate around the feet of Rubha Mor, with Greenstone Point virtually inaccessible by land.

Gruinard Bay and Little Loch Broom are both similar to Loch Ewe in character, while the north side of Little Broom again poses access problems. Loch Broom, with Ullapool nestling on its eastern shore, is only accessible by boat along the steep western shore. The peninsula between the two lochs, culminating in Cailleach Head, is sparsely inhabited, with rocks and sandy coves alternating.

Isle Martin shelters the mainland from the open sea and two or three sandy beaches exist opposite the Isle. Moving north westwards, the Coigach mountains bathe their ancient feet in the sea, with fine sandy beaches and

coves inside the bay and on round to Lochinver, while most of the rock-buttressed eastern shore is almost inaccessible. Inland lies a maze of freshwater lochs and lochans. Do not forget your compass.

The pattern of small, sandy bays among rocky headlands extends northwards to cliff-backed Point of Stoer and eastwards again past Oldany Island, past Nedd to Kylestrome, and further north, through the wettest part of the British Isles where mountains and lochs match each other one for one. Rocky headlands and sandy beaches then extend in jumbled confusion, a map-maker's nightmare, past Handa Island, past Loch Laxford to Loch Ichard. Most of this ground has never been fished from the shore.

The most successful method of exploring along this huge stretch of indented coastline has to be from a boat launched from the sandy beach in one of the many bays. Plenty of suitable beach launching sites exist with the best ones close to villages. Some of the little bays also offer sheltered anchorage.

Northwards from Kinlochbervie the coastline lies outside the sheltering wall of the Western Isles. It becomes progressively more wild and rugged, the little bays backed by sheer cliffs. There is no access at all by road between the surf beach at Sandwood and Cape Wrath. The next nearest access point is at Achiemore at the mouth of the sandy Kyle of Durness. This estuary is flanked by the A838 which runs along the edge of the Durness peninsula, with its cliffs, rock ledges and lovely sandy beaches.

By contrast, the shoreline of Loch Eriboll is fairly tame, on the west side. With much of the A'Mhoine Peninsula inaccessible by road, fishing there is out. The steep rocky ledges on the accessible east side contrast with the sand of Tongue Bay, but the cliffs continue eastwards to Torrisdale Bay, interspersed with sandy coves set between rocky headlands. This bay is very shallow and sandy, and a pattern of steep rocky ledges with the odd sandy bay is found at Clachan, Armadale, Strathy and Melvich and continues eastward to Reay. East of the Dounreay Experimental Reactor Establishment, the cliffs are not very high but the foreshore consists of long fingers of flat rock, this pattern continuing eastward to Thurso Bay,

Highlands

Dunnet Bay, and northwards to Dunnet Head, the temple to which halibut addicts come to worship.

East of Dunnet Head, with its low-lying cliffs giving onto a sandy shore, the flat rock takes over, with the occasional sandy cove, as far as St John's Point. Eastwards from here there is a little more sand and shingle among the outcrops of rock, this sort of ground prevalent at Duncansby Head, with the little village of John o' Groats, and on southwards to the long sandy sickle of Sinclair's Bay, which ends in the twin rocky headlands of Noss Head and, three miles further south, North Head on the north side of Wick Bay. South from here, the shoreline is characterised by rock ledges backed by low cliffs and steep slopes, with a few secret coves in among the headlands, the coves becoming more frequent around Lybster Bay and so on south-west to Dunbeath. After this more stretches of sand and shingle are to be found among the rock ledges. Access along much of this coast is via the A9(T), although in some places it is easier to walk down the steep slopes to the sea, than in others.

South of Helmsdale, the ground eases up. There are still rock ledges, but long sandy bays become more and more frequent southwards to Brora, with the main road and railway sometimes within casting distance of the shoreline. Stretches of sand and shingle are interspersed by very occasional outcrops of rock. The ground becomes progressively more shallow – sandy Loch Fleet largely dries out at low tide, as do the extensive sandbanks and saltings at the mouth of Dornoch Firth. On the south side of the Firth, north of the road that joins Tain with Portmahomack, there exists a Danger Area.

The peninsula of Tarbat Ness is largely rocky, backed by steep slopes, this rock continuing along the south east side of the Ness for as far as Balintore. South from here the shoreline is reached only after a fair hike from the road, and consists of sand, with the odd rocky spur, backed by steep hills and, towards North Sutor, cliffs.

Extensive sands and saltings exist on both sides of the Cromarty Firth and also further south into the throat of the Moray Firth, with just the occasional outcrop of rock. Another Danger Area exists west of the oil platform construction yard at Ardersier, and more and more sand is to be found, with a lone rock outcrop to the west of Nairn, out towards Findhorn. This shallow ground is, in the word of one local angler, pathetic.

Charter boats operate out from several ports. In some places it is possible to hire a boat for the day. However, the dedicated angler is advised to bring his own. Charters from: Gairloch, Ullapool, Lochinver, Thurso, Scrabster, possibly Nairn, Mellon Charles (Loch Ewe), Rhiconich (Loch Inchard) and possibly Brora. Facilities are somewhat thinly spread!

For those with their own boats on trailers adequate slipways exist at the following places (other sites – not listed – require a modicum of muscle power when launching small craft down steps, over walls and among rocks). Check out facilities first with regard to tidal influence, ownership and so on: Fort William (several), Lochailort, Mallaig, Kyle of Lochalsh, Balmacara, Shiel Bridge, Plockton, Shieldaig, Fasag (Loch Torridon), Charlestown, Inverasdale, Gairloch, Ullapool, Kylestrome Ferry, Scourie, Auchuvoldrach, Portnancon, Scrabster, Wick, Lybster, Brora, Golspie, Meikle Ferry, Portmahomack, Invergordon, Cromarty, Inverness (several) and Nairn. In these parts, where so many ferries are used, few objections are raised at using ferry slipways provided your craft is clear in time and your trailer and car do not block access.

Fish species vary around the coastline. Catfish, black-mouthed dogfish, haddock, torsk, halibut, common skate and starry rays are all caught around here. Coalfish, with fewer pollack in these colder latitudes, fewer wrasse, fewer mullet, plenty of the ubiquitous flatfish, cod, codling, rays, sea-trout, summer mackerel, conger eels, some tope, porbeagle sharks (which are quite common in western Scottish water) and one or two other rarities.

Fishing centres are rare around here. Ullapool and Thurso are the best known. There is a vast amount of coastline and offshore water to explore. Although some of the local dealers will be able to guide your footsteps towards good fishing, the commercial fishermen and lobster potters are the ideal sources of information.

Charter skippers also help the shore angler.

1 Mallaig   There is excellent beach, rock, pier and boat fishing around this town set at the mouth of Loch Nevis off the chilly-sounding Sound of Sleat. Beautiful, wild countryside requires a good pair of fell boots as access roads are limited. All local species are taken here either float fishing or spinning from rocks, or hurling a slice of fresh mackerel out on to a sandy area set in deep water. Use small hooks and soft baits for the haddock and do not be in a hurry to strike the first taps.

2 Kyle of Lochalsh   Plenty of sheltered waters here, in the lee of the Isle of Skye. Excellent fishing is to be had from Dornie's shore, near the castle overlooking Loch Duich. Species here include coalfish, pollack, codling, wrasse, small conger eels, dogfish, ling and pouting. The railway pier at Kyle yields good conger on hefty tackle, and likewise from the fishery pier. Herring and mackerel score best on night tides. Details from John MacLennan & Co., Marine Stores, Kyle (Tel: Kyle (0599) 4208).

3 Shieldaig   Former home of a record whiting and current home for many other large whiting – plus a fair selection of the usual local species. Plenty of sheltered water for exploration by boat, but seek advice before venturing out.

4 Gairloch   A useful centre for exploration of the wild coastline. Shore fishing is for the usual local species. A boat from here is likely to find large common skate, porbeagle sharks, and the usual, less glamourous, staple species. Contact Ian and Donald Grant at Aultbea, Isle Ewe for details. Main species inside the lochs are haddock, whiting and codling for the table – an attitude of mind that is common round here. Details from J. MacKenzie, Sea Anglers Aid, Pier Road, Gairloch (Tel: Gairloch (0445) 52116).

5 Ullapool   Plenty of sheltered boat fishing and some excellent shore angling around here for the usual local species – anything from halibut to pouting. The Summer Isles offer protection while fishing open water during onshore winds. Easterlies, as ever, kill the fishing. There are chances of big skate from here, especially in the autumn. Rhu Point, Ullapool pier and Ardmair Bay are popular venues. Find deep water and there is a chance of catching a hake – the shore-caught record is still vacant. Details from: Angie Allan's The Anchor Centre, Ardmair Point.

Also from local charter skippers.

6 Lochinver Excellent mixed fishing offshore. This is the place to come for jumbo haddock up to around 7 lb, also big coalfish (to 25 lb), reasonable ling (to 22 lb), octopus, gurnard, big common skate and so on. The shore fishing is also good if you have the energy. With plenty of boats available here, less agile anglers may plump for the more relaxed alternative and go afloat. Details from Norman MacAskill, skipper of *MV Petrel*, 8 Cruamer, Lochinver (Tel: Lochinver (057 14) 291). Shore marks worth exploring are Rhu Coigach and Point of Stoer, two peninsulas that flank the bay.

7 Rhiconich More excellent unpublicised fishing abounds here-abouts. The best bet is to pay a visit to the School of Adventure, Rhiconich (Tel: Kinlochbervie (097 182) 229) and speak to Captain J. Ridgway. The school runs a 28 foot craft named *Halmatic* which may be chartered. To the north and east of this little village lie some 80 miles of unpolluted beaches and rock marks offering virgin fishing. Lower a bait into a deep-water rock mark and you could tangle with a 200 lb common skate – from the shore!

8 Thurso Together with Scrabster nearby, these two spots have produced more large halibut to rod and line than anywhere else in the British Isles over the past few years. The deep, rocky and turbulent waters of the Pentland Firth attract these monster flatfish. Otherwise, the usual species abound, both from boats and from the shore. The piers and harbours at both towns offer good fishing. Holborn Head and Thurso Bay are generous with varied fishing spots for the beach man. Details from J. Sinclair, 9 Langwell Court, Mount Vernon, Thurso (Tel: Thurso (0847) 2849); A. A. MacDonald, 23 Sinclair Street, Thurso (Tel: Thurso (0847) 2819); Pentland Sport Emporium, 14 Olrig Street, Thurso (Tel: Thurso (0847) 2473); also the Thurso Fish Selling Co, The Harbour, Thurso (Tel: Thurso (0847) 2825). Commercial fishermen know more about both inshore and deep-water fishing than most anglers.

9 Wick Plenty of fish around here and not enough anglers to catch them. Sinclair Sands produce whiting, wrasse, plaice, coalfish, dabs, haddock, cod and so on. There is excellent fishing around the rocks at Longberry and Noss Head, where sea-trout can be taken from the shore on spinners and fly tackle. More information from Wilson & Nolf, 1 Francis Street, Wick (Tel: Wick (0955) 4284). Take particular care to speak to local commercial men because they catch halibut just out from the shore at times and could point a skillful shore caster to water where a suitable bait could claim the shore-caught record halibut.

10 Lybster From Lybster, for many miles south, the water becomes colder, lacking the warming influence of the North Atlantic Drift current which turns away from the American mainland at Cape Hatteras and drifts across the Atlantic. Local grounds around here see a decline in the number of warm water fish – such as wrasse – and an increase in the number of cold water species – such as coalfish.

11 Brora Usual inshore species can be caught on locally abundant bait. The best fishing season is late summer, when the water has warmed up – July to September. Few boats are available, but it is possible to spend a day afloat with a local fisherman for a nominal charge. Details from Lindsay & Co, Main Street, Golspie (Tel: Golspie (040 83) 212).

12 Dornoch Good fishing at Embo from both rocks and pier for the usual local species. Sea-trout are taken around here on spinner and fly, especially on calm evenings when, like mackerel, they herd the fry close to the shoreline. Details from W. A. MacDonald, Castle Street, Dornoch, (Tel: Dornoch (086 281) 301); R. Macleod & Son, 14 Lamington Street, Tain (Tel: Tain (0862) 2171) and the Caravan Holiday Centre with amenities for the travelling fisherman – called Grannies Heilan' Hame(!) – contact the manager, Willie Mackintosh (Tel: Dornoch (086 281) 383).

13 Nairn Nairn offers very poor fishing, but our informant directed our attention to Balintore on the northern coast of the Moray Firth. Find out more from the various Inverness tackle shops: Gray & Co, 30 Union Street (Tel: Inverness (0463) 33225); or Leisuropa Ltd, 6 Inglis Street (Tel: Inverness (0463) 39427); also Sport in Scotland Ltd, Ormiston & MacDonald, 22 Market Brae (Tel: Inverness (0463) 222757) and nearby at J. J. Shanks & Son, Tulloch Street, Dingwall (Tel: Dingwall (0349) 2346).

Bait Areas
Again the coast of Scotland is a Mecca for lugworm, ragworm and various other baits. With so many sandy bays sheltered from heavy seas, all bait forms thrive. Razorfish are freely available along some shores, with or without spring tides to uncover the banks. The lugworm are large and, in some places, require little effort to dig. Soft and peeler crab may be gathered from late June to September among areas of rubble along the shore – peeler is an excellent bait around any rock marks and Scottish cod cannot resist it. Cockles, clams and mussels are also freely available. Mackerel, herrings, sprats, squid and other fish baits can be bought cheaply from fish piers and harbours.

FOR THE FAMILY
There are places of historic interest, and opportunities for walking, riding, bathing and boating, and enjoying memorable Highland scenery. Visit Inverness for shopping and entertainments, and a fine museum and art gallery.
Dunvegan Castle Skye. Ancestral home of the Clan Macleod with fine paintings and furniture. Wooded grounds make a fine contrast to the bare island surroundings. Apr–Oct.
Loch Ness Monster Exhibition Drumnadrochit. A chance to learn more of the monster. Records of 3000 sightings and scientific exhibits. Cruise the Loch from Inverness.
Landmark Visitor Centre Carrbridge. 10,000 years of Highland history in a dramatic theatre presentation. Exhibition, nature trail, sculptures, shop, restaurant, etc.
Strathspey Steam Railway a restored steam line through scenic route between Boat of Garten and Aviemore, the ski centre. Easter–Sept. At Loch Garten Nature reserve is the observation point for ospreys.
Cairngorm Chairlift from Loch Morlich. Stupendous views over Strathspey. At the top is the highest restaurant in Britain at 3,500 ft. Visit the nearby reindeer reserve.
Highland Wildlife Park nr Aviemore. Highland animals and birds – deer, eagles, etc in beautiful Speyside surroundings. Exhibition and children's animal park. Closed in winter.

Western Isles (Hebrides)

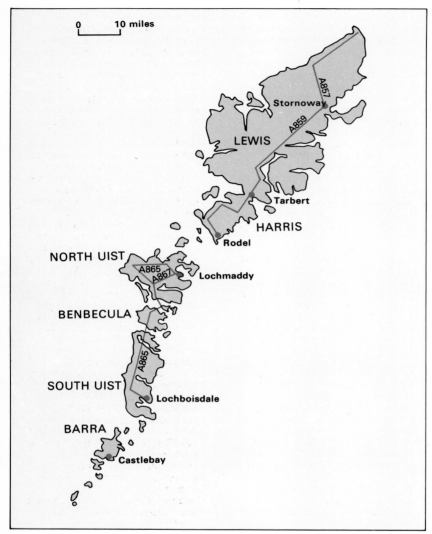

0 — 10 miles

Stornoway

A857

A859

LEWIS

Tarbert

HARRIS

Rodel

NORTH UIST

A865
A867

Lochmaddy

BENBECULA

A865

SOUTH UIST

Lochboisdale

BARRA

Castlebay

This chain of islands receives considerable attention from the multitude of low pressure systems that sweep across the Atlantic. The coastline is etched by Atlantic storms. Pounding waves have produced mile after mile of craggy rock faces and, further south, long surf beaches of shimmering white sand. Rainfall is high and, in parts, you cannot help wondering why geographers have not thought of a term to describe an area that contains as many acres of water as it does of land. Not dry land, note, because such intervening areas are mainly peat bogs with outcrops of granite in between.

These islands, however, offer wonderful fishing, perfect solitude and, when the weather smiles, spectacular scenery that even the most cynical city-lover could not resist. And when a storm is running, the drama of the elements is equally spectacular.

Ferries run between the islands, several of which also have small air fields, and from Scotland: from Uig (Skye), Kyle of Lochalsh, and Oban.

Eastern seaboard
From the Butt of Lewis extensive rocks and cliffs run south east to Port of Ness where there is a little sandy beach. Apart from the occasional sandy cove, this pattern of craggy, heavily indented rocks and cliffs runs round to Cellar Head and to the sands

of dune-backed Traigh Mhor, then out to Tolsta Head. Between Port Skigersta and North Tolsta the shoreline is inaccessible by road.

There are more rocks south to Gress where there is a fine sandy beach, rocks to Coll, sands, then more rocks to Melbost Sands. These extend to the causeway linking Eye Peninsula. Then more rocks each side of Stornoway Harbour, with a few little sandy coves. There is more inaccessible rocky shoreline to Loch Leurbost, then a series of long sea lochs – Erisort, Ouirn, Shell, Bhrollum, Claidh, Seaforth – these watery fingers thrusting deep into mountainous countryside that is liberally scattered with lochs and lochans.

East Loch Tarbert is full of islands, the largest of them Scalpay, then there are more sea lochs indenting the craggy coastline southwards to Rodel, with as many acres of lochs inland as there are acres of bog and moorland.

On North Uist, there is some sand scattered among the reefs and islands of Loch Maddy and inside Loch Eport. The inaccessible crags of the eastern shore continue to the disintegration of islands and islets that marks Benbecula's eastern coast, and on to the islands of Grimsay and Ronay and the reefy islets south to Wiay and the Bagh Nam Faoileann inlet, where there is a lot of sand.

The eastern shoreline of South Uist is mainly rocky and steep to island-dotted Loch Boisdale. Across the Sound of Barra, Barra Island offers more crags and reefy foreshore.

Western seaboard
Moving northwards again, up the west coast of Barra, there are plenty of mountains tumbling to the sea, but with a sandy beach at Halaman Bay, and another to the north of Borve Point, with more and more sands to the duneland around Eoligarry and the sound of Fuday. There is more sand – and a scattering of reefs – at Smerclett on South Uist, this pattern continuing to the long dune-backed surf beaches of A'Mheallach and north to rocky Ardivachar Point. There are more sand dunes – a feature of most sand beaches here, due to the strong winds that often blow – and a few reefy outcrops running northwards along the coast of Benbecula and into the vast flats of Oitir Mhor.

There is more sand to the west of

Baleshare with the huge flats of Traigh Leath Ann and Oitir Mhor to the north, sheltered by sandy Kirkibost Island. The sand continues, with a few reefs and plenty of dunes to Aird an Runair. The sands north of here are interspersed with reef and flat rock as far as Vallay, a small island sheltering Vallay Strand, with sand and dunes running north east, then encircling Oronsay Island and across the Sound of Berneray. The entire western side of this small island is made up of dunes and surf beaches.

South Harris is extensively rocky along its south western shore, but once inside Toe Head there is a wide dune-backed surf beach – Traigh Scarasta – beyond are sandy bays and rock headlands among them, this pattern continuing to Traigh Seilebost on the eastern side of the Sound of Taransay.

Both south and north shores of West Loch Tarbert are extensively rocky. Apart from the odd sandy cove, this pattern continues to Scarp – the end of the road (B887) – then Loch Resort, and Loch Tamanavay, becoming increasingly craggy to Uig Sands. Then more crags run out to Gallan Head.

Loch Roag – in all three parts – has a few sandy beaches on offer, along with a multitude of islands and islets, the largest being Great Bernera. The shoreline northwards is again of rocky crags, a pattern that continues to Carloway, where there is a sandy bay, and north to the Butt of Lewis. There are a few bays and coves en route. Near Carloway lies Dalmore Bay and Dalbeg Bay. Then, working northwards, there is Loch Shawbost, Port Mhor Bragar, Port Arnol and Goile Chroic. Then just a few tiny coves to within four miles of the Butt of Lewis where there are a few dune-backed bays on the western side.

When they run a fishing festival from Stornoway, the catches are measured in tons. During the last European Championships here, 200 anglers caught 13½ tons in three days – fair fishing! Species include haddock, skate, ling, cod, conger, whiting, mackerel, wrasse, gurnard, rays, coalfish, pollack and flatfish – and of course, the ubiquitous dogfish.

Charter boats can be arranged through the addresses given below. These craft are commercial boats that can be hired for set periods. Most of the sea fishing is by boat because of the extreme ruggedness of the shoreline.

The shore fishing remains virtually untouched. It is highly unlikely that the magnificent storm beaches of the south west should contain bass, but surely they cannot be empty? With so much craggy shoreline, there just has to be useful rock fishing; there is probably a halibut or a large skate waiting within casting range of a suitable rock mark. The islands abound in sea-trout, which can be taken from the lochs and some beaches by spinning or fly fishing. Again, little is known about this.

The fisherman with his own boat on a trailer can launch it at one of the many harbours up here. However, it should be large craft as these storm-racked waters are not suited to dinghies. The best months are May to September for fishing as the weather is then at its most settled.

As for bait, the sands and large flats to the south probably contain good lugworm and razorfish. Mussels are abundant, and there is no shortage of herring and mackerel for fish baits. Sand-eels are also probably abundant.

Obtain as much information as possible from the addresses given below, then go there and explore. The people to ask locally are commercial fishermen – both trawlers and crab potters. They will tell you what the sea bed is like, what species are likely to be found inshore and so on. Access is likely to be a major problem to shore marks – and heavy beds of kelp will be a hindrance at times. But the rewards for perseverance could be excellent.

Find out more from the Stornoway Sea Angling Club, South Beach Street, Stornoway, Isle of Lewis (Tel: Stornoway (0851) 2120); W. D. Cameron, The Harris Hotel, Harris (Tel: Harris (0859) 2154); N. Macleod, The Sports Shop, 6 North Beach Street, Stornoway (Tel: Stornoway (0851) 5464). You may care to reflect that a phone call is better at gathering information than a letter because writing is a chore – even for your author – and the two-way dialogue does allow points to be clarified.

FOR THE FAMILY

There are good beaches on most of the islands, especially in the west, lochs, rocky inlets, excellent walking, boat trips, interesting wildlife, Stornoway's busy fishing harbour and the tweed makers on Harris and Lewis. Few conventional holiday amenities, but a chance to enjoy the open air and the hospitable islands.

Standing Stones of Callanish Lewis. Ancient Stone Circle and avenue of megaliths of 2000BC on wild moor.

Lewis Castle Stornoway. Fine wooded gardens and grounds with picnic area, birdlife, ferns and wild flowers. At Arnol see a traditional Hebridean dwelling of timber and thatch.

Kisimul Castle Castlebay. Isle of Barra. On a small island, a remote and interesting 12thC fortress, lately restored.

Loch Druidibeg National Nature Reserve South Uist. Breeding greylag geese and many other species. On North Uist, Belranald Nature Reserve has waders, ducks, etc.

Tourist Boards have lists of recommended walks by shore, loch, hills or cliffs.

Shorbost Museum Lewis. A museum which reflects many interesting aspects of island life – fishing, weaving, crofting.

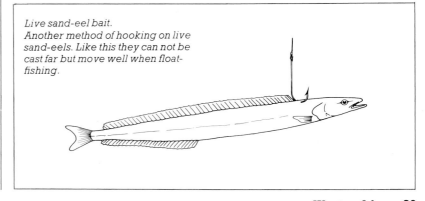

Live sand-eel bait.
Another method of hooking on live sand-eels. Like this they can not be cast far but move well when float-fishing.

Orkney and Shetland Islands

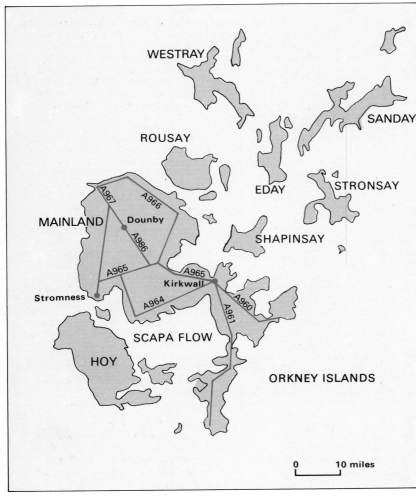

WESTRAY

SANDAY

ROUSAY

EDAY · STRONSAY

A967 · A966

MAINLAND · Dounby

A986

A965

Stromness

A965 · Kirkwall

A964 · A960

A961

SCAPA FLOW

HOY

ORKNEY ISLANDS

0   10 miles

Commercial boatmen can offer very good fresh fish baits.

Charter boats are mainly commercial boats taking the day off. Such craft may be booked from Stromness, Kirkwall, Longhope, Rousay, Shapinsay, and Stronsay. There are also numerous places where both large and small trailed craft may be launched.

Orcadians are friendly people and advice is willingly given, along with directions and suggestions for other sources of information – such as local skippers and anglers.

For more information contact the Orkney Islands Sea Angling Association, Hon. Sec. Leslie Robson, Little Claybraes, St Margarets Hope, Orkney; also, Orkney Tourist Organisation, Information Centre, Broad Street, Kirkwall, Orkney (Tel: Kirkwall (0856) 2856). These two will arrange boat bookings.

FOR THE FAMILY
Apart from good fishing these wild and beautiful islands offer plenty of things to do and places to see, in their moorland and coastal scenery, historic sites, wildlife and in the island centres of Kirkwall and Stromness.
Skara Brae neolithic village with its stone beds, fireplaces, etc, uncovered from beneath the sand dunes.
St Magnus Cathedral Kirkwall. See a fine example of Norman architecture and later styles, with beautiful stained glass. Founded in 1137.
Bishop's Palace and Earl's Palace. Interesting ruins of the 13thC and 16thC near Kirkwall.
Explore the islands by the many boat trips available, to see seabirds, cliffs and remote beaches.
Click Mill nr Dounby. Worth seeing as the only traditional working horizontal watermill of a design introduced by the Vikings.
Scapa Flow visit the deserted but once-great submarine base.

Orkney Islands
Across the Pentland Firth from John o' Groats lies the confused mass of the Orkney Islands, reached by air or by ferry from Scrabster or Wick. The current halibut record is held by a fish from these waters. As with Shetland, the angler coming here to fish for species other than sea-trout is wasting a superb opportunity. The fishing offshore is rich and varied – the species listed for Shetland may all be caught here.

From the shore there are various sites where it is possible to spin above the rough sea bed for coalfish to 2 lb, pollack to double figures, and mackerel. The best season for the coalfish is May–January. The bigger pollack are here during the late winter months. Mackerel are abundant at times from July to September. Wrasse may also be taken on mackerel strip, lugworm or mangled shore crabs from June to September. Some codling, ling and lesser spotted dogfish may also be caught from June to March. Spur dogfish are abundant in warm weather from June onwards. The trouble with bottom fishing here is that the dense swathes of kelp around the shoreline necessitate very heavy tackle. This is not pleasant to use.

However, lugworm cast out a good way from some of the many sandy beaches (with clear water) will produce flounders, small plaice and dabs.

Many sandy beaches yield lugworm and ragworm. There is a fair chance of finding razorfish here too. Crab is abundant in summer from stony areas. Sand-eels can be netted or scraped – or bought fresh.

The Shetland Islands
There is particularly rich fishing around these islands. Halibut, ton-up skate and giant porbeagle sharks are just three of the 40 or so species of fish that appear on the local record list. Others are catfish,

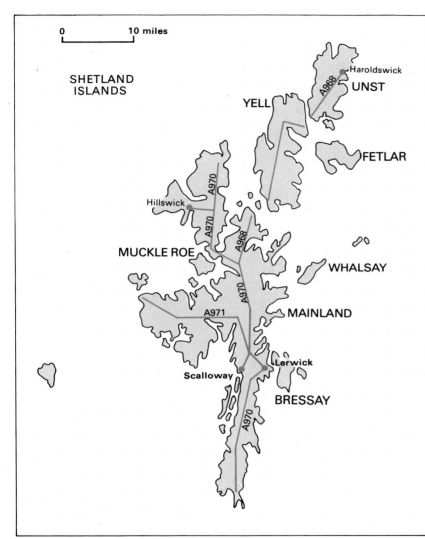

0   10 miles

SHETLAND
ISLANDS

Haroldswick

A968

UNST

YELL

FETLAR

A970

A970

Hillswick

A968

MUCKLE ROE

A970

WHALSAY

A970

A971

MAINLAND

Lerwick

Scalloway

BRESSAY

A970

greater than boat-hire on site.

The Shetland Tourist Organisation is clued-in to local fishing. Contact them at the Information Centre, Lerwick, (Tel: Lerwick (0595) 3434).

Bait is abundant locally. Most of the fishing is from boats and mackerel is the premier bait. It can be obtained virtually anywhere in summer.

Lugworm can be dug at several places. Mussels can easily be gathered from rocks and harbours. Crab can be found during the major part of the season among areas of rubble and sand-eels are abundant. Artificial lures like Redgill sand-eels, spinners, mackerel feathers, cod feathers and pirks are also useful.

It is advisable to take all you will need and more. 30–80 lb class gear is advised for the more powerful beasts offshore, though smaller outfits can be used for the run-of-the-mill species.

Fly fishing and spinning in the sea for sea-trout can provide magical sport when the sea is calm or slightly choppy at evening time and long into the mid-summer dusk. If you take a fly outfit, you may care to fish among the many lochs and lochans for freshwater trout. They make excellent baits for ling.

Access is not allowed to the oil industry's piers.

FOR THE FAMILY

Apart from Shetland ponies and knitwear, you will see fascinating prehistoric sites, seals and vast colonies of seabirds, fishing in the busy harbour towns and have opportunities for sailing, walking, bathing and water skiing.

Fair Isle a mecca for birdwatchers, especially during migration. See the nesting colonies on the cliffs by taking a boat trip from Grutness.

Croft Museum S. Voe, Boddam, Mainland. A museum of the Shetland crofter's history, life and work.

Jarlshof Mainland. Archaeological site occupied by Stone, Iron and Bronze Age Man and Viking and medieval dwellers.

Tingwall Agricultural Museum crofting, fishing, farming and domestic exhibits of Shetland history. Tingwall Loch nearby was an ancient Viking meeting place.

Lerwick visit the Workshop Gallery, where local craftsmen and artists show their work, and the impressive Shetland Museum.

coalfish, cod, conger, dab, dogfish, flounder, grey and red gurnards, haddock, hake, ling, lumpsucker, mackerel, pollack, cuckoo, homelyn and thornback rays, red sea bream, spur dogfish, tope (the record is just under 7 lb), tusk, whiting and wrasse.

From the shore of these deeply indented islands, there is not a great deal of fishing undertaken. Most of the rock marks are buried under dense beds of kelp, while the sandy beaches yield little other than small coalfish, dabs, plaice and other small species. Some rock marks are fishable, though the bottom is generally very rough. The best idea is to get expert guidance on the spot as many marks can be dangerous in

a swell. So jittery can the weather be up here that visitors are advised to come between June and late September.

Charter boats operate out from several ports. These are boats belonging to commercial fishermen and the bookings are best arranged either through hotels or through the Shetland Tourist Organisation. Points of departure are generally Lerwick, Scalloway, Sumburgh, Skeld, Bressay, and Mid Yell.

If you do take your own boat on the ferry from Aberdeen or Wick in Scotland, there are several good launching sites. However, the cost of such extravagance, especially to unknown waters, is likely to be

Grampian

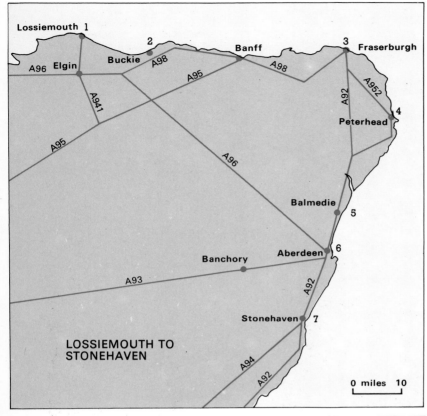

LOSSIEMOUTH TO
STONEHAVEN

0 miles 10

Extensive saltings, sand-bars and marshland between Culbin Forest and the sea make access troublesome – and there is the risk of being cut off by the tide. However, the fishing is poor, so the point is somewhat academic. The large area of sand and saltings at Findhorn Bay is also tough to negotiate and no place for the stranger.

The sandy shoreline continues eastwards to Burghead and ends abruptly there, with sand on the west side, rocky ledges and boulders on the east side. A pattern of rock ledges interspersed by sandy bays continues to three miles west of Branderburgh and Lossiemouth, where sand again takes over and the sweep of Spey Bay runs around to Portgordon. Lossie Forest, between Lossiemouth and Kingston (at the mouth of the Spey) is likely to cause access problems to those who get lost easily.

East of Buckie, shallow reef takes over, cropping up among the sandy bays round towards Findochty and Portnockie. There are some interesting bays and coves to be explored between these two towns – and caves, too. Cullen Bay is sandy, flanked by headlands sloping down to beds of flat rock. This type of rock continues eastwards towards Sandend Bay, and Portsoy, with small, steep headlands jutting between the main ones. This pattern of low headlands, flat rock and sandy bays continues eastwards to Banff, to wide, sandy, stony Boyndie Bay, and Banff Bay, for five miles east of MacDuff to the cliffs of More Head.

East of Gardenstown the shoreline is again of flat rock and rubble with occasional sandy bays, round past precipitous Troup Head and Pennan Head, with the twin sheltered sandy bays at Pennan lying in between, and so on east to Rosehearty with its three-quarter mile wide stretch of sandy beach interrupted by rocky outcrops at Sandhaven, with its one and a half mile sandy bay to the east.

Dune-backed Fraserburgh Bay, lying to the east of the town, offers a good two miles of shallow sands. Although there is some rocky ground around Inverallochy and St Combs, there are four miles of sandy beach backed by dunes. The Loch of Strathbeg lying inland from these dunes makes access hard, though the shore can be reached from the St Combs end or via the coastguard station near Rattray Head.

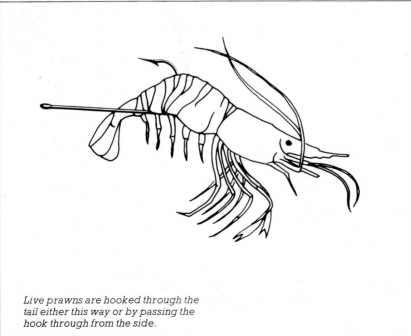

Live prawns are hooked through the tail either this way or by passing the hook through from the side.

Sandy beach backed by dunes extends south from this head for about seven miles to Peterhead with its heavy outcrops of rock and a fine breakwater not far from the prison on the south side of Peterhead Bay. There is another sandy bay just south of here, Sandford Bay, then deeply-indented rocky coves between precipitous headlands, some with sandy beaches at their inland ends, a pattern that continues to the dune-backed Bay of Cruden.

South from this bay are more sandy and rocky coves, not all of which are accessible owing to cliffs behind. But the ground is less hard going than further north, with many of the little headlands easy to negotiate. And there are caves, especially around Collieston.

The rock peters out here, giving way to sand which, over the centuries, has formed the wild and lovely Sands of Forvie nature reserve. Shallow, sandy shoreline continues south past the mouth of the river Ythan, forming one vast sandy beach that continues for some 15 miles from Forvie Ness to Aberdeen.

South from here the shoreline is again comprised of low cliffs, stubby headlands (many of which are easy to negotiate), and small indented bays, some with sand or stones inside, some with caves. There is easy access at Cove Bay, with its picturesque little harbour, Findon, Portlethen, Downies, Newtonhill, Muchalls and Stonehaven. At Stonehaven, a sandy bay is flanked by extensive rock ledges and there are several interesting little bays that are worth exploring for a couple of miles south of the town, though low cliffs and steep slopes make access less than simple.

South to Inverbervie, the shoreline is a mass of little rocky coves, some with sand, small headlands and rock ledges which become more extensive south of Bervie Bay and continue for seven miles to St Cyrus. There then unfolds a five mile stretch of shallow sands backed by golf courses, leading to Montrose and the land-locked sand and mud flats of the Montrose Basin.

Tides around the Grampian area vary from London Bridge by only small amounts of time. High Water at Lossiemouth comes 2 hours before, at Fraserburgh 1½ hours before and at Stonehaven just a few minutes before London Bridge times.

Boats may be chartered from Stonehaven, Fraserburgh, possibly Peterhead, and maybe one or two of the smaller harbours if a private owner is willing. Those with boats of their own on trailers will find reasonable slips at the following places, with the proviso, as ever, to check on availability, ownership and suitability first. Launching sites abound for small craft: Findhorn, Buckie, Findochty, Banff, Gardenstown Harbour, Pennan, Peterhead, Inverbervie and Stonehaven.

Local opinion says that East Scottish fishing is inferior when compared to that available on the West coast, and many local anglers consider the time and money well spent travelling across rather than fishing the local marks. However, there is some fair fishing, especially in boats. There is not so much deep water close to shore hereabouts.

1 Lossiemouth Renowned for the RAF station (from which weather information may be sought); local fishing is for conger, coalfish, flatfish, haddock and codling from the shore; similar, more and bigger fish out to sea. There is good shore sea-trout spinning along here, between Boar's Head Rock and the harbour, from beaches around the estuary mouth, and down the coast at Garmouth, where the Spey enters the sea by the old cement works. Details from The Tackle Shop, 188 High Street, Elgin (Tel: Elgin (0343) 3129); The Tackle Shop, 97b High Street, Forres (Tel: Forres (0309) 72936) and the Angling Centre, Moss Street, Elgin (Tel: Elgin (0343) 7615). Remember the closed season for migratory fish and to buy a licence, even when fishing for them in salt water.

2 Buckie This major commercial fishing port is a useful centre for fish

A fine tope from Scottish waters is returned safely to the sea.

bait and information. There are sandy beaches and massive cliffs along here, with plenty of bait available locally to catch standard inshore species. Try fishing the Deveron estuary, the rocks at Boyne Bay and those east of Macduff to Head of Garness, and other marks around Banff. Also check out Portnockie, the little fishing village on Cullen Bay, and do not overlook Portsoy. More details of some interesting fishing from: Bruce's, 61 West Church Street, Buckie (Tel: Buckie (0542) 32161); Slater Sports, 5 High Street, Buckie (Tel: Buckie (0542) 31769) also Jaytee Sports, 14 Low Street, Banff (Tel: Banff (026 12) 5821).

3 Fraserburgh Yet another area where sea-trout may be taken from the shore in respectable numbers. Indeed, marine sea-trout fishing remains one of the least widespread forms of sea fishing in the British Isles. Rock and estuary marks fish well from July to October, especially during warm weather when the mackerel and coalfish are shoaling. Around here coalfish are also known as saithe. Good fishing here, and fairly swift tides. Details from G. S. Clark, 40 Cross Street, Fraserburgh (Tel: Fraserburgh (034 62) 4427) also Dick's Sports, 54 Broad Street, Fraserburgh (Tel: Fraserburgh (034 62) 4120).

4 Peterhead Local opinion is divided as to whether the south pier is out of bounds, but all agree that even the fishable north pier at Peterhead is no place to go in rough weather when it becomes very dangerous. Under more clement conditions the flood tide produces most codling, flounders, mackerel, garfish, coalfish, pollack, conger, ling, catfish and, once, the Scottish record plaice. Kipper is a successful bait here – the fish are accustomed to effluent from the smoking house. For more details contact local expert R. J. B. Findlay, 49 Henderson Drive, Elrick, Skene (Tel: Aberdeen (0224) 741704); G. S. Clark, 88 Kirk Street, Peterhead (Tel: Peterhead (0779) 2599) also Robertson Sports, 1 Kirk Street, Peterhead (Tel: Peterhead (0779) 2584).

5 Balmedie There are some excellent headlands around here for rock fishing. At Harehill (straight in front of Harehill Terrace, a tenement house near the filling station), there is deep water close in and halibut are occasionally caught here. From the

Bay of Cruden to Collieston a good cast on a rising tide will produce fish, though mainly small ones. Details from local experts who work at, or pass the time of day at, J. Somers & Sons, 40 Thistle Street, Aberdeen (Tel: Aberdeen (0224) 50910).

6 Aberdeen There is fair fishing for flounders, dabs and eels on a rising tide at the mouth of the river Don. Beaches around here fish best in dirty water after a blow when scented baits like lugworm, ragworm, peeler crab and mussel score well. Beaches to the north of the Dee fish well for flatfish on a rising tide, with similar conditions producing cod and saithe around Girdle Ness. Rock marks south of Nigg Bay produce best from October to February, the mixed ground yielding cod, saithe, dabs, flounders, conger, haddock and lythe (pollack). At Cove Bay, the rocks to the left of the harbour fish best for cod on an ebbing tide. Likewise Blowup Nose point. Findon Ness produces cod, lythe, saithe and wrasse on all tides, likewise other headlands further south to Portlethen Bay. And so on south to Downie Point. Remember that the seas here can be very dangerous, so take care when rock fishing. More information from David Wright, 4 Earnsheugh Road, Findon Village, Portlethen, Aberdeen (Tel: Aberdeen (0224) 780313); J. Dickson & Son Ltd., 35 Belmont Street, Aberdeen (Tel: Aberdeen (0224) 20480) also W. Brown & Co., 11 Belmont Street (Tel: Aberdeen (0224) 21692).

7 Stonehaven Fish a falling sea after a blow, but with a rising tide to catch cod, coalfish, pollack, catfish, wrasse, gurnard, plaice, dabs, and flounders around here. This port offers excellent boat fishing. Contact Mrs E. Cargill, who does the booking for all skippers (Tel: Stonehaven (0569) 62483); alternatively, Ian Watson, 16 Castle Square, Stonehaven (Tel: Stonehaven (0569) 63625). More details from R. Millington-Jefferies, 39 New Street, Rothes (Tel: Rothes (034 03) 407). There is good rock fishing hereabouts.

Bait Areas
No shortage of bait along this stretch of the Scottish coastline. Mussels cling to every (or so it seems) pier and rock, while areas of rubble with sand and mud produce peeler crabs in high summer. Lugworm varies in quality around the coast, as also does the size of ragworm, but it seems as

though there is always a bed handy, along with a local who knows either the precise location or the address of somebody who will sell you fresh bait. Many of the mud/sand shores and estuaries produce razorfish, clams and cockles which also score well, especially when crammed on to large hooks for cod. Fish baits are available from fish piers and docksides. Again, enquire locally.

FOR THE FAMILY
There are fine clean beaches, pleasant fishing villages, numerous things to see and do in Aberdeen, ancient buildings, distilleries and Highland Games to visit and some of the most exciting scenery in Britain near at hand. At Fraserburgh and other resorts there are plenty of sports facilities and entertainments.

Dufftown tour two famous malt whisky distilleries and see every process of manufacture. The Whisky Trail takes in visits to several interesting distilleries throughout the county.

Loch Muick Red Deer Reserve. South of Ballater. Visitor Centre and walks in the forests.

Balmoral gardens and grounds of the Royal castle, with an exhibition, shops, restaurant. Open May, June, July.

Elgin impressive ruins of a once-great cathedral in beautiful surroundings. Signposted walks and picnic areas in nearby Monaughty Forest.

Crathes east of Banchory. Enjoy the sight of a Scottish baronial castle with fine interior, paintings, works of art and unusual gardens. Trails.

Aberdeen much to see, including the Art Gallery, St Machar's Cathedral, museums, gardens, beaches and entertainments.

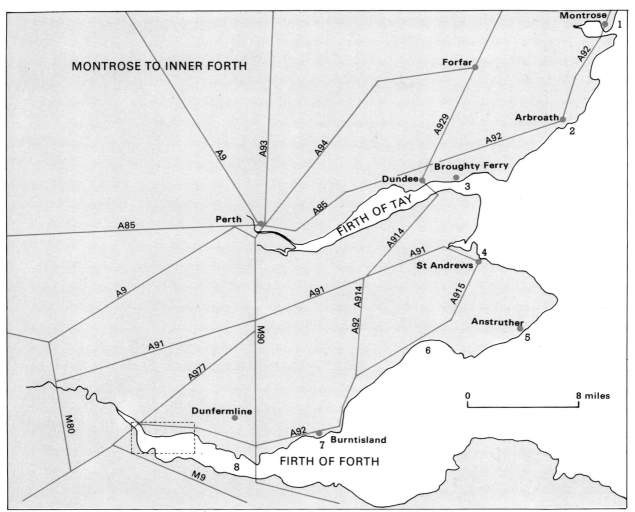

MONTROSE TO INNER FORTH

FIRTH OF TAY

FIRTH OF FORTH

0   8 miles

An area of low-lying rock runs for four miles south of Montrose to Lunan Bay, and more shallow sands. The rocky headland on the south side of this wide bay signals the start of more cove country – little headlands, flat rock ledges, sometimes backed by cliffs, sometimes by easy slopes, continuing south to Arbroath, south of which lies a short stretch of shallow sandy beach before rock ledges again intervene some three miles north of Carnoustie.

Sandy beaches characterise Buddon Ness, a Ministry of Defence Danger Area. Sand and a few patches of rubble are to be found westwards to Dundee, with sand and stones characterising both sides of the Firth of Tay. There is a large area of saltings and mud flats west of Dundee. East of Tayport, extensive sandbanks

stretch for several miles out to sea, with a channel separating the Abertay sands from those marking the shoreline.

A long, shallow beach of sand extends in front of Tentsmuir Forest round to the mouth of the river Eden, with its extensive sand and mud flats, and on towards St Andrews with its rocky foreshore. South east of here the shoreline is largely of flat rock ledges interspersed with patches of boulders and sand. This type of ground extends for 10 miles to Fife Ness, where the coastline doubles back on itself, with similar ground being found southwards to Crail, Anstruther, St Monance, Elie and Earlsferry. Deep water is hard to find around here – the shoreline shelves slowly.

Sandy, south-facing Largo Bay has flat, rocky outcrops at its centre, directly in front of the town. South west of Methil there is an area of sand, but this turns to rock at Buckhaven. This rocky ground extends south west to West Wemyss before becoming sandy again towards Kirkcaldy on the north side of the Firth of Forth. Much of this side is comprised of patches of sand among flat rock, with more extensive sands to be found at Burntisland, Silversands Bay and Dalgety Bay. West of the Forth Bridge there are extensive sands with occasional outcrops of rock, such ground to be found on both sides of the Firth. Wide realms of lugworm-filled sand are to be found along the waterfront of Edinburgh, to each side of the docks.

Tayside, Fife and Central

Boats may be chartered from Arbroath, Anstruther, Pittenweem, St Andrews, Kirkcaldy and Edinburgh. Facilities are how you find them. Members of the Buckhaven and District S.A.C. have their own enclosed boat park on the foreshore. Many members are happy to take out competent anglers with them as it often happens that private owners' regular buddies have domestic duties or work on a day of perfect weather. On such days anybody will do as crew!

Trailed boats may be launched at various sites, including the above club pound, with prior agreement. Such slips are to be found at Montrose, Arbroath, Dundee, Newburgh, Tayport, St Andrews, Anstruther, St Monance, Kinghorn, Dysart, Burntisland, North Queensferry, Aberdour and Grangemouth. Other facilities exist for smaller craft.

Tidal variations from London Bridge are: plus ½ an hour for Arbroath, 1 hour for Grangemouth.

1 Montrose   There is good rock fishing around here, especially at Scurdie Ness Lighthouse, with the usual species prevalent. A breath of easterly wind is liked around here to stir up the sea bed and bring the fish in close. Other rock marks further south towards Arbroath. Details from W. Phillips, 180 High Street, Montrose (Tel: Montrose (0674) 2692).

2 Arbroath   Famous for its smoked haddock – delicious Arbroath smokies – there is good fishing for cod (the major local species all year through), conger, coalfish, haddock, wrasse and ling. Summer species are most prevalent from June to August, while winter species are around from October to February. Local cliffs and other rock marks fish best over the low or high tide periods, depending on where you fish. Bait fishing is best in murky water after a storm; find clear water for summer spinning. Details from R. Herdman, 112 Millfield Road, Arbroath (Tel: Arbroath (0241) 77287, home) also Thomas Clark & Sons, 274 High Street, Arbroath (Tel: Arbroath (0241) 73467).

3 Broughty Ferry   Excellent sheltered boat fishing for middle weight fish. Beaches here and at Tayport across the Firth of Tay produce codling, coalfish, plaice and flounders on locally abundant rag, lugworm, mussel or peeler crab. Good local rock marks, but take care and seek advice – here, and at many

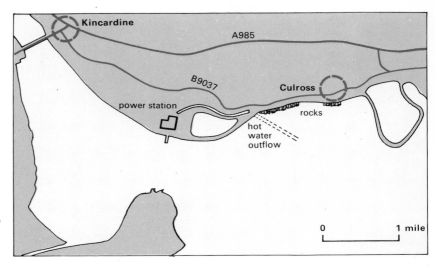

places around this coast, there have been fatal accidents through people ignoring signs and through inexperience of local conditions. Spring tides produce the best results around here. At sea, when boat fishing, the bottom is very snaggy around the most productive codling grounds. One tip is to fix a stone into an old stocking or tights' leg and use that as a sinker. Information from J. R. Gow & Sons, 12 Union Street, Dundee (Tel: Dundee (0382) 25427; P. D. Malloch, 24 Scott Street, Perth (Tel: Perth (0738) 21631); Shotcast Ltd., 8 Whitehall Crescent, Dundee (Tel: Dundee (0382) 25621); Ruthven P. Smith, 287 Brook Street, Broughty Ferry, Dundee (Tel: Dundee (0382) 77351), also DL & DS Ross, 2 Mill Lane, Tayport (Tel: Tayport (082 65) 2518).

4 St Andrews   The boat fishing here is widely considered to be better than the shore fishing, but rocks and sandy beaches hereabouts produce well under the right conditions – rising spring tides and a ground sea running. Check out local details at any of the tackle dealers listed above.

5 Pittenweem   Rock marks are excellent here, but heavy kelp guarantees the loss of plenty of tackle and many hooked fish. There are several excellent locations around here. Anstruther offers good fishing from around the harbour and, as ever, bait is plentiful. Details from: The Anster Gift Box, 44 Shore Street, Anstruther (Tel: Anstruther (0333) 310389). Local anglers have widespread knowledge of their coast and do not overlook crab and lobster fishermen when seeking advice.

They know this coastline well.

6 Largo Bay   There are several good spots around this bay and further west to East Wemyss. Fish for plaice, haddock, codling, mackerel and whiting using easily-gathered local baits. One good local spot is the outfall from the Methil Power Station near the Leven estuary. At Buckhaven there is an area of weedy rock that produces wrasse, codling and so forth, while Leven's flat sandy shore is good for flounders. Some fine sole are caught offshore on the sandy sea bed. Details from James Forsyth, 142 West Street, Buckhaven (Tel: Buckhaven (0592) 713689); Sportshop (Fife) Ltd, 1 Sandwell Street, Buckhaven (Tel: Buckhaven (0592) 712480) also, Davesports, 14a Bridge Street, Leven (Tel: Leven (0333) 25115).

7 Burntisland   Fish the beach at night from the bottom to half flood from November through to March. Bait with ragworm, lugworm, or locally abundant white ragworm (eat your hearts out, Southern match anglers! There is no shortage of white ragworm up here). Long casting scores from the open beach, but leads to tackle losses from rock marks. Enquire for precise marks from: H. F. Greil, 24 James Grove, Kirkcaldy (Tel: Kirkcaldy (0592) 62584); Alex Constables, 39a High Street, Kirkcaldy (Tel: Kirkcaldy (0592) 60770); James Grubb, 367 High Street, Kirkcaldy (Tel: Kirkcaldy (0592) 60441) or Sportshop Ltd, 31 Esplanade, Kirkcaldy (Tel: Kirkcaldy (0592) 69416) also, We're Game, 3 Park Road, Kirkcaldy (Tel:

Kirkcaldy (0592) 54301).

8 Inner Forth West of the Forth Bridge there is good fishing for flat-fish, codling, whiting and other small species from the largely sandy beaches. There are bass – mainly from Cockenzie Power Station near Edinburgh, but also from Torry Burn, spinning with slender silver spoons on the early flood tide. Here are found some excellent winter flounders of high average size (2 lb). Details from local expert Robert Mitchell, 22 Meadowgreen, Sauchie by Alloa (Tel : Alloa (0259) 213415). Also from the many tackle dealers in Falkirk, and D. Crockart & Son, 15 King Street, Stirling (Tel : Stirling (0786) 3443).

Bait Areas
There is plenty of ragworm, lugworm and shellfish from sandy, muddy estuaries. Good razorfish, too, known locally as 'spoots' after their habit of throwing out a spurt of water from their burrow when a heavy-footed digger approaches. Areas of rubble and rock produce peeler crab later in the year – July and August – while white ragworm beds are to be found among the lugworm hereabouts.

Fish baits may be hard to catch – the mackerel have been scarce of late and arrive late in the year – July time. However, there are plenty of local fishing harbours, processing houses, fish docks and markets where really first class herrings, sprats and mackerel may be purchased. Do not overlook strips of small codling, pollack, coalfish or wrasse heads. They all work. A fresh bait is generally more important than an extremely oily or bloody one.

FOR THE FAMILY
One of Scotland's most beautiful regions, it is crossed by great lochs and rivers, bordered by forests, has 50 miles of fine sandy beaches. Every kind of holiday activity and sport in the region and much of interest in Stirling, Perth, Dundee, St Andrews and other historic towns.

Tentsmùir Point National Nature Reserve. A place to watch migrants and many species on the dunes, foreshore and marsh.

Scottish Fisheries Museum Anstruther. The story of fishermen and the fishing industry. Aquarium and fishing craft.

Mills Observatory Dundee. Study the stars through giant astro-telescopes. Lectures and displays. Dundee's six other museums include the Spalding Golf Museum.

Glamis Castle Angus. Ancestral home of the Queen Mother in French chateau style. Grounds by Capability Brown. May–Oct.

Dundee Leisure Centre Landfall. It has four swimming pools, sauna, weight training, table tennis, restaurants, etc.

Scone Palace Perth. Crowning-place of the Scottish kings. Fine interior and collections of furniture, china, etc. May–Sept.

Blair Drummond Castle nr Stirling. A good day out to see lions, elephants, dolphins, in beautiful surroundings. Pets corner, play area, etc.

Landing a large skate. The charter boat was fishing the waters of Scapa Flow.

Lothian and Borders

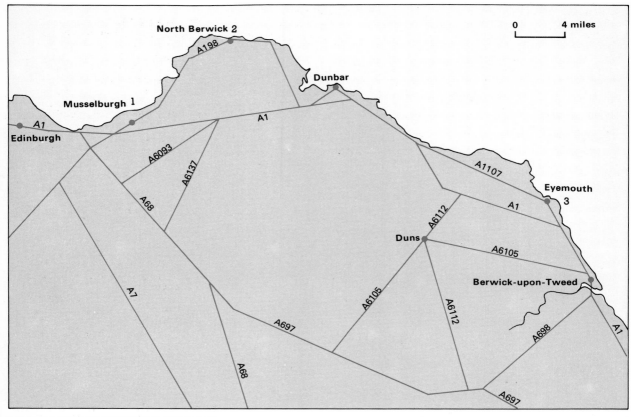

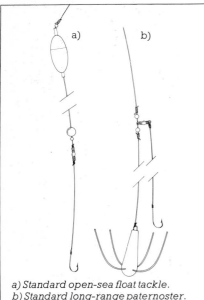

a) Standard open-sea float tackle.
b) Standard long-range paternoster.
Beads are trapped on leader by stop-knots tied with separate lengths of nylon. Swivel rotates freely.

Eastwards from Edinburgh, towards the mullet haven at Cockenzie Power Station, outcrops of rock add interest to the sands. Then there is more sand, with a few rocks and boulders inshore, towards the sand-flats and saltings that constitute the nature reserve of Aberlady Bay. Outcrops of rock and straggly boulders break up the sands westwards to North Berwick and out to the mouth of the Firth to Dunbar. West of the town lies shallow, sandy Belhaven Bay, where marshy saltings restrict access. East of the town is an area of extensive flat rocky outcrops with sands in between. Sometimes the sand predominates, sometimes the rock. Access is no trouble, with the A1 so close by.

South east of Cockburnspath the shoreline becomes more steep, often requiring the visitor to scramble down some steep slopes to the beach – again of rock with sand patches, with' cliffs around the headland formed by Telegraph Hill. The coastline then becomes severe, with cliffs denying access to much of the shoreline towards St Abb's Head and south to the little harbour of St Abb's. There is sand, boulders and rock ledges at Coldingham and round to Eyemouth. Here the cliffs rise up again, stretching towards Burnmouth. Between here and Berwick-upon-Tweed, the shoreline is largely of rock outcrops and boulders with a few patches of sand among them. The railway follows the coastline high up above the sea, but the steepness of the hills and cliffs make access difficult.

Charter boats operate out from Edinburgh, Musselburgh, North Berwick, Dunbar, Eyemouth and Burnmouth. As with many Scottish charter craft, prior arrangements are essential as most skippers make their living from commercial fishing or potting, with charter trips a sideline.

Trailed boats of reasonable size may be launched at Queensferry, Cramond, Fisherrow, Cockenzie, North Berwick, Dunbar and St Abb's. Other facilities are available for those with the energy to drag their craft or trailers to the water's edge.

Tidal variation is about 1 hour after London Bridge times.

1 Musselburgh West of the town, with its busy marina at Fisherrow, the extensively shallow shoreline is populated by sand-loving dabs, plaice and flounders, most of which are available right through the year. Some codling are caught, together with winter whiting, but the better fishing is considered to be east of the town. Excellent sport can be had spinning for bass in the warm-water outflow from Longgannat and Cockenzie Power Stations. While the fishing at Cockenzie is restricted to a small area below the outfall, Longgannat provides an area of several hundred yards. Mullet, too, are taken here on bread and minced fish baits. Details from any of the many Edinburgh tackle dealers: Anglers Corner, 3 Churchill Place (Tel: Edinburgh (031) 447 3676); J. Dickson & Son Ltd, 21 Frederick Street (Tel: Edinburgh (031) 225 4218); Field and Stream, 61 Montrose Terrace, Abbeyhill (Tel: Edinburgh (031) 661 4282); Gun & Fishing Tackle Shop, 28a Haddington Place (Tel: Edinburgh (031) 556 9384); Shooting Lines Ltd, 23 Roseburn Terrace (Tel: Edinburgh (031) 337 8616) or F. D. Simpson Ltd, 28 West Preston Street (Tel: Edinburgh (031) 667 3058).

2 North Berwick Some good shore rock fishing around here and east to Dunbar. Locals like a strong easterly blow to stir up the sea, fishing in the dirty water that rolls in after the wind has died down. Codling (round here a ten pounder is big, even from boats), whiting, coalfish, haddock, plaice and, in mid-summer, mackerel are all taken here, with wrasse and small conger eels also available from heavy rock formations. On night tides after a storm, Belhaven Beach, at the mouth of the Tyne, produces good fishing, even if not for large fish. Long casting is useful. Details from Fisherman's Cove, High Street, Dunbar.

3 Eyemouth Access is denied to much of the foreshore north of Eyemouth by the steep and rugged nature of the coast. Although the scenery is wild and unspoilt around here, the fishing does not justify suicidal scrambles down dripping wet cliff faces. Eyemouth's local beaches and rocks produce as well

Serious consideration of the catch is called for here as the angler poses for the album photo in Stremnell Harbour!

as anywhere else around here, mainly for codling, as the larger fish are offshore where conger, skate, catfish, haddock, plaice, sole and flounders are taken. The rock marks are often very snaggy, necessitating plenty of disposable sinkers instead of pukka lead weights. Details from: R. Grieve & Sons, 26 High Street, Eyemouth (Tel: Eyemouth (0390) 50270). Information is given freely by the professional crab and lobster fishermen who work out from Eyemouth and Burnmouth harbours.

Bait Areas
Southern Forth beaches are alive with ragworm, lugworm and white ragworm. Clams, cockles and razorfish are also available in places. Mussels, peeler crab and limpets may be gathered from the rocks and around piers and harbour walls. Fish baits are likely to be scarce, though a wrasse head or a fresh-caught coalfish or small codling can be processed into acceptable baits. Herring and mackerel are easiest to obtain from harbours and fish markets. Mackerel are not as plentiful around here as they once were.

FOR THE FAMILY
From your holiday location on the Borders or Lothian coast you can tour among heather-covered moors, old coastal towns, visiting historic houses, abbeys and many places of interest. If you're close to Edinburgh you also have the whole range of its entertainments, shopping and sports activities.

Dalkeith Park nr Edinburgh. A day in the Palace grounds. Nature trails, Adventure Woodland play area, riverside walks, tunnel walk. Mar–Oct.

Museum of Flight East Fortune. Jets, Spitfire, historic aircraft, rockets, etc. 1934 autogiro. July–Aug. open days.

Edinburgh Wax Museum the City has 20 museums. This one tells the story of Scottish history in models and waxworks of the famous and infamous.

Manderston nr Duns. Unique Adam-style mansion with silver staircase, gardens and woodlands. May–Sept.

North Berwick take a boat trip round the 350-ft Bass Rock with its gannetry and thousands of seabirds.

Northumberland, Tyne and Wear, Durham, Cleveland

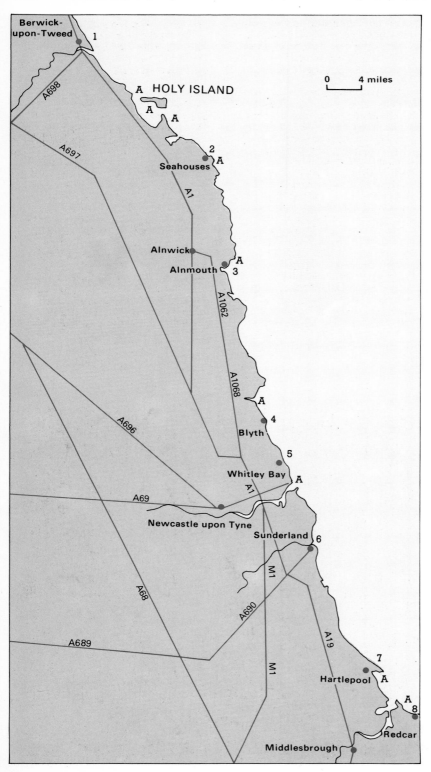

South of Berwick-upon-Tweed there is some sand, then an area of rock outcrops which peters out into the dune country behind shallow Cheswick Sands. These grow into the vast, rippling sand-flats around Holy Island where a spring tide is said to be able to overtake a fit man running. These flats continue south to the dune-lands of Ross Back Sands, which almost lock the muddy saltings of Budle Bay off from the sea.

The Harkness Rocks interrupt the sands just north of Bamburgh and more rocky platforms are to be found at North Sunderland and Beadnell, with flat sandy beaches in between. Rock promontories enclose the two and a half mile sweep of sandy Beadnell Bay. The National Trust owns nearly five miles of this coastline south to Castle Point, a shoreline characterised by rock fingers among the flowing sands.

South of sandy Embleton Bay, the coastline becomes harsher. Rock ledges take over from the sand, these rocky flats running from Craster south to Alnmouth with just three small sandy bays in six and a half miles of coastline.

Between Alnmouth and Amble lie four miles of sandy shore with an outcrop of rock – Birling Carrs – in the middle. There is more sand than rock around the headland at Amble, while sandy Druridge Bay lies in a six-mile sweep before being cut off by the rock scars at Snab Point just south of Cresswell.

Lynemouth Bay is sandy as far south as the cliffs at Beacon Point where more rock scars jut out to sea. Newbiggin Bay is short, sandy, and flanked by rocky outcrops. Then there is more sand – and coal slag – around the mouth of the river Wansbeck and southwards to Blyth. A few rock ledges add character to the town beaches, but the sands return southwards to Seaton Sluice. Here rock ledges and sand intermingle, creating a pattern of shoreline that continues southwards to Whitley Bay and the connurbation of Tynemouth and South Shields. The same pattern – rock scars with patches of sand in between – is also found at Whitburn and Sunderland. Apart from small areas, the rocks peter out south of Sunderland and the shoreline is mainly sandy, backed by low hills between Seaham and Hartlepool. Tees Bay at the mouth of the river Tees, is extensively sandy, a wide sweep from the harbour at Hartlepool round past the Coatham Rocks at Redcar, ending at the precipitous headlands of Hunt Cliff and Saltburn Scar to the east of Saltburn by the Sea.

Here the coastline does another of its dramatic changes, with the Yorkshire Moors falling steeply into the sea. There is a break in the cliffs at Skinningrove, with its stubby pier, then rock scars backed by cliffs continue for four miles to the little harbour of Staithes.

Codling are the staple species for anglers along this coastline. A double figure fish is a good one anywhere, but here it is very special. Coalfish, known locally as billet, are numerous and weigh up to 3 lb, but averaging half that. Whiting, flatfish, eels, mackerel and haddock are taken here. Some places offer mullet fishing and there is also some bass fishing. Boat anglers catch more and better of the above species, plus sole, gurnard, a few conger eels, dogfish, tope, thornback rays and better cod.

Durham beaches are made up extensively of slag from the coal tips. Sometimes it is possible to gather up enough lumps to make a fire and cook your freshly caught fish on the beach – if the weather allows!

Charter boats operate out from various ports. Some are better than others. Check out what facilities are on offer and what you will be paying for before you go afloat. Boats leave from Hartlepool, North Shields, Seahouses, Tees Bay, Seaham Harbour, Redcar, Eyemouth, Staithes Harbour and probably from other little harbours along the coast. Few places offer a regular chartering service.

Those with boats on trailers can launch reasonable boats from various spots. Lesser craft, as usual, have a wider pick of available launch sites. However, small boats should not go far in strange waters. More seaworthy hulls may be launched at Berwick-upon-Tweed, Beadnell, Alnmouth, Foxton Bay, Newbiggin-on-Sea,

Saltburn-by-the-Sea and Staithes.

Tidal variations are as follows: plus 1 hour for Berwick-upon-Tweed, 2 hours for Newcastle and Hartlepool, on to London Bridge tide times.

1 Berwick-upon-Tweed Flounder fishing is productive at the mouth of the Tweed and on nearby sandy beaches early in the year when the fish migrate down-river to spawn. Fish from the North Breakwater, Spittal Beach or the rocks under the cliffs at Bears Head or Huds Head for codling and billet (small coalfish). Details from Game Fair, 12 Marygate, Berwick-upon-Tweed (Tel: Berwick-upon-Tweed (0289) 5119).

2 Seahouses Fish the northern end of Cherwick sands on a flooding tide at night for billet, codling, and flatfish. Similar species are to be had from the harbour arm, and there is fair rock fishing from Saltpan Rocks, The Skerrs, Snook Point and The Tumblers. Ray's Bream, that curious aluminium-coloured fish with the Pekinese face, are caught here and for a hundred

Night fishing for codling from a shingle beach.

miles or so further south in October and November – most of them ending up stranded after drifting into cold water and becoming comatose.

3 Alnmouth Flounders here in the estuary are taken on locally-dug ragworm and lugworm in winter. Rock ledges northwards to Craster, and Birling Carrs, offer good sport with the usual local species on a flooding tide, especially when the water is settling down after a blow. Similar fishing at Hauxley Point at Amble and from both piers there. Details from: Greys of Alnwick, Goods Yard, Alnwick Station, Alnwick (Tel: Alnwick (0665) 602696) also, Murraysport, 2 Narrowgate Street, Alnwick (Tel: Alnwick (0665) 602462). Also from local fishermen and commercial netsmen and potters.

4 Blyth Fish inside the estuary for the usual local species. West pier – which should not be fished in rough weather for safety reasons – produces results and famous Blyth beach is also good, from the town to Seaton Sluice. Long casting is not necessary, but good bait is – crab, lugworm, ragworm or mussel. Rough seas produce the best results, with peak season from September to March. Some bass are caught from Cambois Power Station outfall. Cambois beach produces reasonable fishing, especially in the deeper water by the rocks at the southern end, these rocks also producing good winter cod. Nearby, at Newbiggin, Cresswell Skeer, Lyne Burn, The Beacons and Church Point all produce well at times. Watch out against being cut-off by the tides. Details: M. Cropp, 8 Have Lock Street, Blyth (Tel: Blyth (06706) 2574).

5 Whitley Bay To the north, towards Seaton Sluice, Rocky Island often produces good bags of billet and codling. Rocks towards West Bay fish well during gentle conditions around low water and the rougher the better around high water. St Mary's Island produces cod and the usual local species and loads of mackerel when they are running. Plenty of useful rock scars southwards to Tynemouth Castle. Watch out for rogue swells when rock or jetty fishing. Details from: McDermotts, 112 Station Road, Ashington (Tel: Ashington (0670) 812214); W. Temple, 43 Ocean View, Whitley Bay (Tel: Whitley Bay (0632) 526017); D. G. Aggas, 59 South Frederick Street, South Shields (Tel: South Shields

(0632) 565195) and R. S. Tackle, 36 Collingwood Street, Newcastle (Tel: Newcastle (0632) 25731).

6 Sunderland Two piers and a host of rock marks to north and south make this area popular all year round. Summer codling – the red, maroon-shaded fish – inhabit the kelp tangles while other local species go about their usual business. The river yields plenty of flounders in spring. Southwards at Seaham there is also fair fishing – mainly for the ubiquitous codling. Peeler crab is the number one summer bait for these, with lugworm and mussel best in winter. Details from: Dave Miller, 314 High Street West, Sunderland (Tel: Sunderland (0783) 59666); The Fishbowl, 3 Burdon Road, Sunderland (Tel: Sunderland (0783) 71026); J. Robson, 22 Vine Place, Sunderland (Tel: Sunderland (0783) 4103); Angling Supplies, 5 North Terrace, Seaham (Tel: Seaham (0783) 813962) and Peterlee Sports, 45 Foden Way, Peterlee (Tel: Peterlee (0783) 862396).

7 Hartlepool The Heugh Pier is off

limits, but Red Light Pier, Banjo Pier and Middleton Pier may all be fished. These are excellent places to spin or float fish for mackerel on a calm July–August morning (early) or evening at high water. Streetly Pier is also private, and a permit is required to fish North Gare. Long casting scores from the beaches here, short casts from the numerous rock marks northwards to Easington. There is excellent flounder fishing around South Gare. More information from Anglers Corner (they are very well-informed here), 121 Abingdon Road, Middlesborough (Tel: Middles-borough (0642) 243073); Anglers Services Ltd, 27 Park Road, Hartlepool (Tel: Hartlepool (0429) 74844); F & K Flynn Ltd, 12 Viro Terrace, Stockton-on-Tees (Tel: Stockton-on-Tees (0642) 66473) and J. F. Gent, 161 York Road, Hartlepool (Tel: Hartlepool (0429) 72585).

8 Redcar The beach and scars fish well for cod, coalfish and flounders using crab in summer, lugworm/mussel cocktails in winter. Casting

helps from open beach while some rock gullies involve fishing under the rod tip. Heavy seas score in winter. Less tumultuous water is needed for Marske Beach, fishing around the high water period – same species, plus whiting. Saltburn pier and beach produce cod, whiting and flounders. Long casting from beaches improves results. Around Staithes, the gullies and tangle beds fish well during calm, warm, summer weather and into autumn for the rock cod. Local information is vital here – and indeed for any other unfamiliar rock mark. Details from Anglers Corner (see above); Harry Brough Ltd, 20 West Terrace, Redcar (Tel: Redcar (0642) 482142); D. Smith Ltd, 23 Station Road, Redcar (Tel: Redcar (0642) 486827) also Ward Thompson Bros, 87 Brough Road, Middlesborough (Tel: Middlesborough (0642) 247206).

Catches of codling like this are common in this area from in-shore reefs.

Bait Areas
Informants advise that owing to heavy unemployment in this area there is intense pressure on bait beds. What beds there are are generally small and quality has suffered due to over-digging. Peeler crab is very easy to find from May onwards. White ragworm is common. Plenty of ragworm and lugworm can be found, with major beds around Holy Island, while digging near the Island itself is prohibited. It is the small local beds that have been hammered. Because there are so many small sandy areas set among rocks, it would be impractical to mark them all. Ragworm and lugworm are found in larger quantities inside the estuaries that drain the Cheviot Hills and the Pennines. Some clams can be found in the sand. Mussels are easy to find – and are extremely effective local baits. White ragworm is known locally as white worm.

A Lugworm, ragworm, white ragworm

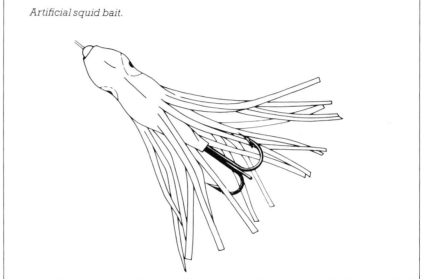

Artificial squid bait.

FOR THE FAMILY
The long coastline from Teesside to the Scottish border, of Northumberland, Tyne and Wear, Durham and Cleveland, provides some ideal walking country, is rich in historical and wildlife interest and offers much in the way of seaside attractions, sport and family excursions and activities.

Hadrian's Wall beyond Newcastle. Explore the Roman wall and enjoy superb views north and south. Visit Housetead's Fort and museum and Vindolanda Fort, museum and gardens.

Bamburgh Castle Northumberland. Norman coastal fortress. Open Apr–Oct. Visit Grace Darling Museum (Mar–Oct) or the Farne Islands seabird reserve and grey seal colony, by boat from Seahouses.

Cleveland Way long distance footpath. 90 miles of outstanding coastal and moorland scenery in Cleveland and Yorkshire.

North Road Station Museum Darlington. Many historic exhibits.

North of England and Open Air Museum Beamish, Co. Durham. Large industrial collection.

Washington Old Hall Washington, Tyne and Wear, 17thC ancestral home of George Washington. Also Washington Wildfowl Park with over 100 species, picnic areas.

Bowes Museum nr Barnard Castle, Durham. Great treasure house of works of art in a splendid mansion with beautiful grounds. May–Sept.

Woodland Visitor Centre Jedburgh. Walks in the Border forests, play area, games, exhibition, tearoom, etc.

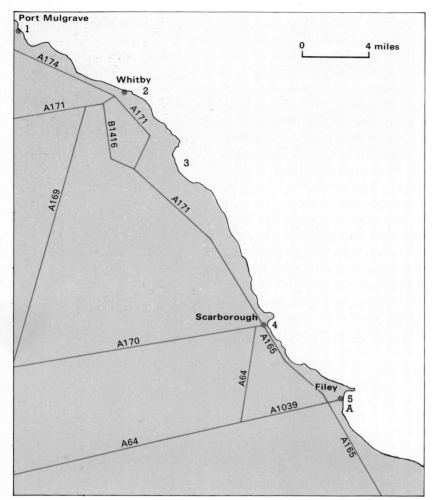

exist at: Runswick Bay, Whitby (several), Robin Hood's Bay (down a very steep, narrow road – park the trailer and inspect it first!), and Filey, where, for some reason, only boats of under twelve horse-power may be launched.

Tidal variation from London Bridge differs between Whitby (add $2\frac{1}{4}$ hours) and Scarborough (add $2\frac{3}{4}$ hours).

Local species of fish are largely cod, codling, small coalfish, plaice, dabs, flounders, rockling, garfish and mackerel. The arrival of the summer mackerel shoals has been getting later and later in recent years, with the shoals becoming increasingly fewer. They show best in hot summers. This applies to a significant portion of the East Coast.

1 Port Mulgrave This old harbour offers a safe footing for those in search of winter cod during heavy seas backed by a stiff nor'westerly wind. Local guidance is essential for access down cliffs and along the foreshore to gullies and tangle beds to the north when fairly heavy northerly seas bring the fish in close. Bait with crab in summer and autumn, worm and mussel in winter. At Runswick Bay, long casting is not essential to catch fish from this steep beach using the usual baits. During rough seas, daylight fishing is as good as at night. Kettleness Point is a good place for red summer cod fishing into the kelp gullies in settled weather, with crab bait that can be collected at low water right there. The best time to fish is two hours each side of low water. The long, steep path down the cliffs is safe – but take care when it is wet.

2 Whitby This harbour burst into the headlines quite recently with the large hauls of pirk-caught wreck cod that are taken here in summer, with August the premier month. Charter facilities are excellent here, with the fleet large and sophisticated, many craft having Decca Navigation. Sandsend Cliff and the adjoining beach to the north offer easy fishing from the flat cliff top and from the steep beach. Cast well out at low water, not so far at high water – the reverse of the usual principle. The piers around Whitby harbour produce well in summer and autumn. There is sand on the west side, rock and kelp on the east side of the harbour. Long casting is no advantage here. Saltwick Bay produces large flounders in summer from the beach

From Staithes south west to sandy Runswick Bay, the rock scars are interrupted by patches of sand and boulders, with easiest access at Port Mulgrave; a pattern of coastline that continues to Sandsend and is joined to Whitby by nearly three miles of sandy beach. There is rock again east of Whitby, tumbling scars backed by steep slopes and, in several places, by cliffs, continuing round to Robin Hood's Bay. Around this bay to the Old Peak (or South Cheek), a foreshore of sand and boulders gives on to rock ledges.

South west of this headland the land falls steeply to sandy beaches that extend for three miles before cliffs limit access north of Hayburn Wyke. Sand, boulders and rock scars form a shoreline backed for the greater part by cliffs that run southwards,

terminating at Scalby Ness. There is easy access around Scarborough where sand and rock scars intermingle, the edge of the land growing progressively steeper as one goes south to Cayton Bay. Here cliffs rear up from the sea and continue south east to Filey Brigg.

Filey itself fronts a beach of flat sand with plenty of simple access points, but the land becomes more steep south of Hunmanby, *en route* to Flamborough Head.

Boats may be chartered out from Scarborough, Filey, Staithes, Whitby and possibly one or two other places. Contact the local fisherman's association at any venue you visit. Those with their own boats on trailers have limited facilities – most boats need to be manhandled. However, slipways for larger trailable craft behind the rocks, and good winter cod in heavy seas. Fish from half ebb to the bottom and back up to full tide. Details from Whitby Angling Supplies, 65 Haggersgate, Whitby (Tel: Whitby (0947) 3855) also from local angling clubs.

3 Robin Hood's Bay Very mixed ground here, beach and scar fishing. Best results come around low water when there is some sea running, but from the sea wall at the village the best winter codding comes around high water, with spring tides producing the best sport, especially if a big sea is pounding in. Nearby, at Ravenscar Headland, some excellent heavy red cod are taken from autumn into winter. The path is safe, even if steep and long. Rationalise your tackle – it will weigh three times as much on the way back! Contact local anglers and clubs via the fishing tackle shop at Whitby (see above) for more information.

4 Scarborough The visitor to this area is advised to stop off here and glean as much local information as possible before heading off to fish. This entire coastline, the eastern edge of the high Yorkshire Moors, offers some of the most challenging shore fishing in England – and it is the environment that provides the challenge. North from this attractive seaside town, according to the maps supplied by Buckleys Angling Supplies (a name familiar to all sea anglers who cast their own lead weights), lie some thirty or so rock scars, with plenty more towards Filey. For up-to-the-minute information on which are fishing best, contact Buckleys Angling, 6 Leading Post Street, Scarborough (Tel: Scarborough (0723) 63202) also Pritchards, 56 Eastborough, Scarborough (Tel: Scarborough (0723) 74017).

5 Filey Famous Filey Brigg fishes best on its north side into the deep water for the usual local species. Access is easy and there are two escape ladders to (or from?) the foreshore. Summer fishing on the bay side does no more than feed the abundant shore crabs, but produces small codling in winter with the occasional better fish.

Filey Brigg is to Yorkshire rock fishing what Inch Strand (County Kerry) is to surf fishing. It has a substantial angling history, and the local shore record cod of 33 lb was taken here. January is the month

when giant cod move in close to the north side.

Northwards, at Cayton Bay, big cod are also the quarry, with reasonable fish providing the bulk of the catch. Do not try this place without an expert local guide. Access is from Flintons Harbour or from a place named Danger Board to the south. Details from Filey Fishing Tackle, 12 Hope Street, Filey (Tel: Scarborough (0723) 513732) also from Ken Carpenter, 18 Ash Grove, Filey.

Bait Areas
Small red lugworms here are called blasties; large black ones, gullies. Neither variety is terribly abundant due to over-exploitation of stocks. Which means that one half of the magic worm/mussel cocktail is harder to obtain than the other, the latter being locally abundant on rocks and around some piers and jetties. Peeler crab, that superb summer and autumn bait for the red cod, is plentiful hereabouts, starting in May. Most shops stock razorfish, along with crab and some worm, but are reluctant to reveal their sources! Digging is prohibited close to the cobble landing at Filey. Big spring tides are virtually essential for the best bait beds to become uncovered.
A Lugworm

Yorkshire cod reefs demand rugged tackle.

FOR THE FAMILY
The North Yorkshire coast has sandy beaches, cliff walking, plenty of seaside attractions. There is the splendid scenery of the National Park and picturesque seaside places.
N. York Moors Railway Pickering Stn. An 18-mile ride through the valleys in a steam train Apr–Nov.
Whitby Lifeboat Museum panoramas of lifeboat history and the last 'pulling' lifeboat in service. This old fishing town has a fine abbey.
Scarborough famous resort with many attractions – open-air theatre, modern planetarium and wide choice of family entertainments and sports.
Castle Howard nr Malton. One of England's greatest houses open to the public. Costume galleries, fine gardens, cafeteria.
Flamingo Park Zoo nr Pickering. Miniature railway, dolphins, boating lake and picnic areas. Pickering is the gateway to the moors.
Gardens visit two on the edge of the North York Moors: Pennyholme and Sleightholme Dale Lodge both nr Fadmoor.

Humberside

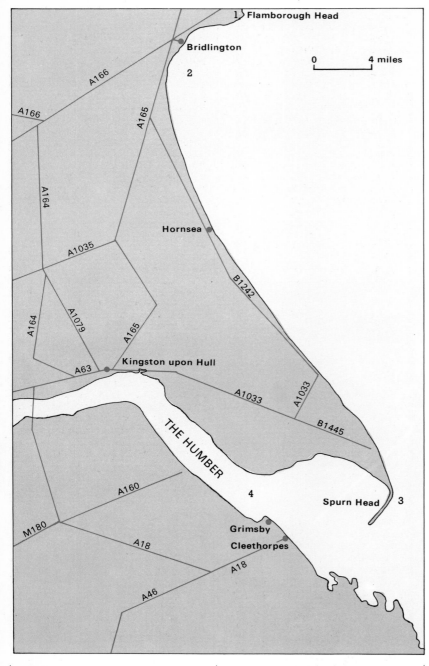

1 Flamborough Head

Bridlington

0   4 miles

2

A166

A166

A165

A164

Hornsea

A1035

B1242

A164

A1079

A165

A63   Kingston upon Hull

A1033

A1033

B1445

THE HUMBER

A160

4

Spurn Head   3

M180

Grimsby
Cleethorpes

A18

A18

A46

westwards to Bridlington. Here the coastline again changes dramatically. Bridlington Bay is one long stretch of sandy shallows that runs for 14 miles to Hornsea, then another 15 miles to Withernsea, and a further 14 miles to Spurn Head – 43 miles of sand, backed by low sand hills.

Extensive sand, mud flats and saltings lie to the west of Spurn Head inside the Humber, and these mud flats continue westwards for over 20 miles to Kingston upon Hull, and east again to Grimsby.

Species are similar to those found in Yorkshire. There are more tope and rays caught offshore, together with more spur dogfish.

Some 20 charter boats operate out from Bridlington, one from Flamborough. Those with their own boats on trailers will find access restricted by the extreme shallowness of Humberside beaches. There is a decent ramp at Bridlington, though a boat insurance certificate is required before permission is granted to use it. There are other facilities, where muscle power – but, in some places, a tractor – is sufficient to drag a boat to the sea. These exposed coasts require experience in launching and beaching through surf; failure to get it right can lead to loss of the craft. Such sites are: Fraisthorpe, Hornsea, Tunstall, Withernsea, Easington and Cleethorpes. Tidal variation from London Bridge: add 3 hours for Bridlington, 3½ hours for Withernsea.

1 Bempton Cliffs   Cod are taken here all year round, also pollack, the best month being September. Fish by day as the walk over the rocks is dangerous. The best local spot is often referred to as 'The Sub' since wreckage from a submarine was washed in there. Plenty of kelp and rocks, so use stout tackle – multipliers. Scarborough reels are losing popularity.

Fishing in several places is from 400 feet up, on the cliff tops. Fishing is generally at night to avoid catching too many sea birds, which fly into the line by day. A 20 foot pole is used with a pulley at one end. Two or three anglers fish together to provide mutual assistance. Fish have to be winched up. Those over 10 lb tend to tear free during the long haul. Details from R. J. Lewis at Filey Tackle Shop (see previous section).

2 Bridlington Bay   Plenty of the usual local fishing from the beaches, rocks and two piers at Bridlington.

Occasional rocky outcrops intrude into the belt of sand that runs south east under Bempton Cliffs, that magnificent landmark where deep water comes right into the rocky edge of the land. These cliffs are a nature reserve and are the seagulls' answer to Hilton hotels, especially during

the breeding season. More rock scars enter the picture from the North Cliff and out to Flamborough Head, the most southerly outcrops of rock scars along the Yorkshire coast, the boundary of a rock fishing tradition. These scars, backed by cliffs and the steep slopes of the Head itself, run

Boat fishing is pleasant in sheltered water even though not spectacular. Lugworm can be dug, along with other bait species, from the extensive local sands. Details from: Linfords, 12 Hilderthorpe Road, Bridlington (Tel: Bridlington (0262) 78045); Mallard's, 5 Harbour Road, Bridlington (Tel: Bridlington (0262) 73103) also D. Burr & Son, 22 West Street, Bridlington (Tel: Bridlington (0262) 71770).

Southwards from here, the vast shallow sand flats produce very little to grow excited at. The occasional thornback ray is caught among the flounders and dabs. There are rumours of bass at Mappleton. Details from the local tackle shops: Chris Barugh, 120 Newbegin, Hornsea (Tel: Hornsea (040 12) 4947) also Mereton Ltd, 58 Southgate, Hornsea (Tel: Hornsea (040 12) 2650).

3 Spurn Head This headland produces mainly cod, together with flatfish, the occasional bass and a few other species. Local knowledge is vital to success, so enquiries must be made to nearby tackle shops.

4 The Humber Dedicated locals plough out through the thick mud at low water to fish into the shipping channel for small codling. The bottom here is extremely glutinous and sticks to clothing with supernatural tenacity. Neap tides are preferred around this part of the world because the currents become too strong otherwise. At high water, on both sides of the Humber, silver eels may be caught and a few flatfish. Goxhill produces better winter cod, with November night tides better than daylight fishing. Doverstrand is considered to be excellent for summer fishing when plenty of silver eels and flounders may be taken. Winter fishing here produces more flounders and a few codling. Similar fishing is to be found at Cleethorpes. Grimsby North Wall fishes reasonably well at night after an on-shore blow. Even so it pays to be able to cast baits out a fair way. More information from D. Boyall, 5 High Street, Barton on Humber (Tel: Barton on Humber (0652) 32706); Castaline, 58 High Street, Cleethorpes (Tel: Cleethorpes (0472) 690256); Duncans, 8 Paragon Square, Hull (Tel: Hull (0482) 28150); E & C Fishing Tackle, 423 Holderness Road, Hull (Tel: Hull (0482) 701384); The Fishing Basket, Beverley Road, Hull (Tel: Hull (0482) 445284); Humberside Armoury & Angling Co,

73 Lady Smith Road, Grimsby (Tel: Grimsby (0472) 52029) and D. Ledger Fishing Tackle, 544 Anlaby Road, Hull (Tel: Hull (0482) 51994).

The North Wall at Grimsby belongs to the Cromwell S.A.C. and to the Humber S.A.C. and permission should be sought from them to fish it. A permit is also required to fish Grimsby's West Pier. Other piers in the Humber are restricted.

Bait Areas
Extensive banks of good lugworm and some ragworm may be found all along this coastline. White ragworm may also be found along here. A permit is required for digging at Cleethorpes. Wherever patches of rubble, junk, or slightly raised rocks are found, a few peeler crabs may be found. Search also in clay banks along the low water marks. They will be hiding in fissures. A survey on long spring tides will show the better bait beds. It is a pity there are so few decent fish to impress with one's labour!

The crew of the Bluebell *have good reason to be cheerful as this 9lb cod comes aboard.*

FOR THE FAMILY
A wide choice of family entertainment and activity on both sides of the Humber Estuary: Bridlington, Scunthorpe, Hull and Cleethorpes, quieter places along the coast, easy reach of the Pennines countryside, the Yorkshire Wolds, the cathedral city of Beverley and many interesting towns and villages. Visit York with its historic buildings, Minster and museums.

Hull watch deep sea trawlers unload their catch along 7 miles of docks. Visit the Transport Museum and Wilberforce House with its 17thC furniture.

Flamborough Head for its spectacular white cliffs and **Spurn Head** for wildlife. Festivals and regattas, as well as a sea angling week, Sept, in nearby Bridlington.

Cleethorpes Marineland and Zoo Humberston. Dolphins, walk-through aviaries, children's farm, etc. Apr–Oct. Good sands and entertainments in this resort.

Hornsea boating, fishing, etc on large freshwater mere. Garden centre and children's amusements, pony rides and tours of the pottery. Village life museum.

Normanby Hall Scunthorpe. A country park. Fine Regency house in wooded parkland with museum, gardens, deer park, playground, zoo, etc.

National Railway Museum York. *The* great railway museum, the whole romance, history and variety of railways.

Lincolnshire

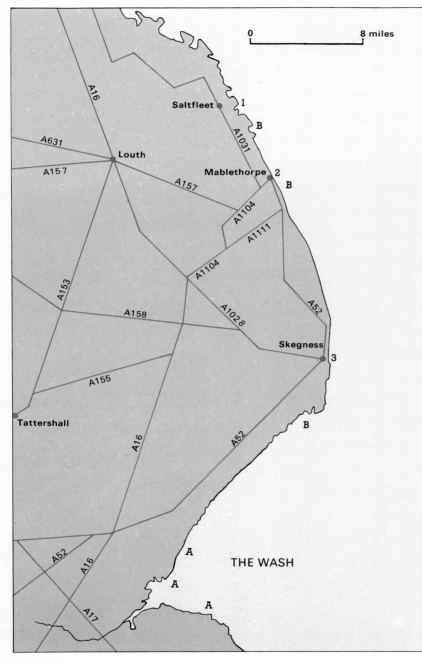

a Ministry of Defence Danger area, so also is the south western shore between Fosdyke Wash and the River Nene.

Although there is good flounder fishing from the channels and drains of The Wash, this country is really the domain of the wild-fowler rather than of the angler. It is unwise to venture onto the extensive sand and mud flats without experience of the routes to follow. Drains and quicksands can trap the unwary, and cut off escape back to dry land. For this reason it is probably a better idea for the stranger to buy his bait locally, unless a digger or another angler allows him to tag along.

No charter boats operate out from here. Ramps suited to larger types of trailable offshore fishing craft are limited to Skegness and Ingoldmells (at Jackson's Corner). Otherwise, smaller craft that can be manhandled on a trailer over soft sand may be launched at Saltfleet, Sutton on Sea, Sandilands, Chapel St Leonards and Skegness. Surf is often running on these sites.

Tidal differences from London Bridge : Grimsby add 4 hours ; Skegness add $4\frac{1}{2}$ hours. Northerly winds pushing extra water into the Wash cause the tide to peak both earlier and higher than charted and to hold back the ebb. Boat owners should beware of sandbanks and overfalls in the Wash. This shallow water requires little provocation to become rough.

Fish species include silver eels, codling and occasional cod, dabs, whiting, plaice, flounders, some sole, bass and mackerel. Offshore are dogfish, tope, rays, and the shore species in greater size and numbers.

1 Saltfleet School bass and flounders are taken around low water, together with the occasional tope, but a walk of two miles is required to reach the fishing mark. Winter cod and whiting, too. Details for this area, and Humberside, contact Tony Burman, 162 Brereton Avenue, Cleethorpes (Tel : Cleethorpes (0472) 67186). Tony is a widely-acknowledged expert on the the area.

2 Mablethorpe With the water so heavily clouded, it makes little difference in winter whether one fishes by day or night. But long casting is vital along much of this coastline – indeed, the new (and some of the old) generation of tournament

At each end of the Lincolnshire coastline mudflats increase in size and stickiness, with samphire (the herb of St Peter) beds more common than fish. Around the Humber local knowledge is essential to avoid being cut off by the tide while out on the flats. Mudflats turn to extensive sands

as one travels southwards to Mablethorpe, these sands continuing for mile after mile, breakwater after breakwater, southwards past Sutton on Sea, Chapel St Leonards and on into the outer reaches of The Wash some four miles south of Skegness.

The northern limit of The Wash is

Fishing for ray in the Bristol Channel at Ogmore Deeps.

casters comes from here. The best time to fish is over the high water period, two hours each side. Details from Belas Sports Shop, 54 High Street, Mablethorpe (Tel: Mablethorpe (052 13) 3328).
The sea wall at Trusthorpe point is considered to be the best local spot for cod, whiting, a few bass and flatfish.
3 Chapel St Leonards to Gibraltar Point (Skegness) The beach shelves quite rapidly along here, and this is the main area where thornback rays may be caught, though perfect conditions must obtain for best results. Long casts with very fresh crab or herring baits will take them, with the sea as flat as a pancake on a warm, muggy summer night. At Chapel Point the fishing can be very productive when the tide starts to flood, though do not count on this – there is no set pattern to this mark. The usual local species are taken here, including some bass. Here a five pounder is something of a miracle. The occasional ray's bream is also taken this far south late in the year – normally they are washed up chilled into a comatose state. Details from Hook Line 'n Sinker, 85b Roman Bank, Skegness (Tel: Skegness (0754) 3623); Palmers, 11 High Street, Skegness (Tel: Skegness (0754) 4404); Storrs, Market Place, Wainfleet, Skegness (Tel: Skegness (0754) 880378); Lakeside Leisure Ltd, Trunch Lane, Chapel St Leonards (Tel: Skegness (0754) 3623).

Bait Areas
A   Lugworm
B   Ragworm
The lugworm is generally the smaller red worm, though there are beds of black, or 'sewie' lugworm, which are best dug individually with a spade. The ragworm is found around Friskney, together with lugworm, for which the Wash is famous.

Shingle beaches stretch for about 100 miles along the Norfolk coastline. This well-equipped night angler is fishing for cod and whiting.

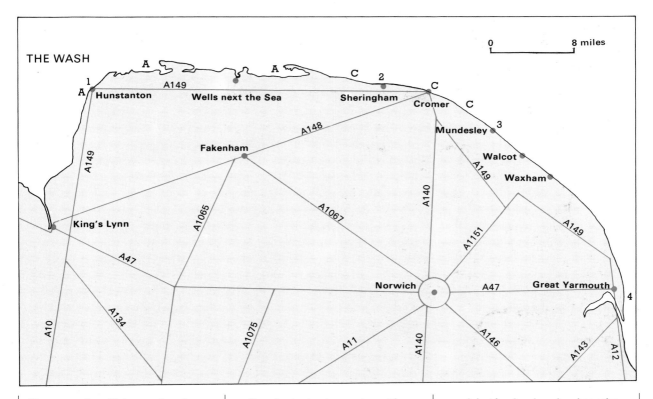

THE WASH

0 ___ 8 miles

A
Hunstanton 1
A149
A
A149
A1065
King's Lynn
A47
A10
A134
A1075
A11
A
Wells next the Sea
A148
Fakenham
A1067
C 2
Sheringham
C
Cromer
C
Mundesley 3
A149
Walcot
Waxham
A140
A1151
A149
Norwich
A47
A140
A146
A143
Great Yarmouth 4
A12

Expanses of mudflats, marsh and saltings extend eastwards from The Wash to Hunstanton and for many miles along the northern part of the East Anglian coast. Much of this is flounder and eel country in summer, although the occasional thornback ray is also taken. Access through the marshes is possible at Thornham, Brancaster, Burnham, Overy Staithe, Wells-next-the-Sea, Stiffkey, Blakeney and Cley next the Sea. Then a sand and shingle beach (and the shingle is more generally gravel than large stones) curves round the East Anglian coast from Cley next the Sea for 100 miles south to Harwich. Apart from a handful of estuaries, the only interruptions to this graceful sweep are man-made – towns, harbours, piers, groynes and breakwaters.

From Sheringham, past Cromer, Mundesley, Happisburgh, Sea Palling, Winterton-on-Sea, Newport, Caister-on-Sea and on to Great Yarmouth, much of the beach is backed by sand hills and low cliffs. This pattern continues south of Gorleston-by-Sea to a mile south of Corton where the cliffs are replaced by the promenade at Lowestoft, south of the Suffolk border.

One charter boat operates out from Wells, and one from Blakeney, but during the summer months only. The main centres are Gorleston and Great Yarmouth.

Because of the extensive inshore shallows hereabouts, slipway facilities for larger offshore craft exist only at Brancaster Staithe, Overy Staithe, Wells-next-the-Sea, Blakeney, Great Yarmouth and Gorleston. However, smaller craft that can be dragged to the water or on a trailer may be launched at many other places where the road encounters the sea and where the sand hills are not steep.

Tides along here occur about 5 hours before London Bridge times at Great Yarmouth, and 5 hours after those times at Cromer and King's Lynn. Check, however, on tidal quirks in the local and angling press.

East Anglian beaches are noted for their winter cod fishing and the prolific runs of whiting which start, in some years, late in the summer, becoming heavier towards October when they start to diminish slightly. Much depends on the location of the venue to be fished. Some thornback rays are taken – many fewer than of

yore – but few local anglers have the patience to catch nothing for night after night in the hope that eventually such effort will pay dividends. Sting rays are caught along here, but again few people have bothered to research this somewhat erratic fish. Dabs are fairly prolific, along with flounders, especially in the estuaries and flanking beaches. Summer fishing is largely for small species, like silver eels and flatfish. A few bass are taken, but with no consistency – there are not enough caught to enable the thinking man to formulate patterns of behaviour. Really, local anglers would rather not talk about the summer fishing, especially since a recent pattern of cold summers has inhibited the mackerel and garfish shoals from building into an appreciable run along here.

Offshore there is some excellent fishing. The sandy flats are nursery areas for immature fish in their thousands (one reason why many commercial men prefer long-lining to trawling). Tope, good bass, cod, conger eels, rays, dogfish and smaller deep-water species like gurnard and whiting are caught in fair numbers. However, the prolific outer Wash grounds are barely fished for major predators. Many experts believe that this area could yield some surprises to anybody with a fast boat to go out the distances required to find the fish.

1 Hunstanton When a north easterly gale destroyed the pier here a few years ago, local anglers believed that it signified the end of their shore fishing. They were right. These very sandy shores, with the tide ebbing a fair way out over the flats, produce little of consequence. But then nobody has really concentrated on the sting ray potential. Details on the fishing of this neglected coast from Norfolk Tackle, 57a Norfolk Street, Kings Lynn (Tel: Kings Lynn (0553) 65534) also Colin Stevens, 55 London Road, Kings Lynn (Tel: Kings Lynn (0553) 5852).

2 Sheringham Small species are caught along here – together with the occasional surprise. The cod shoals take some time to reach here. Contrary to uninformed opinion, they move northwards during the winter months along these beaches, and arrive here quite late, staying well into May most years. Some big bass are taken here on crab each year, from the rocks here and at Weybourne and Cromer, and over the offshore lugworm beds. Such grounds also produce good spring cod fishing. Details from Coastal Supplies Ltd, 15 Beeston Road, Sheringham (Tel: Sheringham (0263) 822587).

3 Mundesley This beach is the start of some 50 miles of excellent winter cod fishing – and for whiting. Summer fishing produces fair sole at night and around dawn, and some good thornback rays. Also at night, the fishing is good from Trimmingham south to Waxham. Flood tides see the best sport, with the cod arriving in late October. Some fair bass are taken hereabouts each summer. Details from the shops listed for Yarmouth information (see below).

4 Great Yarmouth Whiting arrive each year between late July and early September, with night fishing between Southwold and Dunwich (Suffolk) producing the first fish. Cod arrive here from September onwards, moving up the coast to Yarmouth by October – some years it is late October before they come north of the river. North Beach at Yarmouth and Tramp's Alley at Corton produce big cod and are where heavy currents are encountered on spring tides. These

can be a problem. Yarmouth North Beach fishes well on the ebb tide. The South Beach is easier to fish, casting well out on a flooding tide. Caister-on-Sea is less severe on a big spring tide and produces well throughout both ebb and flood tide. The California/Scratby area fishes well for cod in late November through to January; Waxham from November until February. Large cod are also taken.

Happisburgh, Walcot and Bacton beaches between Great Yarmouth and Mundesley fish well late in the year until April (depending on the strength of the run of cod). The last three hours of the ebb and the first three hours of the flood tides produce the best results.

Long casting is often essential, but in severe conditions the line gets buried by sand and tackle is lost. Sometimes the cod move in close. Watch other anglers (these beaches are like Blackpool's Golden Mile with Tilley lamps when the cod are in) and judge how far out the fish are feeding. Ideal conditions are at night, with a warm, gentle south westerly wind, and plenty of fresh lugworm. Do not make long-range trips without consulting any of the dealers listed below for reports. Tony Allen Fishing Tackle, 168a Silver Road, Norwich (Tel: Norwich (0603) 412124); John Wilson, John's Tackle Den, 16 Bridewell Alley, Norwich (Tel: Norwich (0603) 614114); Baker & O'Keefe Ltd, 7/8 Pier Walk, Gorleston, Great Yarmouth (Tel: Great Yarmouth (0493) 62448); Pickards Fishing Tackle, The Hill, Long Stratton (Tel: Long Stratton (0508) 30262); Laurie's Angling Centre, 130 Bells Road, Gorleston, Great Yarmouth (Tel: Great Yarmouth (0493) 601020); Stalham Pet & Leisure Shop, Stonehouse, High Street, Stalham (Tel: Stalham (0692) 81800); Pownall & Sons, 74 Regent Road, Great Yarmouth (Tel: Great Yarmouth (0493) 2873) also Mrs I. R. Flaxman, 3 Tan Lane, Caister-on-Sea (Tel: Great Yarmouth (0493) 728563).

Bait Areas
Plenty of good, firm, juicy lugworm around the north Norfolk coast. Harbour ragworm in some drains and estuaries. Peeler crab wherever you can find a few rocks, but it is very scarce, even though it is the magic bait for big spring cod.
A   Lugworm
C   Crab

FOR THE FAMILY
A peaceful landscape, good seaside places and one main resort, Great Yarmouth, for entertainments, sports. Norwich and King's Lynn not far inland, the Broads for sailing and cruising, and many nature reserves, make Norfolk an area with much to offer for family excursions and expeditions.

Sandringham House   8 miles from Kings Lynn. Visit the royal house, grounds and museum.

Norwich   cathedral, many notable buildings and museums and the Samsby Centre for Visual Arts, University of E. Anglia.

Norfolk Wildlife Park   nr Norwich. Major collection of European animals and birds in near-natural surroundings.

Hickling Broad   a nature trail by water to see Broadland birds and other wild life in the National Nature Reserve.

Windmills   many interesting mills to visit. Berney Arms, the tallest on the Broads, has an exhibition.

Thursford   nr Fakenham. Unique museum of steam road locos and engines, musical organs. Gondola ride, railway, picnic area.

Caister Castle   nr Great Yarmouth. Castle ruins, motor vehicles exhibition, teas and the Battersea Park Tree Walk.

Lowestoft harbour at first light.

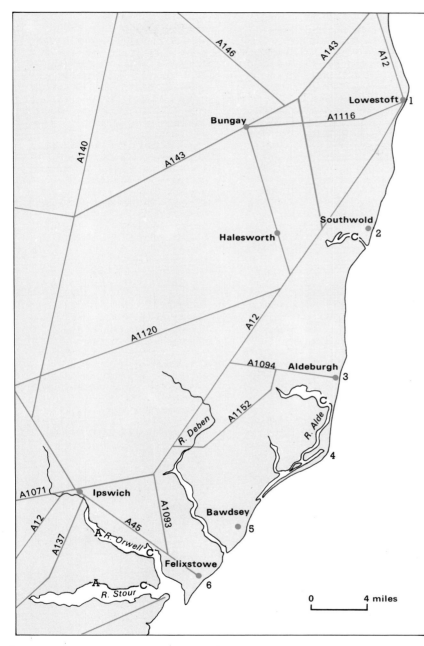

finally tiring of the game at Shingle Street. From the north, access to Orford Beach is restricted by marshland and a government establishment. Locals cross the river in their own boats, though boatmen may be hired to ferry anglers and tackle from the village of Orford to Orford Island, as locals call it. This means marooning oneself for several hours. The area south of Havergate Island produces the best results in both summer and winter.

The shingle continues south from Orford, past Shingle Street to the mouth of the Deben Estuary, and on again to Felixstowe. Inside Harwich harbour, the Orwell estuary stretches north west to Ipswich, while the equally muddy Stour estuary cuts inland for nine miles to Manningtree.

Charter boats operate out from Felixstowe and Lowestoft. More independent boat fishermen may launch at Lowestoft, Southwold, Aldeburgh, Orford, Woodbridge (several sites here on the River Deben), Felixstowe Ferry, and Felixstowe. There are also three sites along the River Orwell at Levington, Woolverstone and Pinmill. Other sites, for boats light enough to be manhandled, can be found at several locations along this coastline.

Tides: Subtract 4½ hours for Lowestoft and 4 hours for Dunwich from London Bridge times.

1 Lowestoft Beaches south from here – such as Pakefield – see the first of the winter cod. These are usually caught by casting well out with fresh lugworm. The night tides produce best, unless the water is clouded after a storm or the fish are thick inshore. Whiting, sole and occasional bass are caught here too – and dabs. Details from: Sam Hook Ltd, 132 Bevan Street, Lowestoft (Tel: Lowestoft (0502) 65821); Ted Bean Fishing Tackle, 175 London Road North, Lowestoft (Tel: Lowestoft (0502) 65832); S & G Gowen, 57 Lorne Park Road, Lowestoft (Tel: Lowestoft (0502) 81943); Lowestoft Angling Centre, 189 London Road South, Lowestoft (Tel: Lowestoft (0502) 3392).

2 Southwold An excellent winter cod and whiting area, this, and where the first of the autumn whiting are taken. The mouth of the River Blythe produces a few bass, especially if king ragworm or peeler crab can be fished around the low water period and when the new tide starts to flood. Some are taken by spinning or fishing

South of Lowestoft, sand-hills then cliffs front the sea at Pakefield, reaching a fair height at their southern end before dropping down to Kessingland and its gravelly, sandy foreshore. There are again low cliffs to the north of Southwold. These beaches are typical of East Anglia.

The River Blythe enters the sea at Walberswick, itself on a pleasant sandy bay, and the shoreline from here south to Dunwich is backed by extensive marshland. There are low sandy cliffs south of Dunwich towards Minsmere, then shingle marshland past Thorpeness to Aldeburgh.

Aldeburgh stands at the northern end of Orfordness, a long shingle spit that for 10 miles frustrates the River Alde from reaching the sea,

Redgills. Bass appear along this shoreline when least expected. More than one angler has arrived at the beach with long-range casting gear and a box of lugworm only to see large bass mashing sand-eels at the water's edge. Such events are rare.

Walberswick Bay, to the south, is about the only place along this part of the East Anglian coastline that is fishable during a nor'easterly gale, when heavy surf effectively rules out the better-known cod beaches. There is just enough lee here to allow comfortable fishing and it can be a deserted, wild, and beautiful place on a sunny winter's afternoon while a big wind is up. Details from Southwold Angling Centre, 64 High Street, Southwold (Tel: Southwold (0502) 722085).

3 Aldeburgh   Northwards to Dunwich and beyond lies winter cod and whiting country. A fair walk from Aldeburgh to the 'dirty wall' produces excellent bags of cod without having to cast far. Sometimes groups of very large fish come in here and the few anglers present have a field day. Though why does it always happen that somebody arrives just as they go off the feed, tackles up with feverish haste, then watches his rods for hours without so much as a bite while the successful lads are busy filleting their piles of large cod?

Sizewell Power Station outfall and nearby beaches produce school bass in summer. Fish early evening around high tide with ragworm or peeler crab. Nocturnal ebb tides produce good sole here, too. Details from Sports Lodge, High Street, Leiston (Tel: Leiston (0728) 830167) also Rod & Gun Shop, 62 The Thorough Fare, Woodbridge (Tel: Woodbridge (039 43) 2377).

4 Orfordness   Spring thornback rays are taken in the estuary here, and good mullet fishing is to be had, too. Some very large bass are caught around the river mouth and the shingle beach on the other side of the estuary produces excellent winter cod. Long casting is often a hindrance, while at other times the fish may stay well out. A boatman is required to ferry anglers and tackle down the estuary to the far bank. For details contact C. Martin (Tel: Orford (039 45) 545) also R. Brinkley (Tel: Orford (039 45) 481).

5 Bawdsey   Some excellent spring thornback rays are taken on ragworm, peeler crab or, best of all, very fresh herring at the mouth of the Alde

estuary. Some of the best fishing spots around here for cod and bass require a stiff walk – only healthy anglers need apply ! More details from Viscount Fishing Tackle, 207 Clapgate Lane, Ipswich (Tel: Ipswich (0473) 78179).

6 Felixstowe   When a cold snap follows a strong wind, and night is falling, the beaches at Felixstowe and Landguard Point produce excellent cod and whiting fishing. The best time is two hours each side of high water, with more of the ebb scoring at Landguard. There is deeper water here, so long casting is not as necessary as is the case at Felixstowe. Shotley Pier produces good fishing on flooding tides. Some bass are caught here in the summer months on ragworm and peeler crab. Flounders are abundant in the estuaries here, with the better fishing around Christmas time and after. Further details may be had from any of the local tackle shops: Bowmans of Ipswich, 37 Upper Orwell Street, Ipswich (Tel: Ipswich (0473) 51195); Breakaway Tackle Development, 376 Bramford Road, Ipswich (Tel: Ipswich (0473) 41393) also Ipswich Angling Centre, 199 Felixstowe Road, Ipswich (Tel: Ipswich (0473) 78004) and other local shops.

Bait Areas
Most shops import their bait from the Wash and north Norfolk. There is some lugworm, ragworm and white ragworm to be dug locally, but most diggers keep the locations of beds a tight secret. Peeler crabs may be gathered in estuaries among junk and rubble early in the summer months.
A   Lugworm and some ragworm
C   Crab

FOR THE FAMILY
In the south the Suffolk coast has the well-equipped family resort of Felixstowe and northwards are quiet seaside towns such as Southwold, with sandy beaches. The county town and port of Ipswich, old towns and villages throughout this peaceful county, offer many interesting places for excursions.
Theatre Royal   Bury St Edmunds. Go behind the scenes in a typical Georgian playhouse. Tours of the theatre, when plays are not in progress.
Kilverston Wildlife Park   nr Thetford. Famous Falla Bella miniature horses and donkeys. Over 600 animals and birds from S. and Central America in parkland.
Somerleyton Hall   nr Lowestoft. Lavishly furnished 19thC Mansion with State rooms. Gardens, miniature railway, nature trail, children's farm, tearoom, etc.
Museum of East Anglian Life   Stowmarket. Fascinating open air museum of buildings, crafts, windmills, etc of E. Anglia. Apr–Oct.
Otter Trust   nr Bungay. Where otters live in semi-natural surroundings in an area of woodlands and lakes.
Lowestoft   bustling fishing port and holiday resort with fine sands, boating lakes and entertainments. Visit the East Anglia Transport Museum at Carlton Colville.

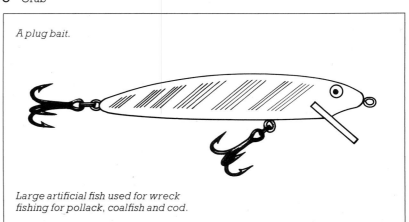

A plug bait.

Large artificial fish used for wreck fishing for pollack, coalfish and cod.

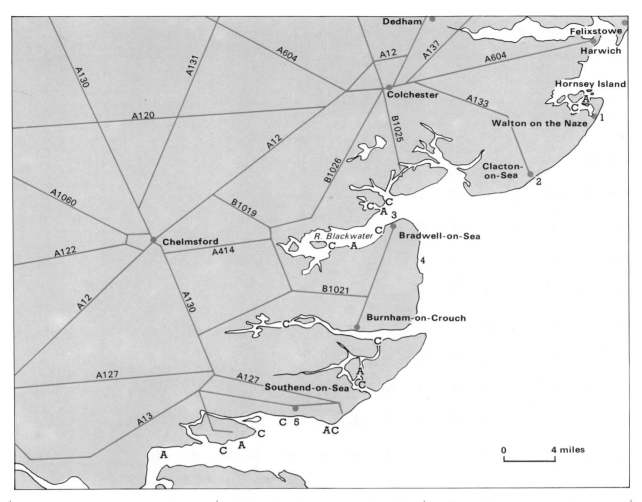

South of Harwich, the sandy, shingly foreshore continues for a few miles to the mass of drowned saltings and marshland north west of Walton-on-the-Naze, with its marvellous wooden pier. Then there is more sand and shingle at Frinton, Clacton-on-Sea and St Osyth. It becomes more muddy as the coastline bends north into Brightlingsea Reach at the mouth of the River Colne.

Mersea Island boasts mudflats on its seaward side – and mudflats on its other three sides. Similarly, the outer reaches of the River Blackwater are of mud, while the shore to the west of Mersea is extensively clay flats, with gravel along the high water mark, right up to Maldon.

Likewise along the south bank of the Blackwater Estuary. Clay flats, with a sticky covering of mud, characterise the shoreline from Maldon to Bradwell, except where the banks have been shored up with rocks and concrete slabs. Such ground extends east of Bradwell Power Station out to the sands, the fissured clay flats, and the drifts of gravel and sun-bleached cockle shells that mark the vast Dengie Flats. These extend for over seven miles south to the mouth of the River Crouch and the tidal creek known as the River Roach.

From Foulness Point south west to Shoeburyness and westwards to Southend-on-Sea, the shoreline consists largely of fine shingle and sand with heavy admixtures of mud in sheltered areas and throughout the extensive creeks. From Southend, the shoreline westwards becomes increasingly muddy, with junk and human debris proliferating towards Tilbury and on to the City of London.

Charter boats operate out from Harwich, Walton-on-Naze, Brightlingsea, West Mersea, Burnham-on-Crouch, Bradwell-on-Sea, Thorpe Bay and Southend-on-Sea. There is a central booking agency at Thorpe Bay : Mr B. Hooper, Charter Boat Association, 27 Fermoy Road, Thorpe Bay (Tel : Southend-on-Sea (0702) 587721). Charter skippers around the estuary areas fish extensively inside the estuaries and advertise in the angling press. This is particularly the case with Bradwell boats. The visitor may care to obtain details of the shore fishing from them, as well as local tackle dealers. They are, after all, out there nearly every day and know what fish are moving in what areas.

Those with their own boats on trailers can launch at Walton-on-the-Naze, Frinton-on-Sea, Clacton-on-

Essex

Sea, Brightlingsea, Alresford, Rowhedge, West Mersea, Tollesbury, Maldon, Bradwell-on-Sea, Wallasea Island, Burnham-on-Crouch, North Fambridge, Woodham Ferrers, Southend-on-Sea, Leigh-on-Sea, Canvey Island (several) and Pitsea. This area is over-run with sailing folk in summer, so anglers are advised to check out a suitable launch site well in advance and try to be first in the queue to get off. Other facilities are available for small craft.

Fish species are very similar to those found around East Anglia. There are many more bass and mullet caught around here than further north. Add smooth hounds to the list – both varieties – sting rays in greater numbers, but fewer shore-caught cod. Golden-grey mullet are taken from Southend Pier. Thick-lipped mullet are found in most estuaries.

This area also contains some of England's premier custom rod-builders – Going Brothers at Southend-on-Sea, and Essex Angling Centre at Leigh-on-Sea.

Offshore fishing over the Thames Estuary sand-banks can be excellent for bass, thornback rays, smooth hounds and cod. Bradwell charter boats were the first to start the renaissance of up-tide boat casting, a technique that is now universally accepted by anglers and skippers who fish offshore sand-banks where disturbance of the water by the boat's hull and anchor warp inhibit fish from coming too close.

Tide times: subtract 2 hours from London Bridge times for Clacton, 1½ hours for Southend-on-Sea.

1 Walton-on-the-Naze An excellent place for shore fishing, with a pier that is second to none. Bass – and very large ones at times – are caught spinning along the pier piles when small garfish are about. Bait fishing on the sea bed produces cod, flatfish, smooth hounds, thornback rays, sting rays, whiting, pouting and good sole. More details from John Metcalfe, 15 Newgate Street, Walton-on-the-Naze (Tel: Frinton (025 56) 5680) also, for fishing closer to Harwich, from Sherwood Tackle, 6 The Kingsway, Dovercourt, Harwich (Tel: Harwich (02555) 4602).

2 Clacton-on-Sea Similar species to those found at Walton-on-the-Naze are caught from the sea wall here, at nearby Holland-on-Sea and Jaywick. Long casting often helps. Smooth hounds provide an exciting

fight, being very fast fish, but peeler crab is vital to success. Some very good winter cod fishing, too. Sting rays, which are caught towards Colne Point at St Osyth, have a passion for king ragworm – the larger the better. Details from: E. J. Porter, 43 Pallister Road, Clacton-on-Sea (Tel: Clacton-on-Sea (0255) 25992) also John Metcalfe, Clacton Pier, Marine Parade, Clacton-on-Sea (Tel: Clacton-on-Sea (0255) 25295).

3 Bradwell-on-Sea There are some fine mullet in the marina here, but there is better fishing all around these drowned estuaries and saltings. Bass work up inside them, together with sting rays which like to sunbathe in the sun-warmed shallows. Ragworm and peeler crab should be used to

catch them. Cod are sometimes taken up the estuaries where deep water comes close to casting range. Smooth hounds – often big ones – are taken from the shores around here, always on crab. Flounder fishing in winter can be excellent as the fish move down to the sea to spawn. Bradwell Power Station attracts very large bass, and loads of school fish. Some may be taken, along with sting rays, by casting well out from the shore towards the warm water outfall. When crabbing hereabouts, make sure that all rocks are replaced exactly as they are found. The charter skippers rely on them for bait for offshore trips. Details from Keltex, 155 Station Road, Burnham-on-Crouch (Tel: Maldon (0621) 784189).

A good sting ray, tempted by king ragworm. Sting rays enjoy the warm waters of estuaries and saltings and even the warm water outfall of Bradwell Power Station.

4 Dengie Marshes Bass are the main quarry here. During the summer months when the weather is warm and there is not too much wind, the bass may be taken on peeler crab fished on very light tackle cast into the clay gullies at around high water. Easterly winds, which stir up the sea bed, deter the fish from coming close into the dirty water. Some smooth hounds and sting rays are taken here, too. September is the best month for large smooth hound hereabouts. Details from : Anglers Corner, 114 Wantz Road, Maldon (Tel : Maldon (0621) 52885) also from some of the Chelmsford tackle dealers and from those listed for Southend-on-Sea.

5 Southend-on-Sea Similar species to those found further north, but the water is extremely shallow here and boating activity in summer deters better quality fish. Excellent mullet fishing is to be had near the cockle sheds at Leigh-on-Sea. In winter, good cod and whiting are taken from the Thorney Bay – Scars Elbow area of Canvey Island. Most of the fishing from the shore is at around high water. The pier fishes well at any state of the tide, especially at the very top. Details from : Going Brothers, 8 High Street, Southend-on-Sea (Tel : Southend-on-Sea (0702) 66439) ; Jetty Anglers, 47 Eastern Esplanade, Southend-on-Sea (Tel : Southend-on-Sea (0702) 611826) ; Sea Tackle, 5 Pier Approach, Southend-on-Sea (Tel : Southend-on-Sea (0702) 611066) ; Essex Angling Centre, 109 Leigh Road, Leigh-on-Sea (Tel : Southend-on-Sea (0702) 711231) also, The Tackle Shop, 52 High Street, Shoeburyness (Tel : Shoeburyness (037 08) 3683).

Bait Areas
Plenty of bait locally available, especially lugworm and ragworm which may be dug in estuaries – but check first that such activities do not infringe any Water Authority byelaws. At Southend a permit is required from the Pier and Foreshore Offices, costing £1, to dig bait there. Even so, digging is not allowed within 500 yards of the beach – penalty £30.

A Lugworm and ragworm
C Peeler crab

The smooth hound is a species that is generally on the increase and likely to be found in unusual areas.

FOR THE FAMILY
The deeply indented Essex coast offers the busy holiday scene of Southend or Clacton-on-Sea, the smaller more peaceful seaside towns and deserted estuaries, and many interesting places to visit inland.

Vale of Dedham Shire Centre   see the great shire horses, ponies, and many horsy exhibits in the midst of some typical Constable country.

Mole Hall Wildlife Park   Widdington. Rare woolly monkeys, breeding otters, snowy owls. Elizabethan house.

Colchester's museums   besides the County museum, of outstanding interest, there are special features like Grandad's Photography Museum where you can have an Edwardian-type photo taken.

Historic Aircraft Museum with over 30 aircraft of great historic interest – one of Southend's many attractions.

Audley End   Saffron Walden. Magnificent house and gardens. Miniature steam railway through woods.

Evening river and harbour cruise 2 hours of exploration from Felixstowe or Harwich.

Colchester Zoo and Aquarium Stanway Hall. Fine collection of animals, birds, fish, etc. Amusements and restaurant.

Dublin and Wicklow

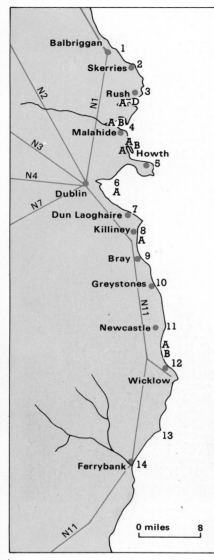

southwards to Bray Head and for many miles beyond with the railway running very close to this rather uninteresting shoreline down to Wicklow.

There are rocks at Wicklow Head, then a pattern of gentle headlands at Long Rock, Seapark Point, Ardmore Point, The Castle Point, all interspersed with sandy beaches, culminating at Brittas Bay. There are some patches of rock around Mizen Head at the southern end of this bay, with the coastline curling south past Ferrybank in a series of sandy bays punctuated by the rocky headlands of Arklow Head, Clogga Head, Kilmichael Point and others along the Wexford coast. Between each lies a bay of sand and stones.

Charter boats operate out from Balbriggan, though the fishing there is poor, Skerries, Dublin (poor), Dun Laoghaire, Bulloch Harbour, Bray,

Greystones, and Wicklow. Those with their own boats on trailers may launch reasonable craft down ramps at Dublin (several), Skerries, Loughshinny, Rush, Bullock Harbour, Bray, Greystones, Wicklow (several) and Arklow. When they can be carried to the water, boats can put to sea at several other sites.

Tidal variations from Dublin times: subtract 18 minutes for Skerries, 41 minutes for Wicklow and 2 hours 35 minutes for Arklow.

As with everywhere else in Eire, make enquiries to the Central Fisheries Board offices in Dublin about the fishing and facilities available wherever you intend to go. Their address is Balnagowan, Mobhi Boreen, Glasnevin, Dublin 9 (Tel: Dublin (0001) 379206). They have a continuous programme of development, the information provided is completely up-to-date.

A prized catch of turbot out of Keem Bay, Co Mayo.

For several miles north of Balbriggan lie extensive sandy beaches. But at Balbriggan itself there are rocks, with a few sandy bays. The rock is low-lying, and this pattern of flat outcrops of rock interspersed with sandy beaches extends to the wide, sandy bays around Malahide, opposite Lambay Island, with the Velvet Strand running south to Howth, yet another of Ireland's almost-islands, on the north side of sandy Dublin Bay. The south side, at Dalkey and on southwards consists of shingle and sand with some areas of flat reef.

Killiney Bay consists of sand and rubble, this pattern extending

1 Balbriggan Flounders, a few bass, and some sea-trout may be caught from the beaches flanking the River Delvin to the north of the town. The mullet fishing in Balbriggan harbour can be excellent, using bread or minced fish to interest the fish. Long casting from nearby beaches in winter produces codling at times, dabs and whiting.

2 Skerries The pier here produces small pollack and coalfish, mackerel and some fair mullet fishing at times. From the rocks on Red Island there are small pollack, garfish, mackerel and some wrasse to be had.

3 Rush To the north, at Loughshinny, the pier offers summer mackerel fishing in fine weather, together with garfish and small pollack when the fry are inshore. Similar fishing is to be had from the pier at Rush. To the south, the Rogerstown estuary fishes well during the summer months for bass over the sand bar at the mouth. Live sand-eels score best, but king ragworm and peeler crab also work fairly well. The sand-eels can be collected on site from the bar. On the southern side, where the estuary channel is most easily reached, similar baits also work for bass. Flounders can be taken inside the estuary. Further south, the strand produces codling, whiting and dabs in winter. Long casting is an advantage. There are some plaice in early summer.

4 Malahide Flounders and bass can be taken at several places in this estuary – where it enters the sea, school bass from the tidal pool just inside the mouth, and flounders too. Mullet are common, especially in the pool to the west of the railway line. Further south, at Portmarnock, the rocks near the martello tower produce some bass and sometimes flounders are plentiful.

5 Howth Another martello tower, also with a rocky base, produces small pollack, mackerel and flounders. The pier at Howth is not very productive. When the weather is fine and the fry are inshore, mackerel, small pollack and garfish are sometimes plentiful. Bottom fishing produces a plague of lesser weevers at times, so be careful of this fish with its poisonous spines. On the western side of this peninsula, the channel behind Dollymount enters the sea at Red Rock. Bass and flounders use this channel. Dolly-mount beach yields a few bass and the odd plaice.

6 Dublin Bass, mainly school fish, silver eels and flounders are the mainstays of the fishing hereabouts. There are several marks along this very sandy shoreline where they may be taken, especially into the mouth of

Casting for surf bass. Along the sandy shoreline around Dublin, school bass are the main catch, together with silver eels.

the River Liffey. The hot water outfall from Pigeon House Power Station is often alive with juvenile bass and also attracts some fair mullet.

7 Dun Laoghaire   Night fishing from the west pier produces whiting, pouting, small pollack, plaice, codling, dabs and small conger eels. The mullet fishing, using bread, can be very good here. The east pier produces similar results, with some bass and, once in a while, the occasional tope while fishing on the south side of the bend. Mackerel come in close on calm summer evenings and early in the morning. Some of the most consistent fishing here is for whiting and codling in winter.

8 Killiney   To the north, Bullock Harbour has a large rocky outcrop from which wrasse are to be had. Bottom fishing produces small conger eels. At Colliemore, reefy ground under the pier produces small conger eels and, in winter, codling on peeler crab with night the best time for both species. Small pollack and mackerel can also be caught here. Long casting into Killiney Bay produces plaice and flounders in summer, codling, whiting and dabs in winter. Further south, at Shankill, there is mixed fishing for small species during the flood tide and over the high water period. Cast either in front of or behind the offshore sand-bank. Species include codling, whiting, dabs, plaice, flounders, school bass, and lesser spotted dogfish.

9 Bray   Bray Head can be fished for small pollack, mackerel and small conger eels. Access is tricky and not suited to the unfit. There are two piers at Bray which produce small pollack, lesser spotted dogfish, codling, whiting, small conger eels and, at times, plagues of poisonous lesser weevers. The strand here also produces good results, especially for small bass and flatfish. The beach to the south of Bray Head produces fair fishing at times. Tope have been caught here, together with dogfish, dabs, plaice, flounders and other flatfish species. Codling and whiting can be taken here in winter, with long casting scoring.

10 Greystones   The occasional bass is taken from the south side of the pier, but the fishing here is not worth much of a detour. Small pollack, winter codling and whiting, pouting, some plaice, dabs and flounders are taken here and from rock ledges to the south of the pier.

11 Newcastle   The shoreline along here is steep shelving and very similar in nature to East Anglian beaches. The beach is made up from sand and gravel rather than heavy shingle, and the tides run hard over

The unusual catch of a fine crayfish by rod and line from Youghal Bay.

a sandy bottom. Neither is there a great range between high and low water hereabouts – 9 feet on spring tides and about 6½ feet on neap tides.

The fishing here, however, is reckoned to be about the best there is along the eastern seaboard of Ireland, an 11 mile stretch running from Greystones in the north to Wicklow in the south. There are plenty of easy access points along here, though the main marks are the Point, Kilcoole, Newcastle and the Breeches. Night fishing produces the best results with the low water period and the high water period preferred by local anglers. However, it would be interesting to see what an East Anglian tournament angler would make of this shoreline. Species to be found here are codling, whiting and dabs in winter and into the spring, pollack, gurnard, rays, dogfish, plaice and flounders in summer. Tope have been taken from this shore.

12 Wicklow To the north, the ragworm, lugworm and mussel beds of the Broad Lough can be raided to provide bait for plaice, flounders, codling, whiting, dabs, pollack and small thornback rays. Fish off the east pier at the mouth of the harbour – the estuary of the Vartry River.

The tide off Wicklow Head can be too uncomfortable to fish, and the sea bed around there is extremely rocky. To the south, the Silver Strand produces bass, flounders, dabs, some plaice, whiting and codling. Lesser-spotted dogfish are taken here, together with spur dogfish at times.

13 Mizen Head To the north of the headland, Brittas Bay offers fishing for flounders, bass, whiting, codling and dogfish. A surf helps here to get the fish going. To the south of the head lies another long, steep-to shingle beach with the Ennareilly River flowing through it. At the river mouth and for a quarter mile south-wards to the rocks, fish around high water time at night for bass, flounders, plaice, dabs, whiting, codling and, of course, lesser-spotted dogfish.

14 Ferrybank The usual local species can be taken around high water from the rocks called Porter's Rocks and from the beach to the south. There is similar fishing to be had at Ferrybank itself and further south at Clogga Beach. There is a rock outcrop along here where float-fished or legered peeler crab can score well with good bass in spring and early summer.

Bait Areas
This shoreline is sheltered from the prevailing winds, but even so the best bait collecting is to be found inside harbours and estuaries, mainly for lugworm and ragworm. There is plenty of crab wherever you can find a patch of suitable rubble, and some of the sandy areas produce sand-eels and shellfish.

Fish bait may be a problem at times, so it will pay to visit the commercial fishing ports or fish markets and make arrangements if a steady supply of mackerel is hard to come by in summer.

A Lugworm
B Ragworm
D Sand-eels

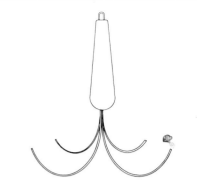

Gripping lead.
Grapnel torpedo lead – for beach and boat casting in fierce tides.

FOR THE FAMILY

The coast of **County Dublin** is well known for its gently shelving sandy beaches, ideal for children. There is ample opportunity for sport and good excursions inland. All the variety of Dublin City's entertainments and many places of interest are easily accessible.

Dublin visit Phoenix Park, the 50-acre Botanic Gardens, the Zoo, and the National Museum with its fine art collections. See the Book of Kells.

Aeronautical Exhibition Dublin Airport. A fine display of historic aircraft from wood and wire to the present day.

Malahide Castle nr Dublin. Visit the ancient fortress and grounds, and the National Portrait Gallery there.

Three Rock Mountain forest walks and panoramic views south of Rathfarnham.

Falconry of Ireland Robertstown. The largest falconry in Europe. Open daily. Barge trips in beautiful surroundings.

Howth Castle Gardens spectacular gardens famous for rhododendrons. From the Harbour take a boat trip to Ireland's Eye island, good for picnics.

Irish Horse Museum at the National Stud. Evolution of the Irish Horse in an interesting display. Also delightful Japanese gardens to visit. Known as the Garden of Ireland, **County Wicklow** offers beauty and variety of scenery, the cliff walks around Bray's Head, its spectacular mountains, leafy glens, valleys and lakes, and beautifully situated coastal resorts where you will find good beaches and seaside attractions.

Russborough Blessington. In a superb setting in the Wicklow mountains, a great Georgian house with a famous collection of paintings and other works of art. Open Easter–Oct.

Castleruddery Transport Museum Donard, Wicklow. For transport fans – a great collection of trams, trolley-buses, buses, fire-engines. Open Apr–Sept.

Glen of the Downs nr Greystones. A beautiful glen in which you can follow the Bellevue Forest nature trail.

Powerscourt Estate Enniskerry. Walk among Japanese and Italian gardens. Tearooms. Easter–Oct. 400 ft waterfall.

Loughs Tay and Dan take the SW road from the Sally Gap to the two loughs, the Glenmacnass valley and on to Glendalough – some of the finest scenery in Eastern Ireland.

Mount Usher Gardens Ashford, nr Wicklow. Fine gardens designed around the Varty river. Panoramic walks at nearby Devils Glen. Tiglin adventure centre organises courses in adventure sports.

Avondale House and Forest Park Rathdrum. An elegant house to visit and walks in the forest park. Nature trail and picnics.

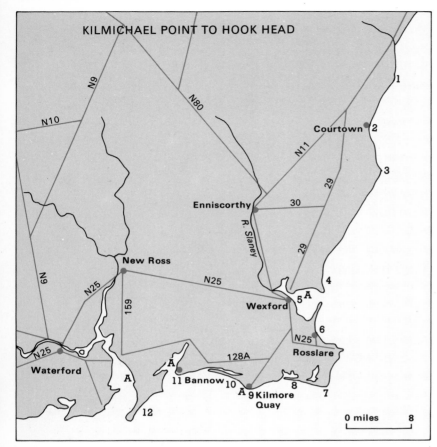

KILMICHAEL POINT TO HOOK HEAD

To north and south of Kilmichael Point the coastline curls in a series of long sandy bays punctuated by rocky headlands; Kilmichael Point itself, Duffcarrig Rocks, Breanoge Head (at Courtown), Pollshone Head, Glascarrig Point and Cahore Point. Between each is a beach of sand and stones. South of Cahore Point, the coast runs in a long sandy line for many miles to Wexford Bay, backed in some places by low hills. On south to Raven Point where the bass fishing can be very good – if you do not mind a long walk.

Raven Point faces Rosslare Point, on the south side of wide Wexford Harbour. This is largely of sand flats with mud in more sheltered areas. Rosslare Bay is largely sandy, a curving sweep of sand that is interrupted by hill-backed Rosslare Harbour before swinging south east to the rocks of Greenore Point. There is more sand, with small bays, south to the rocky headland of Carnsore Point.

There is even more sand to the west of this, Ireland's most south eastern part, the shoreline largely inaccessible in front of Lady's Island Lake and Tacumshin Lake, unless you care for a long hike, and yet more sand westwards towards Kilmore Quay and Forlorn Point. North east from here lies the sandy sweep of Ballyteige Bay, with the Burrow Shore a noted beach for bass when there is a surf running, and pack tope when there is not.

The western end of the bay is largely rocky towards Baginbun Head and round to Hook Head, with a few patches of sand among the rocks. In many places low cliffs deny access to the foreshore, while in others there is a fairly safe scramble down.

Charter boats operate out from several of the small harbours. These belong to commercial fishermen and potsmen and prior agreement must be made. Those with their own boats on trailers may launch their craft at Courtown, Wexford, Carne, Kilmore Quay, Saltmills, Fethard, Duncannon, Arthurstown and Ballyhack. As ever, there are plenty of other locations where light craft may be manhandled over the beach.

There is very varied fishing around this corner of Ireland. The shore species include bass, flounders, plaice, small turbot, rays, sea-trout. tope, codling, pollack, conger eels, silver eels, whiting and dogfish. Many estuaries and rock coves contain thick-lipped mullet.

Sea fishing offshore is largely for more of the same, with more tope, rays and dogfish than are caught from the shore.

As for Dublin, make enquiries to the Central Fisheries Board. See previous section for address.

Tidal difference from Dublin: subtract 5 hours 35 minutes for Wexford Harbour.

1 Kilmichael Point The rocks here provide fair fishing for bass and mackerel, with quite good plaice fishing on lugworm during the summer months. There is a chance of codling and whiting here in winter. To the south, a flooding tide on Clones Strand provides opportunities to catch tope, whiting, codling and bass. Flounders are common, particularly in winter. The beach shelves quite steeply along here, which must be why the dogfish come so close.

2 Courtown Some bass and a few flounders are taken from the strand outside this sanded-up harbour. Inside is some excellent mullet fishing, where bread scores well – in experienced hands. Around Poll-shone Head to the south there is clear-ground bottom fishing for flatfish and gurnard – and some codling and whiting in winter – while nearby rough bottom produces bass on peeler crab.

3 Cahore Point Rocks close to the pier here produce bass, while the sandy beach is good for flatfish. Four miles south lies Mauricecastle Strand, which produces bass, tope – and flounders – during the late spring. Night tides in winter are good for bull huss, using fish baits. The occasional ray – sometimes a sting ray – is taken here. Cast either in front of or well beyond the offshore sand-bank. Similar fishing is to be found at Tinnabearna, to the south, with the odd tope preferring dark tides.

4 Raven Point To the north, at Blackwater, there is some very good night fishing to be had on a flooding tide for bass, tope, flounders and winter bull huss. Other species are there in summer. The Blue Pool south of Cush Gap is a recommended location. Along this shore, May is the best time for the tope and rays. Raven Point itself can be excellent for bass, especially when the weather is creating surf. Fairer conditions produce a few tope here, too, from the channel that empties Wexford Harbour, much of which dries out at low water. Take care not to be cut off by the tide when fishing sand-banks around low water.

5 Wexford   Flounders travelling down the Slaney river during the early months of the New Year may be caught in good numbers from Ardcavan Strand, Ferrybank beaches and from Cats Strand. This last is very marshy and anglers risk being cut off by the tide. Various piers and jetties around the harbour produce fairly well for flounders, bass and the occasional thornback ray.

6 Rosslare   The pier close to the ferry terminal produces flatfish, dogfish and a few bass, conger eels and rays. Outside on the surf strand is some fair bass and flounder fishing, the best of it around Rosslare Point. To the south, at Greenore Point, the adventurous may find a rock finger from which to fish for tope in the tide race here, otherwise a south easterly blow is needed to encourage the bass to feed along these beaches. There is no shortage of flounders. At St Helens, on the south side, there is a small pier and another at Carne.

7 Carnsore Point   From the rocks here bass and small pollack may be caught by spinning with a slim silver spoon. Bait fishing with a float produces wrasse (on crab, prawn or lugworm) or pollack on prawns, king ragworm dug from Wexford Harbour, or strips of mackerel flesh – these fish can also be caught here at times. Legering on the sea bed produces bass, codling and flounders. Dogfish also take fish baits legered for other species.

8 Lady's Island Lake   This area of drowned marsh has access to the sea a couple of miles west of Carnsore Point. Sometimes storms build up the sands so that the mouth is closed. The beach from the point westwards provides good bass fishing, with tope, codling and flounders also available. Bass may be caught when Lady's Island Lake drains into the sea with the ebbing tide, casting king

ragworm, peeler crab or artificial lures (flies and spinners) into the overfalls. Tacumshin Lake to the west offers similar opportunities, especially spinning for bass and sea-trout at the White Hole, where the lake drains into the sea. The beach in front produces bass, tope and flatfish and is quite steep.

9 Kilmore Quay   From here you can take a boat fishing around the rocky pinnacles of the Saltee Islands and catch good pollack on trolled Red-gills or feathers. Or cast spinners to each side of the boat, especially at dawn and dusk when the fish are high in the water.

Bottom fishing produces tope, rays, conger eels and spur dogfish. Fish for bait may be bought, at times, from boatmen operating out from this harbour. It may be possible to hire a boat here for fishing around the Saltees Islands. The shore fishing is generally for small species, though the bass spinning can be excellent from St Patrick's Bridge, an outcrop of rock to the east of the harbour.

10 The Burrow Shore   Fish with peeler crab to the west of Forlorn Point on a flooding tide for bass, especially at night around late May or June. Surf conditions on this beach in front of Ballyteige Lough produce bass, flounders and quite a few tope. Fish the outlet of this lough, at the western end, for good bass in the overfalls when the tide is ebbing back to the sea. The tides are fierce here, and be careful of being cut off on a flooding tide. Fishing into the lough around the flooding tide produces excellent flounders. Peeler crab is a good bait for the bigger specimens.

11 Bannow   The channels flowing out from Bannow Bay produce good bass, also some fine tope fishing and plenty of the omnipresent flounders. Inside the bay there is some bass fishing, while areas where the bottom is sandy produce excellent flounders when the seas outside are too rough to contend with. Much of this bay dries out at low tide, so fish into the channels at that time for the flounders as they will be concentrated into a small area. When the water floods out from these channels as the tide rises, the flounders disperse over the sand flats and are less easily located.

12 Hook Head   The shoreline is very rocky on both sides of the headland. Access is difficult along much of its length, but can be managed at

Baginbun Head, Slade, near Hook Head Lighthouse, and at Churchtown. Float fishing with lugworm dug inside Bannow Bay produces wrasse, while live sand-eel, fish strips or king ragworm fished under a float will bring in pollack. Spinning is also excellent here. Where there is sand close to the rocks, some rays and dogfish – even tope – may be taken.

Bait Areas
If mackerel are a problem, see what local boatmen can do to provide suitable fish bait. There are crabs to be gathered where there is some rubble inside the creeks and harbours around here, but very little along the open coast. However there is plenty of lugworm and quite a few ragworm and clams to be gathered in the natural harbours. Mussels are abundant.

A   Lugworm, ragworm and sand-dwelling shellfish

FOR THE FAMILY
Some of Ireland's finest bathing beaches and resorts lie along the coast of Wexford, providing relaxation, sport and entertainment for the family. There are good tours inland through hilly countryside, river valleys and farmland. In Wexford itself are entertainments, historic places and festivals.

Wexford Maritime Museum reminders of Wexford's maritime history housed in a disused lightship. Wexford town has a famous opera festival and ballad singing in its hospitable inns.

Johnstown Castle   south of Wexford. 19thC Gothic. Visit the gardens, museums of agriculture and rural life, enjoy the lakeside and nature trail. May–Oct.

John F. Kennedy Park   New Ross. Forest garden dedicated to the US president. Fine view from the heights of Slieve Coilte. From New Ross there are river cruises with refreshments on board.

Saltee Islands   south of Kilmore is Ireland's most famous bird sanctuary. Boats trips from Kilmore Quay.

Enniscorthy County Museum archaeology, local history and a good folk section. Open summer. Climb to Vinegar Hill for a fine view of the River Slaney valley.

Courtown   a popular resort with plenty of summer seaside amusements and sport.

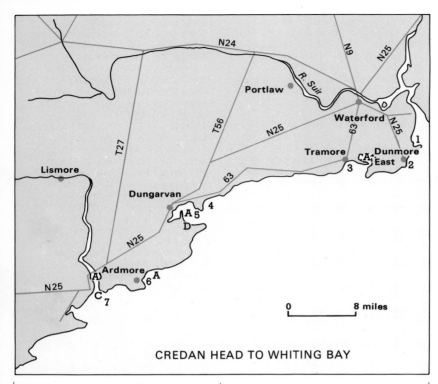

CREDAN HEAD TO WHITING BAY

flounder fishing, especially early in the year and around Christmas time.

2 Dunmore East   There is a major commercial fishing port here, an asset which can alleviate temporary inshore shortages of mackerel and other bait fish. To the west lies Swines Head, where there is some excellent pollack fishing, best approached via Rathmoylan Cove, reaching it on foot over the cliffs. Two coves produce fish, one with a rock ledge extending out at low tide, the other with a large rock at its seaward end shaped like the superstructure of a ship. Many double-figure pollack are taken here when the fish herd sprats and sand-eels into the cove. Mackerel, too, are abundant at times. Flatfish may be caught inside several of the coves along here.

3 Tramore   Dig a canful of lugworm from the back strand inside The Burrows and use them to good effect on the handsome surf beach when there is a wind blowing life into the waves. Bass and flounders are then caught. Around low tide, fish in the channel that feeds the back strand for bass – and more flounders. When the tide is full, both species will be exploring the flats for food, but move back seawards with the ebb. Under clear water conditions the bass will be found in the overfalls where this draining-off joins the sea. Fish the tide back using either reservoir trout tackle or slender spoons on spinning tackle. Pollack, mackerel and fair wrasse may be taken from the rocky headlands to each side of Tramore Bay.

4 Clonea Bay   Much of the coastline west of Tramore is cliff-bound. Where access is possible, deep water is likely to be found close in. Although virtually unexplored, this is tope country, with rays and dogfish likely to attack baits put out for the tope. Conger eels are also likely, as the water is fairly deep close in. Rock spinning for pollack is bound to be productive, with mackerel plentiful during the summer months. Wrasse, too, will be found where the rocks are rugged. Clonea Bay used to produce fair catches of bass, though these have fallen off of late. Fish among the rock patches for flounders and other flatfish and, possibly, the occasional dogfish if your luck is out. Ballynacourty Point is also worth exploring. Lying at the northern edge of Dungarvan Bay, there is a chance of tope and rays from rocks near the

Inside Waterford Harbour, the estuaries of the River Nore and River Suir, lies sandy Woodstown Strand to the north of Creadan Head on the western shore. South of here the foreshore is largely rocky with low cliffs and a few sandy coves extending towards Dunmore East. There are more low cliffs, with but few sandy coves westwards to sandy Tramore Bay with its marshy strand. West of here the picture of steep rocks and gentle coves continues to sandy Bunmahon Bay at the mouth of the River Mahon, and on west to Clonea Bay, just north east of Dungarvan Harbour.

The steep rocks of Helvick Head reiterate the pattern of low cliffs and occasional sandy coves. Some of the cliffs can be scaled, while others are too steep. Thus the shoreline continues south west to Mine Head and on westwards to the two sandy bays at Ardmore. There are more rocks between Ardmore Head and Ardoginna Head at the mouth of Whiting Bay, and even more rocks from Cabin Point westwards to Youghal Harbour.

Charter boats may be found at Dungarvan and Youghal, while smaller harbours offer small boats for hire – at times – and possibly a boatman too. Those with their own boats on trailers may launch their craft at Tramore, Passage East, Dunmore East, Annestown, Dungarvan, Helvic Head, Ballynagaul and Ardmore. As always, there are other places where small boats can be dragged down to the waters edge. Just be careful and remember that a small boat is like a shuttlecock when the sea is up, or tides are running hard.

As for Dublin and Wexford, make preliminary enquiries about fishing in Eire to the Central Fisheries Board in Dublin. The address is given in the Dublin section.

Tidal differences: subtract 5 hours 31 minutes for Waterford Bridge from Dublin time.

1 Credan Head   From here you can watch the salmon netsmen going about their business out in the tideway. Close by, to the north, Woodstown strand offers some good bass fishing in a surf, especially close by the rocks of the head. The tide forms an eddy that sweeps close in to the rocks at Credan Head during the flood, and bass may be caught here. There is a lesser eddy on the south side when the tide is ebbing. Further inside the harbour, in the estuaries, there is fair lighthouse, where access is possible.

5 Dungarvan Charter a boat here for some excellent light tackle fishing for blue shark during the peak of the summer months. From the shore, the fishing is less exciting. The beaches here are extremely shallow, with much of the sand flats drying out at low water. However, some bass and flounders may be caught in the channels, especially from Abbeyside, to the east of the town, or at high water from the extreme end of the Cunnigar sand-spit. Around Helvic Head, small conger eels may be taken from the piers of the harbour, together with rays if you care to hurl a bait a fair way out to sea. As ever, there is fair pollack fishing and mackerel to be had from rocks around the headland. Dungarvan also hosts shoals of bass later in the year; and at other times they may be caught on live sand-eels fished over the sand-banks.

6 Ardmore Head Southwards from Mine Head the shoreline is largely inaccessible because of the cliffs. Ballyquin strand offers fair fishing for bass and flounders when a wind from the south or south east rolls in some surf. Similar sport may be enjoyed around Ardmore Bay. There is a rocky outcrop to the north called Black Rock which offers facilities for spinning for sea-trout and bass. Casting with worm baits catches flounders and other flatfish. A long cast with a fish bait may produce tope and rays. Between Ardmore Head and Whiting Bay lie many excellent rock platforms from which to fish for pollack, mackerel and wrasse in the usual way. Again, it is likely that a cast on to clean ground around here could produce tope and rays.

7 Whiting Bay A bass of 17lb was taken here in 1977 and maybe its grandmother is still waiting for somebody to catch her! There is fair fishing around here for painted rays, especially early in the autumn. Calisto Bay and the rocks around towards Ferry Point, at the mouth of the harbour, produce bass when casting into the surf, when spinning from the rocks, and when fishing with the tide with live sand-eel from a drifting boat.

Bait Areas
There is no shortage of mussels in these latitudes. Many anglers neglect this easily collected bait, but the fish are keen to take them at times. Plenty of lugworm, and some ragworm and clams, may be dug from the harbours and from some of the sheltered surf beaches. Sand-eels may be scraped from coarse sand-banks inside Dungarvan Harbour – but keep your eyes open. As usual when fishing in Eire, there is more than can ever be detailed in guide books.

A   Lugworm, ragworm and some sand-dwelling shellfish
D   Sand-eel
C   Peeler crab

Angling boats at Cork Harbour. The harbour itself offers good mixed bottom fishing for bass, flatfish, rays and tope.

FOR THE FAMILY
County Waterford has Ireland's leading seaside resort – Tramore – and offers a wide choice of safe, sandy beaches and seaside attractions. The county is steeped in history, has interesting places to visit including the old town of Waterford itself, and scenic beauty of countryside and coast.

Curroughmore House Portlaw. Fine gardens and a Shell House. Open Thurs.

Waterford Glass watch the manufacture of the world-famous glass. Visits by appointment. No children under 12.

Reginald's Tower Waterford. A high circular stone fortress, once a Viking stronghold, now a museum. Apr–Oct.

Tramore a day out for the children, with miniature railway in a 50-acre amusement park. 3 miles of golden sands and a lagoon for boating.

The Nire Valley for fine hill walking, motoring or pony trekking – enjoy its lakes, mountains and woodlands.

River cruise from Waterford, 2-hour trip with afternoon tea.

Knockmealdown Mountains scenic drive along the L34 between peaks rising 1000 ft above the road to the Gap, one of Ireland's most renowned viewing points.

Cork

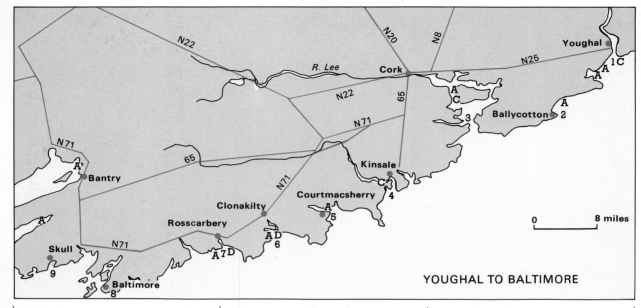

YOUGHAL TO BALTIMORE

There are extensive rocks around Youghal Harbour and Youghal Bay out to precipitous Knockadoon Head. From here more rocks, cliffs and small coves are to be found, the southern edge of a line of low hills, extending westwards to the sandy flats of Ballycotton Bay. There, the rocky foreshore continues westwards to Roches Point at the mouth of the Cork Harbour.

Inside the harbour lie extensive sand and mud flats together with harbour installations and a few rocky outcrops. South and west of the mouth of the harbour lie more rock promontories, low cliffs and little sandy coves – some, like Carrig Adda Bay, being larger than others. This pattern of countryside continues towards the mouth of Kinsale Harbour, nestling among the hills, and out to the extremely rugged Old Head of Kinsale.

At Garrylucas there are two small strands, then more rocks and the sands and stony mud of Timoleague, with Courtmacsherry on the southern shore of the estuary. There is more rugged country to the south among the Seven Heads, with a little sandy beach at the pretty inlet of Dunworly Bay. Then more rock and sandy coves – but fewer cliffs – towards the sandy harbour at Clonakilty.

More rugged countryside intervenes with occasional coves here and there towards Dunowen Head, around Dirk Bay to Galley Head. To the west of this headland lie the surf strands of Rosscarbery, with rocky promontories and narrow inlets towards picturesque Glandore Harbour and similar heavily indented coastline on to Castle Haven, Toe Head, and so to the estuary of the River Ilen at Baltimore Bay.

There then appears a maze of small islands, inlets and tiny coves around Cape Clear to Roaringwater Bay, to Skull and south west to the sheltered harbours of Crookhaven and Barley Cove, with cliffs barring access to most of the shoreline along to precipitous, spectacular Mizen Head.

Dunmanus Bay is extensively rocky with little sand except at its landward end. Once round Sheep's Head, Bantry Bay has a similar foreshore with muddy sand among the little promontories at its landward end. There are rocky headlands around Grengariff Harbour, Adrigole Harbour and Bear Haven nestling among the mountainous northern shore.

This peninsula terminates in steep rock headlands and precipitous cliffs towards Dursey Island and Cod's Head to the north. Similar rugged foreshore stretches into Kenmare Bay, except at the little harbours of Ballycrovane, Ardgroom and Kilmakilloge up to Kenmare at the mouth of the Kenmare river.

Fish species around here comprise just about everything to be found on the Irish list, from cod to porbeagle sharks to blennies. They are all to be found along this rich and varied coastline.

Charter boats operate out from Ballycotton, Cobh, Glenbrook, Crosshaven, Kinsale, Youghal, Courtmacsherry, Castletownshend, Baltimore, Skull and Kenmare. Trailed boats of fair size may be launched from ramps at Youghal Knockadoon, Rostellan, East Ferry, Cobh (several), Passage West, Monkstown, Crosshaven, Summer Cove, Kinsale (several), Harbour View, Courtmacsherry, North Ring, South Ring, Rosscarbery, Glandore, Baltimore, Goleen, Bantry (several), Glengariff (several), Adrigole, Castletownbere and Kenmare. Several other sites may be used with smaller craft, though the advisability of using such small craft in for fishing in strange waters is open to question.

As ever, address preliminary enquiries about the fishing in Eire to the Central Fisheries Board (the address is given in the Dublin section). As their research is continuous, there is a high probability that you could be the first to learn of a superb new fishing spot. In the absence of well known ones still produce superlative sport.

Tidal difference from Dublin times: add 6 hours 8 minutes for Cork; 5 hours 22 minutes for the Bantry Bay area.

A crock of bass at the end of this rainbow? Beautiful scenery at Ballinrannig Strand, Co. Kerry.

Cork

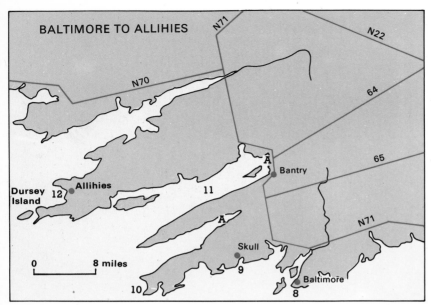

BALTIMORE TO ALLIHIES

N71
N22
N70
64
65
Â
Bantry
N71
Allihies
Dursey Island
12
11
Â
A
Skull
9
10
8
Baltimore

0   8 miles

1 Youghal Several jetties and waterfront installations around the town offer fishing for flounders, bass and some other species. Southwards towards Knockadoon Head there is fair surf fishing for bass and flounders, though a wind from the south east is required to put body into the waves. There is some good dinghy fishing for bass and general bottom species in this bay.

2 Ballycotton This town must be the original deep-sea fishing centre. It was here that the infant British Sea Angler's Club centred its efforts and broke so many European records many years ago. There is still good fishing to be had from both boat and beach. The rocks west of Knockadoon Head offer good pollack, wrasse and mackerel fishing, with dogfish, rays and conger eels where there is some sand within casting range. Access is possible at Ballymakeagh, and here some winter fishing for flounders, codling and small coalfish is possible. The strand which stretches from Ballycrennane

to Ballycotton offers surf fishing for bass and flounders, though a wind east of south is required to build up the waves. Ballycotton harbour offers mullet and conger fishing, while the cliffs give access in the west to pollack and wrasse. The beach at Ballycroneen offers fair bottom fishing for bass, dogfish, and the occasional ray and tope.

3 Cork Harbour There is a lot of excellent mixed bottom fishing for rays, flatfish, bass and tope inside this sheltered harbour. However, traffic can be heavy and the tides at the mouth very fast, so watch out. To the west of Roches Point at the harbour mouth lie two small beaches, Trabolgan and Inch strands where bass and the ubiquitous flounders may be had. From Cobh, excellent mixed fishing is available for large species, shark, skate, tope, rays, pollack etc.

4 Kinsale This sheltered port, with handsome houses and expensive boats around the harbour, is one of Ireland's premier deep-sea angling centres. There are even several well stocked tackle shops around the small town. Offshore lies light-tackle fishing for ling and pollack over the Ling Rocks and, during the peak of the summer months, excellent fishing for blue sharks. The shore fishing is not too hot. There are thick-lipped mullet in the harbour, but they are

Bass fishing in a tide race at Credan Head.

very hard to catch. Shoals of herring show up as thick clouds on the echo-sounder of the fishing boats during the autumn months, right up to the main harbour. From my bedroom window I once watched a large shoal of mackerel working fry in the water immediately below me – a handline would have sufficed to catch a few stringsfull.

Although the various arms of the harbour, like the major one of the river Bandon estuary, look as though they should be swarming with fish, they are not. Some bass and occasional spring thornback rays are taken from Jagoe's Point to the west of the town. In June the rocks here yield plenty of peeler crabs. There are lots of flounders in winter to catch. At the Old Head of Kinsale, mackerel, medium wrasse and small pollack are plentiful, with access fairly easy to a mark on the east side – just follow the path, while a mark on the west side offers similar fishing. Mackerel are thick around here in summer. The rocks around the lighthouse are shale and are treacherous; a scramble down there is not worth the effort.

5 Courtmacsherry As at Kinsale, large skate can be caught around here from deep-water boats. The Irish learned a lesson of conservation in this area some thirty years ago. Masses of big skate were killed and brought to shore for weighing, photographing and publicity. But these slow-growing beasts do not travel far and stocks were quickly thinned out, with no influx from other areas to replace those taken out. Few are captured nowadays, and the angler who wants a skate is advised to take a camera, photograph his catch then slide it back.

Mullet are plentiful in Kilbrittan creek, and flounders and bass may be taken from the surf strands at Flaxford and Broadstrand Bay. At Timoleague, the author was once ferreting about in the ruined Abbey and unearthed a human thigh bone. The bridge there over the river Arigdeen can be fished on both sides for bass and flounders. The bass congregate at low tide in the estuary mouth and may be caught on spinners or bait. As the tide floods, they move up the river and can be intercepted at various points. Success depends on the angler's ability to read the water on spring or neap tides and judge how far and how fast the bass shoals are likely to move.

Fishing into surf on dramatic, unspoilt beaches is, to many sea anglers, one of the chief attractions of the Irish coast.

As ever, there is fair rock fishing from several places around here for pollack, wrasse, mackerel and, if sand can be found close to deep-water rocks, conger eels and rays.

6 Clonakilty Fish into the eastern channel at the Ring Head end around low tide for bass, then move to Curraghane at half flood, where the pier at Arundermills permits easy access to the channel. Or, at low water, fish from the sand-spit at the western end of Inchydoney Island. The surf beach around this 'island', fronting the mouth of the harbour, fishes well during stormy conditions. More settled weather allows bass spinning from the rocky outcrop known as Virgin Mary's Point. Bait fishing from here also scores. On the opposite shore, at Muckruss Head, fish from the flat rocks there with bait or artificial lures.

7 Rosscarbery Bass fishing on the strands outside the narrow mouth of this inlet used to be magnificent and there are reports that stocks are again building up around here. Best surf fishing on the sou'west-facing surf beaches of Long Strand, Little Island Strand and Owenahinchy Strand is for the first half of the tide. Little Warren strand, to the west of the mouth, fishes very well at times. Spinning into the channel around low water and during the first part of the flood tide can produce good bags of bass. This channel would benefit from an extended trial with live sand-eels,

On each side of the causeway across the upper part of this inlet are mullet – plenty of them. To the east lies a tidal lagoon at low water where the fish are to be found by the hundred. They will take bread after heavy groundbaiting. Salmon also become marooned in this pool.

8 Baltimore This is a somewhat arbitrary nomination. Much of the coastline from Rosscarbery to Baltimore – and beyond – has been only lightly fished. There is tremendous variety, with plenty of the usual inshore species to be found. The main interest in this area lies at Lough Hyne, a sheltered salt lake where, on a warm summer night, the angler can lie on his back under the oak trees waiting for the first gentle pulls of a big conger somewhere out there in 30 fathoms of water – a strange feeling. The western side is deepest and produces wrasse, whiting, pollack, ling, mackerel and mullet. It is a beautiful place, worth a visit.

At Roaringwater Bay an angler once set sea fishermen talking by describing in a leading fishing magazine a catch he made of giant bass. Some said it was possible, others decided it was a hoax. If you stand on the cliffs here and survey this mysterious bay, you may decide he was telling the truth.

9 Skull There is excellent dinghy fishing around here for tope, rays, dogfish, pollack, wrasse and so on in the shelter of the numerous islands. Charter boats operate out from here and catch just about everything in the book. As ever in this part of Ireland, there is plenty of good ground to explore from beach and boat.

10 Mizen Head Despite the holiday camps at nearby Barley Cove, there is fair fishing from the rocks in the centre of the cove, on the eastern side, for pollack, wrasse, dogfish, rays and, possibly tope. The author once hooked a 30 foot basking shark that swam within a few feet of the rock on which he was standing, using a spinning rod, 10 lb line and a 5/8 oz spinner. The shark did not even notice. Fair size shoals of sea-trout are also to be found around these rocks at times. A well equipped angler is likely to find explorative fishing pays off here. The rocks around the headland into Dunmanus Bay are often too fierce and precipitous to fish. From the road, Dunmanus Bay does not look too attractive, although the author watched another basking shark cruising about only a few yards out from the shore.

11 Bantry Bay Notwithstanding the oil terminal at Whiddy Island, the coastline is very beautiful hereabouts, but lightly fished. This is yet another of Ireland's largely unexplored areas. There are plenty of sheltered areas for those with their own boat on a trailer to fish, especially for the prolific (at times) rays in Bere Haven, with reef fishing for good pollack, and clear-ground fishing for a host of other species. The shore angler will find no shortage of rock marks for mackerel, wrasse, pollack and . . . who knows what else?

12 Allihies Again this area is but lightly charted, mainly because of the proximity of the fabulous Kerry fishing. The mountains of Slieve Miskish fall dramatically to the sea, and the tide that roars between Dursey Island and the mainland is a suitable reminder of the majesty of the countryside hereabouts. This peninsula is well off the beaten track, so the visitor who comes well armed with technical expertise is likely to find fishing areas that are not only unknown to other anglers, but which are unlikely to be fished again until he returns there next year. North and west of Kenmare, the fishing is better known.

Bait Areas

There is never any need to go without good bait along the Cork coast. Several fishing harbours can supply fish baits when the seas are too rough to allow mackerel fishing from the rocks. Lugworm beds are plentiful.

Sand-eels may be scraped or raked from several places. Mussels are very common around some rock marks and inside the sheltered waters of several of the many inlets. If you do get talking with any of the lobster or crab fishermen, do not forget to enquire about the nature of the sea bed around many of the interesting promontories here. They set their pots over rough ground generally, and will be familiar with both the sea bed and likely access points.

A   Lugworm and some ragworm
C   Crab
D   Sand-eels

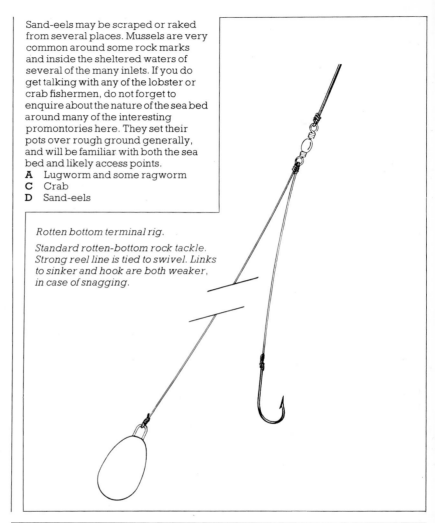

Rotten bottom terminal rig.

Standard rotten-bottom rock tackle. Strong reel line is tied to swivel. Links to sinker and hook are both weaker, in case of snagging.

FOR THE FAMILY

In the north and east of County Cork you can enjoy pleasant country and coast and the friendly City of Cork. West Cork is an area famous for its scenic beauty – mountains, lakes and rivers; the coast offering bathing, walking, riding, festivals and many other holiday attractions.

Garinish Island   a short boat trip from Glengarriff takes you to this lovely island with its wonderful 37-acre subtropical gardens. March–Oct.

Bantry House   truly magnificent 18thC house with tapestries, furniture, works of art. Terraces overlook the Bay. To see the sights of Bantry Bay take a 1½ hour cruise from Bantry Pier.

Ballad sessions   and musical events in hotels and pubs in many centres.

Blarney Castle   nr Cork. Do not miss the famous Blarney Stone. The castle has impressive battlements and an 85 ft keep.

Dursey Island   from Dursey Sound, nr Allihies, you can take a cable car trip to visit this island on the tip of the wild Beara Peninsula.

Cork City   much to see and do in this elegant and historic city with its miles of good beaches nearby and delightful country on all sides.

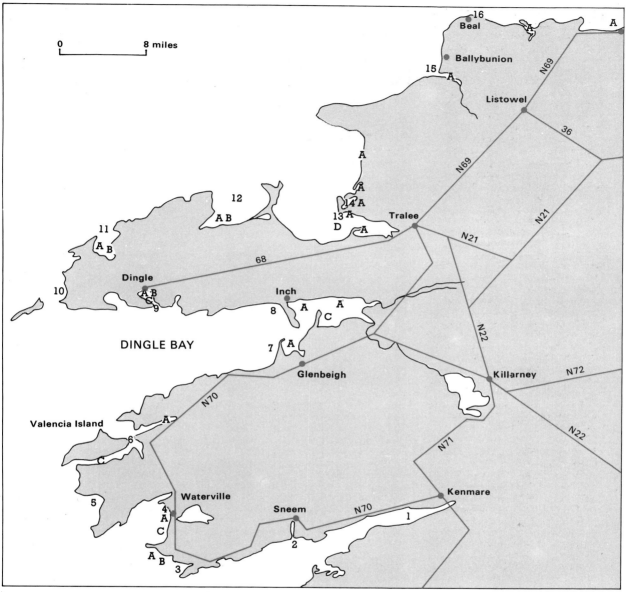

Small sandy bays are to be found around the mouth of the Kenmare River. The north side of the estuary is similar, with Coongar Harbour and other inlets frequent towards Lamb's Head. There is a fine surf beach of coarse sand at Derrynane, with large rocky outcrops like small islands at each end. The rocks proliferate towards Hog's Head on the south side of Ballinskelligs Bay, with a shoreline of sand and rubble near Waterville, becoming sandier on the western side out to precipitous Bolus Head. This entire bay may be surveyed in spectacular manner with a pair of binoculars from the top of Coomakista Pass.

The northern shore of the Bolus peninsula is extensively rocky, with a tiny – but extremely good – surf beach at St Finans Bay. There are more rocks westward to Puffin Island and steep cliffs lie to the north. The shore of Valencia Harbour (sometimes spelt Valentia) is a mixture of sand, low rocks and rubble. Much of Valencia Island is very steep and rocky on its seaward side. It is reached via the bridge at Portmagee.

Much of the shoreline to the south of Dingle Bay to the east of Doulos Head is inaccessible and steep. The White Strand at Rossbehy and Inch Strand to the north bound the seaward side of Castlemaine Harbour, which has a foreshore of rubble becoming muddy sand.

The north shore is steep and rocky, but with a few small sandy bays among the rocks – Minard and

Kerry and Limerick

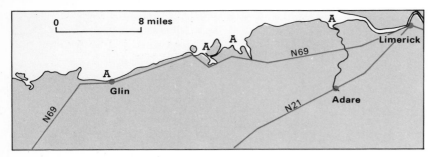

Trabeg Strands, for example – going towards sheltered Dingle Harbour – with its rubbly foreshore and Ventry harbour, which is largely sandy. There is more steep rock westwards to Slea Head and the headlands overlooking the Blasket Islands. Small surf beaches are scattered between heavy rock headlands at Clogher Head, Sybil Point, with the cliffs at Sybil Head denying access to the sea.

Smerwick Harbour is rocky on its western side, with some access points, and with a fine surf beach of white sand at its southern end (Ballinrannig) and others along its eastern shore. West from Ballydavid Head more cliffs deny access to the shore where Mount Brandon falls steeply to the sea.

Access to Brandon Point requires the visitor to retrace his route via Dingle and the magnificent Connor Pass. Brandon Bay encompasses some superb surf beaches out towards the Magharee Islands with sheltered Tralee Bay equally sandy, but lacking the surf. There are a few outcrops of rock and patches of rubble among the sands that curve round to Fenit. To the north lies the surf strand of Carrahane.

The eastern shore of Ballyheige Bay is sandy; rocks and cliffs extend along both sides of Kerry Head, dropping to clear blue Atlantic water. Along the north side of the head are a few tiny coves with sand deep inside them, this pattern continuing north eastwards to the strand at the mouth of the Cashen River, south of Ballybunion.

Northwards lie rocky headlands with several bays between them, largely of low rock, extending into the mouth of the Shannon estuary. The southern shore is largely of sand with just the occasional rocky or stony outcrop towards Tarbert, with sand proliferating to Limerick.

Charter boats operate out from Derrynane, Ballinskelligs, Sneem,

Valencia, Caherciveen, Dingle, and Fenit. As ever, there is a fair chance that a boatman at any of the other harbours along here may agree to take you out or to hire out his boat.

Those with their own boats on trailers will find suitable launching ramps at Kenmare, Templenoe, Gleesk, White Strand, Castlecove, Bunavalla, Coonanna, Ventry (and at nearby Cuan Pier), Ballydavid, Brandon Harbour, Fenit, Barrow, Tarbert, and Foynes. Small boats may be launched at many other sites, but their use is not advised. The weather around the Kerry coastline can deteriorate at a dramatic speed. Caution is advised to all comers. Never attempt to fish into surf from a boat. Surf has a habit of starting to break 200 yards, say, from the shore, this pattern may continue for a short while, then waves will start to break 400 yards out. A boat caught in this is likely to be lost, even though the life-jacketed crew make it to the shore.

Preliminary enquiries about the fishing in this area may be directed, as in previous sections, to the Central Fisheries Board. (The address is given in the Dublin section.) There are branches of the Irish Tourist Board throughout England to whom enquiries about accommodation should be addressed. There are also local boards that serve small areas. The main tourist office in London's Bond Street can supply plenty of information but somewhat skimpy angling intelligence.

The Kerry coastline is justly famous for its fishing. Practically every species in the book is caught from it or around it. It boasts magnificent mountainous scenery, making surf fishing on Brandon Bay, for example, an aesthetic experience whether the bass are there or not.

Tidal differences from Dublin: add 5 hours 20 minutes for Tralee Bay; subtract 5 hours 9 minutes for Limerick.

1 Kenmare There are several places along the southern shore of this estuary, called the Kenmare River, from which general fishing may be practised.

Buna Pier produces conger eels to fish baits around high tide at night. The beach at Ardea offers flounder fishing, with a few dogfish and the odd bass thrown in for good measure. From Reenafreach Point pollack, wrasse, dogfish and the occasional tope may be caught from the rocks and bass – and sea-trout at times – may be had by spinning from the rocky outcrop under the road bridge that crosses the Kenmare river.

2 Sneem To the east, the shore west of Blackwater Pier, and the pier itself, offer fair fishing for conger eels and rays – together with sea-trout and small pollack caught by spinning. There is good mullet fishing at Oysterbed Pier, together with ray, conger, wrasse and pollack fishing, though not of the highest quality, with similar fishing at Gleesk.

3 Lambs Head An arduous walk from the little harbour at the end on the north side over to the sheltered south side is not worth the small congers, pollack and wrasse to be taken here, especially since the fishing closer to the mainland is to be had with greater ease. At the end of the head lies a large rock and the sound between the land and this rock is extremely deep, but the fishing is not very good here. However, the coarse sand at the surf beach on the north side of the head is well stocked with sand-eels. Bass may be taken here all through the year, with Christmas time especially good for fat, well fed fish in peak condition. Often sand-eel is the bait that scores best of all. At high tide it is safe to maroon oneself on the grass-topped rock islets at either end of the beach. However, the first four hours of the flood tide seem to produce the best results. Lugworm may be dug from Derrynane harbour, along with razorfish.

4 Waterville To the south, the southern side of Hog's Head offers good fishing for pollack, wrasse and mackerel. This has not been over explored, so there is a fair chance that a bait launched out onto sand would be found by rays, dogfish, conger eels and possibly tope. Inside the bay, sea-trout may be had while spinning at the mouth of the short river that drains Lough Currane. To the north, the mouth of the River Inny is set between good surf beaches which produce well for bass and flounders at times. Fish well away from the river mouth if heavy rain has fallen as the fish dislike the cold, peat-stained water. The sandy beaches out towards Bolus Head produce nothing of any note. To the west of the car park on Bolus Head, fishing the northern side of the rocky promontory produces excellent pollack and wrasse, though the sea bed is too fierce to allow bottom fishing.

5 St Finan's Bay   The little surf beach here, with fingers of flat rock among the sand, produces good bass (and, of course, flounders) late in the year. When surf is running in here at an angle, fish fairly close to the rocks at whichever side the wash is pushing the food for the fish towards.

6 Valencia (or Valentia)   While the coastline from St Finan's Bay to Portmagee is unfishable from the shore due to the mighty cliffs over-looking Puffin Island, the outer side of Valencia Island has limited access points – and these are not thoroughly explored. One well-tried mark is Cooloo, where the wrasse, pollack and mackerel fishing is excellent. Where sand comes to the rock edge, rays may be taken, together with tope : This outer edge looks really promising – a record halibut was caught here years ago.

At Cahirciveen, long casting from the rocks around Valencia harbour – and on the Valencia side, will produce thornback rays which are very common here. Turbot, too, are likely. There is a fish pier at Cahirciveen. Large shoals of mullet are attracted to the outfall behind the processing house where fish viscera are washed through a pipe into the sea. Thornback rays also come scavenging here. A local mink farm collects the small fish that are cleaned out of trawl nets. There are some excellent bait species to be found in the boxes of fish awaiting collection. The small pier where the trawlers tie up produces thornback rays, while float fishing or spinning produces nothing but diminutive pollack. Rays are also available from the shore at Lough Kay, inside Doulos Head.

7 Glenbeigh   Cliffs eastwards from Doulos Head deny access to the shoreline except at Cooncrome Harbour, which has rock platforms on the western side from which

mackerel, pollack and wrasse may be taken ; Coonanna Harbour, where a few rays may be had from the little pier ; and at Kells where Kings Head produces pollack, mackerel and wrasse.

Rossbeigh strand runs for three miles from Glenbeigh and produces excellent bass and a few tope when a surf is up. The tope are found early and late in the year around the low water period, waiting to run with the tide to feed on the flatfish inside Castlemaine Harbour. Long casting with fresh fish baits among some sort of rubby-dubby trail at the end of this sandy peninsula should produce well. It may be possible to perform the same feat at the end of the Cromane Peninsula.

At Ballycasane, two miles north of Killorglin, the River Laune may be fished from half tide up for bass, though some experienced anglers have found that the estuary bank opposite this place fishes better. Netting in the area has severely reduced the numbers of fish available here.

8 Inch   On the northern side of Dingle Bay, Inch strand produces excellent bass fishing at times, especially near the car park by the caravan site. A good surf is required for them here. When there is no surf the bass hunt around the weed-covered rocks on the northern side but may be taken from the sand by night. The best times are early and late in the year. High summer sees the bass working sprats and sand-eels well offshore. The south end of Inch produces some tope.

Under severe weather conditions, fishing some four and a half miles east of Inch into the estuary channel of the River Maine produces bass that run up with the tide. Flounders too, of course.

Driving towards Dingle from Inch, the road bends inland where the Anascaul River joins the sea. Here there is fair night fishing with crab for bass, or they may be had by spinning – sea-trout too. Further west, at Minard, rays and bass are taken around high tide from the stony beach.

9 Dingle   A few miles to the east of the town lies Lough Trabeg. Spinning around low water from either side of the entrance to the lough produces bass and sea-trout. Dark tides produce rays and bass – the beach here shelves fairly steeply. Rocks to the

west produce wrasse and pollack.

Dingle harbour holds a few thornback rays which may be reached from the beach. Rock marks inside it yield wrasse and pollack. There are large shoals of mullet at times – thick-lipped – and these will take mashed bread or minced fish groundbait and then be waiting for your baited hook. One of the best places to fish is around the fish pier. Do not overlook this commercial fishing port when after good quality fish for bait. It pays to arrange with a skipper for him to reserve fish for you.

Five miles further west lies Ventry Harbour. The rocks between the two harbours are inaccessible, due to the cliffs. Ventry produces masses of lesser-spotted dogfish at times, with flounders. However, when the wind veers south easterly and builds up a big surf here, the bass fishing can be excellent, especially for fish fish of good size.

10 Slea Head   The cliffs east of Ventry are largely too steep to be scaled. At Slea Head, on the corner opposite the little shrine there, the car may be parked without blocking the road and the cliff scaled to sloping ledges just above the sea. The author did the climb once and decided that there are safer, more relaxing areas to fish. If a big wave sweeps in here, you do not stand a chance. However, the agile – and the foolhardy – will catch the standard Irish rock species – wrasse, pollack and mackerel.

A mile to the north lies Coomeenoole strand, noted home of lesser-spotted dogfish and the occasional large bass when the surf is pounding in. This beach lies on the south side of Dunmore Head. The western extremity of this headland produces excellent wrasse, pollack and mackerel fishing, with conger fishing on the bottom. Good conger can also be had from Dunquin Pier, while the rock ledges to the north are good for pollack, wrasse and mackerel. There is another pier, unused, a little to the north of here with a rock finger jutting seawards : pollack and wrasse are abundant here. Clamber down the rocks below the well signposted village school (built for the film *Ryan's Daughter*) and you can catch pollack and wrasse.

Clogher Strand is a disappointing and strangely dismal beach. Rocks on the northern side are quite unprotected so calm weather is required before they can be fished.

They produce mackerel, wrasse and pollack. Close to the sandy beach of Ferriter's Cove, bass may be had by spinning. Bottom fishing here is likely to produce bass, rays and possibly tope. Flounder fishing here can be excellent, especially at the end of the year and early in the New Year.

11 Smerwick Harbour The cliffs of Sybil Head deny access to that part of the shoreline. On the western side of Smerwick harbour, a long walk along the cliff tops eventually leads to a few places where you can clamber down and fish for wrasse and small pollack. Of the three strands inside this bay, Ballinrannig is reckoned to be the most consistent for bass and flounders, while the Black Strand and White Strand also fish well at times when there is a fair surf running. A few miles to the east conger eels, wrasse and small pollack may be taken from the pier at Ballydavid and from the rocks at Brandon Creek. There are also fair mullet to be caught from the creek – locally named Cuas.

12 Brandon Bay East of magnificent Mount Brandon lie the fabulous surf beaches of Brandon Bay. At least, from a fisherman's point of view, they used to be. Nowadays trammel nets are reported along some sections and trawlers can be seen ploughing the sand behind the surf. However, there are still bass to be caught here, especially from late October to Christmas, when the weather is mild, and in March and April. The summer months see most bass activity well offshore. Develop a feel for surf. If it is too heavy, with curtains of sand suspended in the water by the pounding wave action, the bass are unlikely to be in it. Brandon Bay curves round from Cloghane to Fahamore. The western side is the most exposed, so when there is little surf at Fermoyle or Stradbally, then the outer areas may hold the fish. And if bad weather makes the surf barely fishable at Kilcummin or Stradbally, conditions can be perfect at Cloghane or around the Black Rock.

When is the best time to fish? Some anglers reckon that low tide is the best period at the Black Rock and Fermoyle, the middle part best at Kilcummin where the two tiny streams drain across the sand. Never take a car onto the sands – it will swiftly sink. Fahamore, where rocks are found among the steeper part of this beach, also produces well at times.

Flounders are numerous and will also relish lugworm and clams dug from the back strand at Cloghane. Peeler crab may be gathered from around the black Rock.

There is fair fishing into the estuary channel from the west bank of the estuary for bass, rays, dogfish and flounders. Mullet are abundant inside the harbour, and sea-trout may also be taken here by spinning.

From the Magharee Islands round to the southern part of Tralee Bay and Derrymore Island the fishing is pretty unexciting, though some fair bass have been taken where Lough Gill drains in to the sea. Tope can be caught in settled weather from Brandon Bay, when there is no surf, as far as the Magharee Islands.

13 Fenit This pier used to provide a good chance of a common skate, but the absence of a conservation policy has reduced such chances virtually to nil. Rays, conger eels and a few monkfish are taken here, with mullet common. The deepest water is at the extreme end on the southern side. Fenit pier is justly famous for its lesser-spotted dogfish.

Tralee Bay is very sandy and offers excellent boat fishing for a variety of ray species, tope, common skate (a few) and monkfish. Flatfish, like turbot, enjoy this environment, while plaice are abundant.

14 Barrow Harbour Flounders, bass, small turbot, rays and tope may be taken from the mouth of this small harbour, much of which dries out at low tide. Bass come to live sand-eels

Preparing to fish the autumn surf on Brandon Bay.

collected at low tide near Fenit Pier. Similar fishing for bass and flounders – with the chance of one of the other species – can be experienced at Carrahane Sands, a similar harbour. A few miles to the north, bass and flounders may be taken from the surf beach, with Black Rock an excellent spot to spin for the bass. To the north, around Kerry Head, there is excellent fishing for wrasse and pollack. Tope and rays may be expected where sand comes close to the rocks. Access can be tricky to some of the better looking marks.

15 Ballybunion From the surf beaches at the mouth of the River Cashen bass can be taken at low water on bait and also by spinning across the estuary channels as the tide starts to flood. Up-river is some good flounder fishing. To the north, at Black Rock, there is good bass fishing along the strand and, as is common with many Kerry surf beaches, fine settled weather sees an influx of small turbot along the sands. Flounders just cannot be avoided. The same applies to the beaches between the various headlands to the north, while bait fishing from Doon Point and Leck Point produces dogfish, conger and rays. Spinning brings in pollack, float fishing or legering produces wrasse.

16 Beal Beal strand produces some good bass fishing at times, especially into the channel off Beal Point. Littor Strand also produces a few bass. Small turbot, flounders, plaice and bass may be caught all round this outer limit of the Shannon. At Tarbert it is possible to spin or float fish live sand-eels in the warm-water outfall from the power station or from the pier that marks the cross-Shannon ferry terminal. East of Tarbert the fishing is for dogfish, flounders and small species mainly – not very exciting when compared to the catches that can be made to the south.

Bait Areas
Good fishing and plenty of bait.
A Lugworm
B Razorfish and clam
C Crab
D Sand-eels
Not all bait areas are marked on the map because even in Kerry it is possible to fall into the routine of digging bait and fishing marks that one knows well.

FOR THE FAMILY
With some of the finest mountain and coastal scenery in Ireland – the Ring of Kerry, Killarney's Lakes, and the Kenmare valley – **Kerry** caters for walkers, bird-watchers, wild-flower lovers, golfers, motorists and bathers. There is much of archaeological and historical interest and wildlife to see.

Muckross House 3 miles from Killarney. This fine 19thC mansion is now a museum of Kerry Folk Life. You can see all kinds of craftsmen at work and enjoy the gardens.

Killarney National Park beautiful lakeland estate with waterfalls nearby, deer, nature trails and viewpoints. Killarney itself has all the tourist amenities.

Gap of Dunloe 7 miles of breath-taking scenery. For a new experience go there by jaunting car, one of many such trips from Killarney.

Blasket Islands take a boat trip from Dunquin to 'the last outpost of Europe'. Further north, from Knightstown you can visit *Skelligs Rocks* with their ancient monastery and bird sanctuary.

Kenmare a good centre for Kerry hills and Killarney's mountains, Macgillycuddy's Reeks and the south west. See the Shean Falls and local lacemaking.

Sing-songs and traditional ballad sessions are popular in many hotels.

See the sights of **Limerick** itself, a historic city with Georgian houses, modern shops and entertainments. You can explore a countryside and coast of outstanding beauty and variety and see the Shannon estuary by boat.

Clare Glens waterfalls, scenic walks, nature trails in woodland of conifer, oak and ash. A good picnic place.

Adare Manor and gardens. Great hall, minstrel's gallery, formal gardens. May–Sept. In one of Ireland's most attractive villages, with thatched cottages.

King John's Castle Limerick. Explore the castle, built in 1210, and try an evening of Irish entertainment, laid on twice weekly in one of the towers.

Glen of Aherlow from Kilmallock you can tour the Galtee, Ballyhoura mountain country and woodlands and see the caves of Kilbeheny and Tipperary.

Lough Gur a small lake in the south east, surrounded by prehistoric remains – dolmens, Stone Age dwellings, stone forts and tombs. Lakeside walks and visitor centre, picnic area.

Beagling country Beagles hunt (on foot) from Oct to March and hunts welcome visitors. A good family day outdoors.

Massive boulders dwarf this angler as he fishes for wrasse from Clogher Head.

Clare

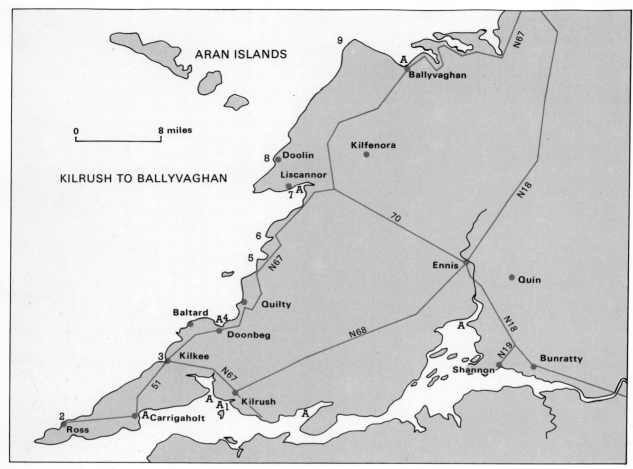

ARAN ISLANDS

KILRUSH TO BALLYVAGHAN

0 — 8 miles

Ballyvaghan

Doolin 8

Kilfenora

Liscannor

7 A

6

5

N67

Quilty

Baltard

A4

Doonbeg

3 Kilkee

51

N67

Kilrush

A A1

2 Ross

A Carrigaholt

A

Ennis

Quin

N18

N67

70

N68

Shannon

N19

N18

Bunratty

9

The north shore of the Shannon estuary consists largely of sand, with mud and stones in more sheltered areas. There is a group of islets around the River Fergus Estuary. The sand, with a few patches of rubble, extends to Clonderalaw Bay and westwards to Kilrush, then on to Carrigaholt Bay. Here rocks again assert themselves, especially around Kilcredaun Point.

To the west lie two sandy bays, then a rocky foreshore with low cliffs behind extending west to Loop Head. The north side of Loop Head consists of tall, majestic cliffs. The little bay at Bridges of Ross allows access to the foreshore and a fine view of this spectacular scenery. Further north, there is the sheltered sandy bay at Kilkee with another small bay beyond to the north.

Apart from stony Ballard Bay, the shore between Donegal Point and Killard Point is largely of flat rocks with low cliffs behind. There is a fair

amount of this type of reef among the sands of Rayoganagh Strand, but the White Strand to the north is pure dune-backed sand.

Northwards to Spanish Point lie headlands of flat rock with gentle sandy beaches in between. There is less sand north of the Point, the outcrops of rock extending to Lahinch (or Lehinch) inside Liscannor Bay. There is a sandy beach here at the mouth of the River Inagh near Spanish Point, with more flat reefs west of Liscannor and out to Hags Head.

The massive cliffs of Moher – 700 feet above sea level – stoutly deny access to the sea here, falling sheer to the water and for some way under water. Porbeagle sharks feed along here within yards of the base of the cliffs. The cliffs gradually subside to the north east giving way to the sandy beach at Fisherstreet, with flat rocks flanking the beach at Doolin Point.

More cliffs back the flat reefy foreshore northwards to the little strand at Fanore, just south of the heavy cliffs around Black Head. To the east along the southern shore of Galway Bay, the cliffs fall away to a sandy foreshore with extensive flat outcrops of rock around Ballyvaghan, with similar ground of mixed sand and reef extending around the eastern side of Galway Bay.

Charter boats operate out from Quilty, Liscannor, Ballyvaghan and Seafield. Other harbours may be able to offer boat-hire facilities. Trailed boats of decent size may be launched at slipways at Cappa, Kilkee, Quilty, Milltown Malbay, Liscannor and Doolin. Lesser craft can be manhandled at several other sites.

Tides along this coastline occur some 5 to 6 hours before Dublin times (see also local press).

The coastline of County Clare is populated by a wide variety of species, but they all seem to pale to insignificance alongside the porbeagle shark potential, both from boats and from the rocks. It was under the cliffs of Moher that the techniques were developed for trolling for them. Many years ago Jack Shine developed techniques for catching them from the rocks – Green Island, to be precise – but more of that later.

1 Kilrush The small pier at Cappagh offers excellent conger fishing from the western and southern side. Fish at night, for preference, and use perfectly fresh fish baits. The problem is the dogfish which often get to the bait and shred it before a conger finds it. For this reason groundbaiting, a trick that is often so successful when conger fishing, is not advised. The occasional monkfish is caught here, too.

To the west, the inlet of Poulna-sherry should be fished at its mouth during the early stages of a flooding tide for rays, bass, tope and the chance of a monkfish. This is a place where groundbaiting with minced mackerel is likely to score. Fish also for the bass towards the end of the ebb tide. This mark is worth bearing in mind when heavy weather makes others outside the Shannon estuary unfishable.

2 Ross Few places can rival this for magnificence, especially when the setting sun is low over the water and the water is flat calm. There is good rock fishing for pollack, wrasse and mackerel around here. The bottom is very rough, so bait fishing is not advised. Even though congers are present, the chances of getting them out are slim.

3 Kilkee Fish the rocks to the south of the sandy beach for mackerel, pollack and wrasse. Float fishing in a choppy sea with mackerel strip is an effective and lazy way of catching the pollack, with the bait set to fish about six feet above the bottom. From the surf strand here some large bass have been taken. Fish close to the rocks for the best results, using large baits of mackerel, shellfish or soft crab.

4 Doonbeg North of the town for five miles lie a series of surf beaches which produce fair bass under the right conditions. Rays also may be caught around the high water period, and there is the chance of a tope or two when the weather is set fair and the water is calm. There are outcrops of reef set among these sands, and these should be explored as suitable

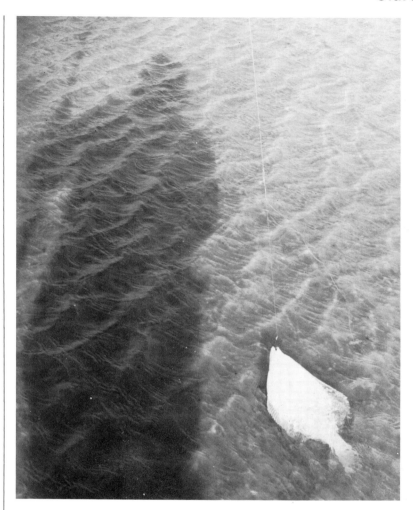

fishing places. At Seafield, a ridge of reef runs out to the west of the pier and can provide fair bass spinning at times, though small pollack are more numerous.

5 Spanish Point From the exquisite surf beach here some good bass fishing is to be had, together with flounder fishing. Tope have been taken from this beach under calm, settled conditions. At the mouth of the River Bealaclugga you may spin for bass and sea-trout or fly fish into the surf. At Black Rock, bass may be caught on baits fished on the bottom together with dogfish. Spinning is productive at times, especially in the evening when fry are close to shore.

6 Green Island The south western tip of Liscannor Bay, north west of Milltown Malbay, is called Green Island. It was from here several years

Shadow angler and his good-sized estuary flounder.

ago that Jack Shine spent a great deal of time and patience to catch several porbeagle sharks, his largest 145 lb on 31 lb nylon, a large Alvey side-cast reel and an ordinary beachcasting rod. The sharks are abundant here in July and August, and will venture close to the rocks when the weather is fine and settled. Jack reported at the time that he had to move his bait before any takes were forthcoming. Obviously a float-fished live mackerel – or two on one hook – would score well. Nowadays we have the benefit of big game techniques imported from America to use against this most noble of quarries. At times Jack was pestered by tope – nice pests!

While waiting for sharks, pollack,

mackerel and wrasse may be caught. The mackerel can be converted into rubby-dubby. The bottom is very rugged here, and bottom fishing is not advised. The sharks are caught by float fishing using a lightly inflated child's balloon for a float.

7 Liscannor Lahinch (or Lehinch) strand fishes well for bass and flatfish to either side of the Inagh estuary. Upstream at Liscannor Harbour are large shoals of thick-lipped mullet which will take standard baits.

To the north, the Cliffs of Moher impose a shore fishing challenge that is as daft as the nearby porbeagle potential is exciting. 250 yards of line is needed just to reach the water!

8 Doolin On the strand here there is often a good surf running, even in calm conditions. Flatfish and dogfish may be taken here, together with bass, though these have thinned out a great deal of late. The beach is quite steep, so long casting for the bass is not required. Pollack and bass may be caught by float fishing or by spinning from the rocks at the northern end of the beach. Northwards for 10 miles to Fanore are several good rock marks that offer wrasse, pollack, mackerel and tope fishing. Rays and dogfish may also be taken and porbeagle sharks have been sighted close in.

The surf beach at Fanore produces bass and flounders, especially when fishing close to the rocks at the southern end. Rays also come into this sandy mark and may be caught, by the usual means, mainly at night. Peeler crab is probably the most effective all-round bait from this mark.

9 Black Head Fish from the rocks near the lighthouse for wrasse, pollack, garfish, mackerel and dogfish. Conger eels are also taken here, together with the occasional ray. There is a fair chance of a tope coming out of Galway Bay with the ebb tide. At Ballyvaghan, the fishing is mainly for flounders and other flatfish; similar fishing is to be had further east into Galway Bay.

Bait Areas

There are plenty of digging grounds inside the more sheltered harbours and estuaries. Mackerel are plentiful from rock marks during the warmer months, and may linger as late as November in an Indian summer. As with most Irish shore areas, the bait beds are not over dug or over publicised. There are likely to be more than are listed on the map.

A Lugworm and other sand/mud dwelling bait species.

Above: A dedicated task – digging for lugworms by flashlight.
Below: A sprint up the beach to avoid a drenching!

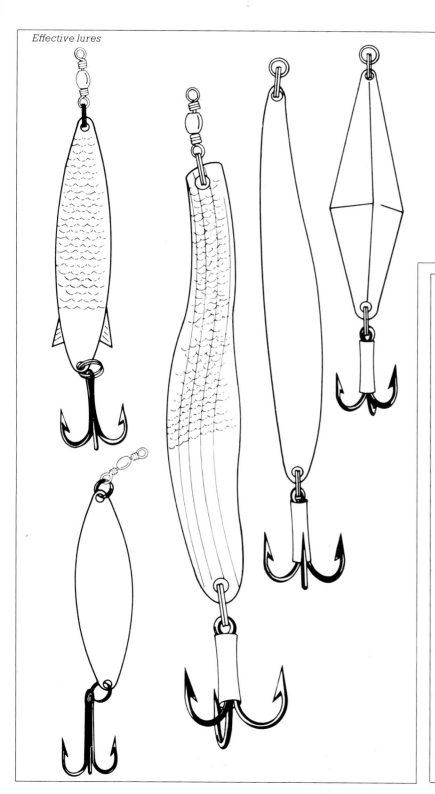

Effective lures

Spinners and small pirks are both useful for long casting and fishing deep water from rock marks. Large pirks score best over wrecks.

FOR THE FAMILY

There is much to see in this varied and beautiful county. The coast has sandy beaches, inlets and coves. There are mountains and lakes, the interesting limestone area of the Burren, and castles, ancient churches and prehistoric sites.

Cliffs of Moher nr Liscannor. Nearly 5 miles of towering cliffs. Tremendous views from O'Brien's Tower (777 ft) observation and tourist centre.

Bunratty Castle and Folk Park on the Ratty River. 15thC fortress with fine art collection. In the Park are traditional dwellings, craftsmen at work, teas, etc. Try Bunratty Folk Village for an evening of folk music, dancing, wine and Irish stew.

Aillwee Cave nr Ballyvaghan. Stalagmites and stalactites in a prehistoric animal's lair. Open April–Oct.

Burren Display Centre Kilfenora. An unusual series of displays on the natural history and history of this interesting area will help you to enjoy an exploration of the region itself. Easter–Oct.

Killaloe hire a bike – or a cruiser – to explore the lovely Shannon area. Both available from the cruise operators.

Craggaunowen nr Quin. A fascinating complex of reconstructed Bronze Age and Medieval buildings. Teas.

Kilrush forest walks and picnic area (420 acres) 22-mile waterside route from Cappagh Pier. Boat trips to Scattery Island with its ruined monastery.

Galway

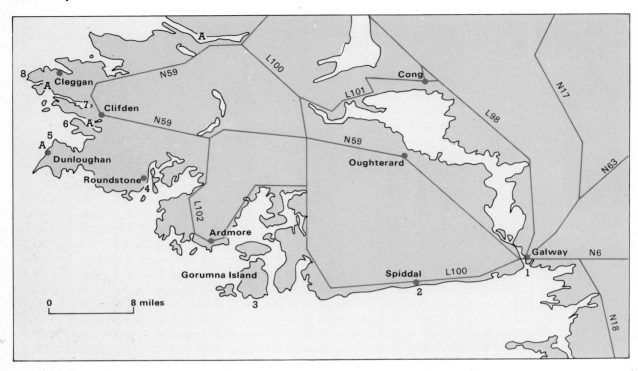

The eastern shoreline of Galway Bay is complicated by a mass of little islands and heavily indented bays. The beach consists largely of sand, rubble, boulders and outcrops of reef round to Galway itself. West of the harbour, along the northern shore of Galway Bay, lie extensive sands to Barna, increasing to Cashla Bay. North and west from here the land crumbles into the sea in a confused mass of islands, islets, rock stacks, sandy bays and coves – with flat rocks and reef in between. Here and there low cliffs rise up – the place is a maze. To the north the land is also a mass of loughs, rivers, streams and marshland.

North again from Slyne Head the coastline becomes no less complex – deep inlets are to be found: Mannin Bay, Ardbear Bay, Streamstown Bay, Cleggan Bay and Ballynakill Harbour, all adding greater complexity to Clifden's islands, reefs and sandy bays. Thus the coastline continues with Inishbofin Island and Inishturk Island lying off a coastline of sand, rubble and flat rock.

There is a lot of good boat fishing off this coast, especially for the small boat man who will find sheltered water in the lee of islands and inside bays. The shore fishing is not so good,

however, though there is some good hunting to be had from several marks.

From a boat conger, porbeagle shark, blue shark, skate, rays, pollack, tope, turbot, plaice, flounders, bass, dogfish and mackerel may be caught.

Charter facilities exist at Galway, Clifden, Leenaun, Cleggan, and Spiddle. Boats may be hired, together with a willing boatman, from smaller ports by enquiring on site. The trailed boat may be launched from a slipway at Roundstone, and at several other spots where the craft is small enough to be dragged down to the water's edge. Such sites exist at Spiddal (or Spiddle), Kilkerin, Callowfeenish, Mynish, Moyrus, Clifden, Letterfrack, Omey and Cleggan.

Tide times are some 6 hours after the times advertised for Dublin.

1 Galway Bay The fishing at the eastern end of Galway Bay is far from spectacular, though the visitor who wants a few fillets of flounder for dinner will find plenty along the sandy beaches hereabouts and inside the various estuaries. At Galway, the promenade to the west of the town produces large numbers of mackerel when the weather is fine. Inside the harbour are good mullet which are taken on bread or diced fish.

2 Spiddal (or Spiddle) About a mile east of the harbour is some rock fishing where small pollack and mackerel, garfish and wrasse may be taken. West from here lie extensive sands which, although beautiful to view, are also restful on the fishing rod. Deep sea fishing can be excellent for a wide variety of species, from shark to large pollack.

3 Gorumna Island While much of the fishing in this area is made impossible by extensive belts of bladderwrack among the numerous islets and inlets, such shallow water producing little more than shore crabs and frustration, there is a little harbour called Trawbawn near the outer reaches of Greatman's Bay. Here there is a bottom of pure white sand, with clear water over it, and catches of plaice and flounders may be made on shellfish and worm baits. At times, and with the help of polarised glasses, it is possible to watch the flatfish take the bait. Fish from the harbour jetty or from the rocks opposite.

The wide fringe of bladderwrack along these stony shores effectively precludes fishing for a fair way north towards Slyne Head, where much of the shoreline is inaccessible.

4 Roundstone Fish from the rocks on the north side of Gorteen Bay for pollack, mackerel and wrasse. There are some sandy patches around Ballyconneely Bay from which flatfish may be taken. From the harbour at Bunowen flatfish, small rays and small conger may be taken.

5 Dunloughan There are plenty of large lugworm here, and they can be used to good effect on the flounders and plaice on the little sandy beaches round about. The turbot require mackerel strip, and although they are small, they are abundant at times. The mackerel bait may be caught from the rocky headlands that separate these beaches, together with small pollack and wrasse. On the eastern side of Knock Point, inside Mannin Bay, plentiful sandy beaches may be fished for flatfish. The most western beach produces a few rays and dogfish. The north shore of this bay is largely unfishable.

6 Erislannan Peninsula A large white concrete marker called the White Lady marks the outer limits of Clifden Bay. To the west, round to Boat Harbour, the rocks fish well for large wrasse, with pollack and mackerel spinning to be had. Eastwards to the Hawks Nest lie several small rock promontories from which fair catches of thornback rays have been made. Just south of Clifden, fish the southern side of the inlet at Salt Lake for wrasse, pollack and small conger eels. Mullet also travel through here but are not catchable.

7 Clifden This harbour is becoming one of Ireland's major deep-sea fishing ports. Even when the weather is foul it is possible to fish sheltered waters and to catch something large – like a common skate or big monkfish.

Driving along the cliffs north of Clifden Bay, there are two spots where it is possible to scramble down to the rocks and fish for pollack, wrasse and possibly mackerel. These are called Sloper's Cliff (where some rays are also taken on mackerel strip) and Beleek. On the northern side of this peninsula there is some conger fishing into Streamstown Bay when the tide is not running hard.

8 Cleggan With plenty of reefs off the coast here, the fishing from boats is largely for pollack, though turbot and rays are caught from sandy areas. To the southwest, it is possible to drive over the beach at low tide to Omey Island and fish the beach at the opposite side for flounders or from the rocks on the southern side of the beach for pollack, wrasse, conger

eels and dogfish. From the rocks near Aughrusbeg Lake, more rock ledges can be fished for pollack, mackerel and wrasse. At Cleggan itself, the pier sometimes yields a large conger, while flounders and mullet are available from the harbour itself. From Cleggan Point to Ballynakill Harbour the coastline is largely inaccessible and, where access is possible, a fringe of shallow bladder-wrack-smothered rock prevents practical fishing. Similar conditions obtain to the north of this harbour, around the steep rocky headland to Rinvyle Point. Pollack and wrasse may be caught at Ardnagreevagh and at Gowlaun.

Bait Areas
Plenty of lugworm in several suitable locations. Mussels are relatively abundant. Crab may be gathered from extensive areas of rubble, starting in June.
A Lugworm and possibly other sand-dwelling bait species

The sandy beaches and estuaries of Galway are excellent fishing grounds for flounder. Large lugworm are plentiful here and can be used to good effect for catching specimens like this one.

FOR THE FAMILY

A long, indented coastline with sheltered sandy beaches. Great scenic beauty and variety of lakes and mountains. There are old towns and villages steeped in history islands to visit, opportunities for riding and pony trekking and plenty of family holiday activities.

Dunguaire Castle Kinvarra. 16thC castle perched on a rocky promontory of Galway Bay, where medieval banquets, music and drama take place. Apr–Sept.

Gorumna Island explore this Connemara island with its ancient churches. It is joined to the mainland by bridge.

Clonbur climb Mount Gable for a breathtaking view. Walk and picnic by the lakes and in the forests.

Thoor Ballylee nr Gort. The Tower House which inspired the poet W. B. Yeats. Rare editions of his works on show. March–Oct.

Portumna Forest Park bordered by Lough Derg. Forest walks, wildlife sanctuary, deer, ponds for wildfowl, nature trail.

Kylemore a beautiful valley with three lakes. The Abbey, now a convent, welcomes visitors to this lakeshore setting. There is a pottery, chapel and restaurant.

Coole Park Gort. Once the home of Lady Gregory now a national forest and wildlife park. Woods, yew walk and autograph tree bearing many famous names.

Caves of Cong a series of fascinating caves, with underground streams. Cong lies between two great loughs – Mask and Carrib.

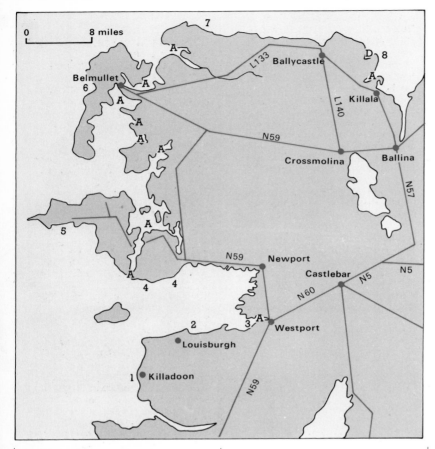

There are several fine sandy beaches at Tallaybaun, around Srumore Point, at the mouth of Roonagh Lough, northwards to Roonagh Point. The southern shore of Clew Bay is largely rocky, with several patches of sand among the outcrops of reef. The eastern shore is made up of some 30 square miles of drowned islands, islets, sands and boulders. It is said that there is an island here for every day of the year. Westport Bay and Newport Bay shelter behind this barricade.

The coastline becomes more rugged towards Achillbeg Island at the end of the Corraun Peninsula Sand flats separate Achill Island from the mainland, with a channel in between. On Achill Island the rock lets up for two miles south of Keel and, west of the twin headlands of Gubalennaun Beg and Gubalennaun More, to the beach at Keem. The cliffs then become more and more severe to Achill Head, with Mount Croaghaun falling over 2000 feet from its summit

to the sea within half a mile

On the north shore of the island there are two small bays set among the cliffs, with the shoreline mellowing somewhat as you travel east to Doogort, Ridge Point and Blacksod Bay. The shoreline north from Owenduff is largely of sand, boulders and rubble on the outside, with sand and mud proliferating inside the many sounds. Sand, boulders and the occasional outcrop of flat rock characterise the eastern side of Blacksod Bay, with extensive sands inside it as far north as Belmullet. There are a few outcrops of flat rock on the eastern side of this bay, but sand dominates. The peninsula to the west of the bay ends with fingers of flat rock and a little strand at Portmore. There is more low rock to the north on the western side of Blacksod Bay, but this gives way to extensive sands with occasional patches of reef. Much of the shoreline along here is backed by dune fields.

North of Annagh Head lies a series

of bays with precipitous promontories between each one, towards the cliffs around Erris Head. Rock surrounds the outer reaches of Broadhaven Bay, with extensive sands inside the sheltered parts of this bay. Around Benwee Head and to the east lie extensive rocky headlands, many of them extremely steep, with deep sandy coves in among them. This pattern continues to Belderg Harbour and on to Downpatrick Head with extensive reefs on its north western shore. Less severe rocks line its north eastern shore. There is sand at Lackan Bay, and more rubbly foreshore of low rock extending into Killala Bay. On the west side there is more sand situated amidst the low lying rocks.

Charter boats operate out from Westport, Newport, Achill Sound, Clare Island, Belmullet and Killala. As with all Eire fishing, preliminary enquiries should be addressed to the Central Fisheries Board in Dublin (their address is given in the Dublin section). They will be able to inform you of new developments.

Trailed boats may be launched from ramps at the following locations: Old Head (near Louisburgh), Westport, Rosmoney, Rosscahill, Newport, Mulranny, Achill Sound, Cloughmore, Purteen Harbour, Belmullet, Ballyglass, Ballycastle, Killala and Ballina.

Tides times for round here may be estimated by adding 6 hours to the times given for Dublin.

There is a tremendous variety of fish species around here, and once again the list here contains almost everything on the Irish list. There are fewer bass up here, but those that are caught are generally big ones. At Westport there is a thriving club which centres round the Westport Sea Angling Centre, The Quay, Westport (Tel: Westport 251). It can fairly be said that the visitor here is likely to receive a warm welcome from the members.

1 Roonagh Lough   Some six miles of surf beaches lie along here where flounders, the occasional tope and large bass may be taken. When going for tope it is wise to bury weighted paper bags full of rubby-dubby in a line from the low water mark and to cast fish baits over them.

2 Louisburgh   The beach here may be fished for flounders, with a chance of a big bass. Around the Old Head and at Lecanvey there is some rock fishing for small pollack, wrasse and dogfish, with the possibility of rays on fish bait cast well out on to sand.

3 Bertraw Island From the mainland a narrow strip of land sticks out into Westport Bay. Spinning into the tide race from the western side produces a few bass and some mackerel when they are inshore. Bottom fishing with large fish baits has produced bass, monkfish and rays.

4 Corraun Peninsula Access from the road to a number of rocky sites is easy because the rock slopes quite gently to the sea. Pollack and wrasse may be taken here, together with mackerel when the weather is settled in summer. Long casting with fish baits on to sand will produce rays, with the chance of tope or monkfish.

5 Achill Island There are some fine rock marks along the southern shore, though access is less than easy to most of them. However, a careful climb should produce pollack, mackerel and, if there is sand, rays, monkfish and tope. Keel Strand can be fished for flounders and there is a fair chance of a bass. The Irish record sea-trout was taken here, so spinning from nearby rocks may produce another. Further west, via a road that was carved out of the 800 foot high cliffs, Keem Strand can be fished for bass, flounders and, in autumn turbot. There is the possibility of a sea-trout on a carefully cut slice of mackerel. Moyteoge Point, on the western side of this bay, offers good rock fishing. The shore fishing has not been over explored here, to say the least, thus offering opportunities to the man who likes to find things out for himself.

6 The Mullet Peninsula The southern side of Annagh Head has fine fishing for pollack, mackerel and wrasse. There are plenty of other rock marks around this peninsula that produce similar fishing. Where a reasonable sea bed is to be found, conger eels, tope, monkfish and rays are likely to be caught. The south western part of this peninsula is one vast surf beach and offers great potential for bass, rays, sea-trout and who knows what other species? It is unlikely that the visitor will see anybody else fishing here. This is one of Ireland's more deserted areas.

7 Benwee Head The north eastern edge of Broadhaven Bay is largely unexplored for shore fishing, and the same goes for the shoreline for many miles east of Benwee Head to Lachan

Bay. Some places, as where Mount Glinsk falls 2000 feet to the sea, are inaccessible. However, the determined explorer will find many places around here that offer fine fishing. After all, boats out from Broadhaven and Killala make excellent catches close in of many large and interesting species like pollack, cod, ling, haddock, coalfish, conger, gurnards, turbot, tope, brill, rays and skate.

8 Killala Bay (west side) At Lackan bay, scrape some sand-eels from the sand at the mouth of the river and fish into the surf with them for small turbot, flounders and possibly bass. Other sandy beaches inside the bay offer flounder fishing, while nearby rock promontories may be fished for wrasse, pollack, conger eels and possibly rays.

Bait Areas
This heavily indented coastline has been but lightly explored by the sea angler. With so much excellent freshwater and game fishing nearby, local anglers fish for salmon and sea-trout – a picture that is widespread throughout Ireland. Therefore not all the bait beds have been publicised. There is no shortage of lugworm which can be dug with ease and a little energy from many sandy areas. There is also the chance of finding some excellent razorfish and clam beds. Peeler crab may be gathered in fair numbers during the summer months from areas of rubble, which are quite common hereabouts, and inside some harbours.
A Lugworm and possibly other sand-inhabiting bait forms
D Sand-eels

Imitation sand eels for use on fly fishing tackle for bass, mackerel, coalfish and pollack.

Sligo and Leitrim

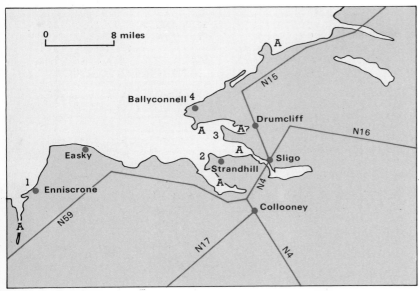

The eastern side of Killala Bay is made up of extensive flat reefs and rocks, with a few sandy beaches, like the one at Enniscrone (or Inishcrone). East of Lenadoon Point along the shore of Sligo Bay, the foreshore is largely rocky as far as Aughris Head. There is some sand on the west side of the Head, but Dunmoran Strand lies on the east side, then more flat rock continues round to Ballysadare Bay. On the eastern side of this bay, across the narrow entrance, lies a fine west-facing sandy beach, and beyond the extensive sand flats of Cummeen Strand situated to the west of the town of Sligo.

There is a rocky headland north west of Drumcliff Bay, with sand making up most of the foreshore along here and north east of Roskeeragh Point, with some rubble around Altmore, then the extensive sands at Grange, Cliffony and Banduff Strand before shallow reef and low lying rock takes over on the southern shore of Donegal Bay – with, of course, a few sand patches.

Charter boats operate out from Enniscrone, Mullaghmore, and, possibly, from other small harbours hereabouts. Anglers bringing their own boats are likely to experience problems along this part of the coast as launching facilities are limited and slipways for boats will have to be hunted out. Unfortunately this lack of offshore facilities does no justice to the fine fishing to be had out from Sligo Bay, much of which is undeveloped. Tope, good pollack, coalfish, flounders, good turbot, brill, ling, rays, cod, haddock, skate and blue shark all hunt off this section of the coast – the sort of fishing that many anglers would love to have off their nearest bit of coast.

The shore fishing is quite good here. There are plenty of flounders on the sandy beaches, with small pollack, small coalfish, mackerel, garfish, some wrasse and other small species around what few reasonable rock marks there are. But then, little detailed exploration has been undertaken for the tope potential. There are masses of tope around the inside of Sligo Bay at times – the salmon netsmen complain, and the riparian owners demand their blood. What could one of the Lowestoft tournament casters do with a slice of fresh herring or mackerel at one of the inlets inside Sligo Bay?

A fine reward for a day's patience, a good bull huss. One of the joys of fishing in Ireland is the wide expanses of unexploited coastline.

As with all Eire fishing, make preliminary enquiries to the Central Fisheries Board in Dublin (their address and telephone number are to be found under the Dublin section).

Subtract 6 hours from Dublin times to find out the times of the tides.

1 Enniscrone (Inishcrone) The flatfish here are small and numerous – easy to catch, too, if you have a young son who demands a crack at sea angling and cannot cast very far. Just occasionally large bass are encountered along here. Flatfish may also be caught from the pier here, and from nearby rocks, where small conger eels and smaller pollack may be had.

2 Strandhill Flounders may be caught from the surf beaches hereabouts, with the possibility of some tope, especially around the mouth of Ballysadare Bay early in the year on the first part of the flood tide and the middle of the ebb. Quite a tide tears through here – which the tope like – and so grapnel leads are a must. Groundbaiting with a mess of pulverised mackerel, sprat, herring or whatever is handy mixed with pilchard oil, horticultural dried blood, bran, and similar evil concoctions should cast a suitable spell on the fish.

3 · Rosses Point Mackerel spinning is the mainstay of sport here, together with small flatfish. This area is a nursery for immature flounders, plaice and dabs, all of which are willing to commit suicide on a choice

length of lugworm. There is plenty to be dug locally.

4 Ballyconnell On the southern side of Cloonagh Bay is a rocky area from which pollack and, sometimes, mackerel may be taken by spinning. At Mullaghmore, the harbour yields a few fair conger at times, with small wrasse and small pollack also to be taken. On the north western side of this headland wrasse, pollack and mackerel may be caught from the rocks. The coastline in between these two points is not particularly inspiring and, as yet, largely unexplored. Again, there are opportunities here for the adventurous to break new ground.

Bait Areas

Lugworm can be dug at a number of sites, and there are probably good razorfish beds to hand, too. The visitor may care to do some investigating for himself as fresh razorfish is a premier bait, both from the shore and from a boat. Crabs can be uncovered among areas of rubble and around piers.

A Lugworm and possibly other sand-dwelling baits

FOR THE FAMILY

An area of great scenic beauty and variety, ideal for family touring when not fishing. Much to do and see in 'Yeats Country' and Carrick on Shannon, with its fine marina. There is boating, walking, golf, tennis and music, festivals and other events around the source of the Shannon.

Gleniff Horseshoe north of Sligo. Spectacular scenic drive in mountains and glens with splendid views of Truskmore, 2113 ft.

Lissadel House Drumcliff. A fine house in classical style overlooking Sligo Bay. Yeats associations. May–Sept except Sunday. At Grange you may see craftsmen making Sligo hand cut crystal.

Glencar Lough nr Sligo, astride the two counties Sligo and Leitrim. Two waterfalls cascade down from the mountains in a superb setting.

Lough Gill cruises 2½ hours. Explore the lough on a luxury cruiser. Readings of Yeats's poetry and a visit to Innisfree.

Lough Key Forest Park nr Ballymote. A day in one of Ireland's most beautiful forests. Gardens, nature trail, viewing tower, boat trips, swimming, restaurant.

Carrick on Shannon is the centre for cruising on the River Shannon, has a wide range of sporting facilities and festivals and open air events in summer.

The Redgill rubber sand-eel. The most deadly lure for sea fishing yet devised.

Donegal and Londonderry

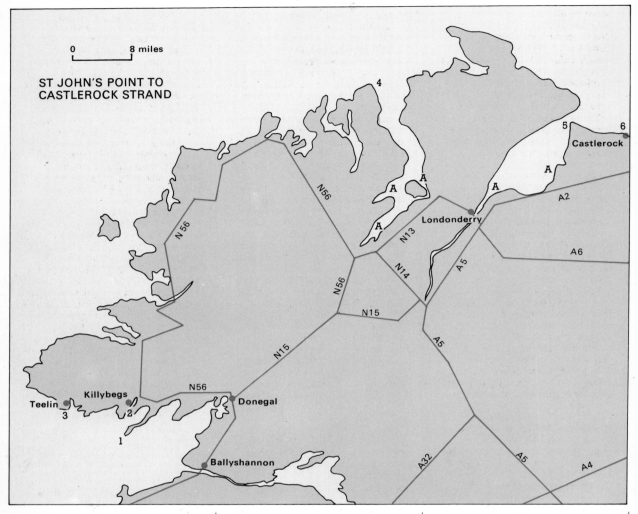

ST JOHN'S POINT TO CASTLEROCK STRAND

The eastern shore of Donegal Bay consists largely of sand. Tullan Strand is separated from the others to the north by three miles of low rocky reef. This reef can also be found along the northern shore, with small sandy bays in between, especially along the peninsula that terminates at St John's Point. Sandy McSwyne's Bay is separated from the sand of Killybegs Harbour by rocky Carntullagh Head. Likewise Fintragh Bay by Drumanoo Head. Then there is more sand among the flat reefy ground that extends westwards to Muckros Head.

There are sandy beaches inside Tawny Bay and Teelin Bay, then rocky headlands westwards to Carrigan Head, with the massive cliffs of Slieve League to the north. There are a couple of sandy bays at Malin Beg,

though the coastline here is very rugged, with rocks and cliffs continuing round to Doonalt in Glen Bay, where there is a short strand at the estuary mouth.

There are more cliffs north and east of here, with severely restricted access to the foreshore, especially to the north of the Slievetooey mountain. The cliffs continue into the twin bays each side of rocky Loughros Point.

Maghera Strand lies at the mouth of the Bracky River, which flows into Loughros Beg Bay. At the mouth of the twin estuaries of the river Owentocker and Owened, flowing into Loughros More Bay, is Ballinreavy Strand.

Rocks skirt Dawros Head to the sands inside Gweebarra Bay, with the almost land-locked Trawenagh Bay,

then the strands run north west to rocky Crohy Head. Northwards from here the coastline disintegrates into a jumble of rocks, islets and sandy beaches called The Rosses. Aran Island (not to be confused with the three Aran Islands off Galway Bay), is the largest of several lumps of Donegal that Atlantic breakers have separated from the mainland.

Most of the coastline here is easy to get to. Sands, with occasional outcrops of rock, are to be found around Inishfree Bay, Gweedore Bay and northwards to Bloody Foreland. The cliffs from here stretch for three miles to the east, then the coastline softens again with the sands of Ballyness Bay, opposite the three islands of Inishbofin, Inishdooey and Inishbeg. The sands in this bay extend for several miles north eastwards to the headlands of Crockagarran and Black Burrow, with another rocky headland at Horn Head on the western side of Sheep Haven. There is a lot of marshland separating this headland from the mainland. Inside the Haven are wide sandy beaches separated by rock promontories.

The east side of this bay is also virtually an island, called Ros Rosguill, the seaward side of which is a jumble or rock tumbling to the sea with small promontories, offshore islets and little sandy coves.

To the east, Mulroy Bay reaches inland to a labyrinth of sheltered water, with coves, little headlands, islets and rubble arranged in a higgledy-piggledy manner around the Fanad Peninsula. There is sand inside Ballyhiernan Bay, with rocks becoming more frequent to Fanad Head.

The shoreline of Lough Swilly is more organised. There are patches of rock with sandy bays on the north west side with sandy Ballymastocker Bay nestling among the green hills. There is more rock – and coves – south to Mill Bay, then extensive sand-flats that extend southwards to Inch Island and into the Swilly estuary and, on the eastern shore, northwards past Buncrana. The shoreline then becomes more rocky towards Dunree Head. Crummies Bay lies to the north, and the shoreline here skirts the feet of the Urris Hills and is extensively rocky, but with a picturesque strand at Lenan Bay, sheltered by Lenan Head, with more rock northwards to Dunaff Head with its sheer precipices.

Rockstown Bay, to the east, is aptly named. The place is a jumble of boulders and rubble – but with some sand. Tullagh Bay, around rocky Tullagh Point, has a wide sweep of shallow sand-flats. This is bounded to the east by the foothills of Mount Binnion, with Pollan Bay thereafter. Doagh Isle is separated from the mainland by low lying marshland. Inside Trawbreaga Bay the shore is sandy, with stony mud in sheltered places. Northwards from here the country becomes increasingly rocky towards Malin Head, though there is a rather stony cove called White Strand Bay just south of West Town.

The rocks around Malin Head are extensive and sheer, with a scattering of sandy coves. Such ground terminates at the massive cliffs of Glengad Head, with the coast mellowing towards Culdaff Bay. East of Dunmore Head are small rocky headlands and a few sandy coves towards the precipices of Mount Crookback. There is a pleasant bay of sand and reef at Kinnagoe Bay before more cliffs run round to Inishowen Head.

Sand and rocks intermingle on the west side of Lough Foyle, becoming increasingly sandy south west of Moville towards the mouth of the River Foyle – vast flats of sand and mud that gradually diminish on the east side towards Magilligan Point. There is a fine sandy beach east-wards from here to Coleraine, then rocks again and little headlands to Portrush. A sandy beach lies to the east of the town, then rocks towards Bushmills.

Charter boats operate out from Rathmullan (Lough Swilly), Portrush, Portstewart, Burtonport and Bunbeg (Donegal Bay), Downings and Port Na Blagh (Sheephaven Bay), Culdaff, Greencastle and Moville.

Trailed boats may be launched from ramps at a large number of harbours, the principal ones being those from which charter boats operate. There are numerous inlets where the road comes close enough to the shore to allow lighter craft to be dragged down to the water.

Along this northern coast, cold water fish are to be found mingling with those that prefer warm water. Bass are scarce, though the ones that are taken tend to be very large. Offshore fishing is for haddock, dogfish, tope (plenty), common skate, rays, conger eels, ling, cod, coalfish, pollack, gurnard, turbot, plaice and blue shark. The shore fishing is rich and varied for wrasse, pollack, tope, bull huss, sea-trout, flatfish, conger eels, rays and so on. Unbelievably, a great deal of the shore fishing along this huge stretch of coast has never been tried. There are beaches and rock ledges that have never felt an angler's boot. This seems a severe oversight because the seas off here are rich in fish. The probable reason is the rich coarse and game fishing inland. Local anglers are happier fishing from a sheltered river bank for good salmon and sea-trout rather than brave the elements for an inedible 60 lb tope or two.

A technique that works well around here is spinning or fly fishing into the surf and tideways for sea-trout. Some large fish are taken, especially at night. Although this is not easy fishing, it can be as rewarding as mullet fishing with large bags of fish taken when conditions are right and the best techniques have been discovered for a specific mark. Unlike sea-trout when in fresh water, the mouth of this fish when at sea is hard and bony. Sharp hooks are required, and it is essential to bang them in hard if the fish is not to come loose during its spirited fight. High summer is the best time to find them close to the shore, especially when the fry and small fish are close in. Mackerel weather is ideal.

Tide times are some 5 to 6 hours earlier than at Dublin.

1 St John's Point Fishing from the rocks near the lighthouse here, one can easily get the impression one is fishing in the middle of the Atlantic. There is no land between this point and America, so a heavy swell is often to be expected here, partly due to the tide running around this headland. Large pollack, mackerel, wrasse and good conger are taken here. If you can find some sand, try for tope, rays and monkfish. Or, who knows, a large common skate?

This angler on his comfortable tree trunk perch has plenty of time for contemplation.

Donegal and Londonderry

2 Killybegs Excellent conger fishing is to be had inside this commercial fishing port, and the mullet fishing, using bread or fish, can be very good during periods of settled weather. Mackerel come up this inlet in summer and may be caught from the quays, together with small pollack.

3 Teelin This is another commercial fishing port and fair conger can be caught here, too, fishing from the pier. Mullet also abound inside here, the Owenteskiny estuary, and flounders are, as usual, almost inevitable.

4 Fanad Head Wrasse, mackerel and pollack are taken here. Inside Lough Swilly there is good tope fishing. If you can find a suitable rock ledge giving on to a clean bottom, it may be possible to catch tope here at some time during the tide while they enter or leave the lough. Bottom fishing could also produce rays and turbot. Coalfish, while small, can be abundant here, and sea-trout may be taken by spinning off the rocks.

5 Magilligan Point Just inside the point there is fair fishing for dabs, flounders and dogfish. From the point, a long caster armed with fresh mackerel bait and some sort of rubby-dubby might persuade a tope or two to depart from the main channel. On the opposite bank, at Moville, there is fair rock fishing for coalfish, pollack, wrasse and mackerel at Dunagree Point and also to the south of the town.

6 Castlerock Strand Fish from the walls on each side of the River Bann for flounders, bass, sea-trout and the chance of a conger eel. The strand itself fishes well after a storm for small turbot, bass, flounders and other small species. Portstewart Strand produces similar fishing, with small coalfish abundant in autumn.

Bait Areas

Bait is abundant inside most of the inlets and estuaries. Areas of sand offer lugworm, ragworm, razorfish and clams. It is highly likely that, in western Donegal at least, your questing spade will be the first to be dug down into these untouched bait beds.

Obviously, only experienced shore anglers are likely to undertake their own exploration, so keep an eye open for sand-eel banks and for peeler crab beds, too.

A Known lugworm beds, also offering clam, razorfish and possibly ragworms

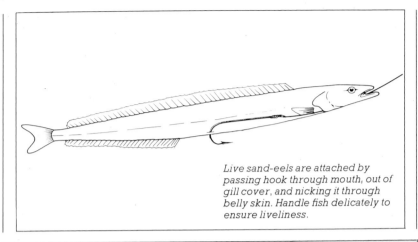

Live sand-eels are attached by passing hook through mouth, out of gill cover, and nicking it through belly skin. Handle fish delicately to ensure liveliness.

FOR THE FAMILY

South **Donegal** has sandy beaches, quiet coves, the popular resort of Bundoran, old fishing ports and handwoven tweeds. In the mountainous north is a contrasting landscape of hill country, cliffs and good beaches – a spacious and beautiful area for sport and open air activity.

Arranmore Island one of several islands to visit on the north coast, for sea and lake fishing and enjoyable exploring.

Belleek nr Ballyshannon. A guided tour of the factory making the famous Belleek porcelain (closed first 2 weeks August). At **Ardara** you can visit handweaving centres.

Glenesh Pass a superb scenic drive in a mountainous area. Walks and picnic places. Also explore the magnificent coastal area to the west.

Rossnowlagh the Donegal County Museum of local history is worth a visit. Also a beautiful beach with surfing facilities.

Ards Forest Park nr Creeslough. A good family place for swimming, walks, wildlife and picnics, Adventure centre nearby.

Grays Printing Press Tyrone. Visit Strabane's ancient printing shop which had close links with United States in the 18th Century. National Trust.

The old walled city of **Londonderry** has much to interest visitors. At Portstewart and Castlerock there is plenty of seaside entertainment and sport. Throughout the county there are scenic drives, parks and houses to visit, the Sperrin Mountains,

interesting villages and small towns.

Ness Country Park nr Londonderry City. 46 acres of woodland and Ulster's highest waterfall. Nature trail. Picnic sites.

Mussenden Temple and Bishops Gate. Built in 1783 on the clifftop. Cliff paths, woodlands, and the Glen Hill nature trail.

Springhill Moneymore. Visit an elegant 17thC house with fine interior, paintings, costume museum and kitchens. Apr–Sept.

Ulster-American Folk Park Camphill, Tyrone. Exhibits of Ulster's links with the United States. Covered wagons, etc.

Drum Manor Forest Park Cookstown, Tyrone. Spend a day in an unusual garden, specially designed to attract butterflies.

Londonderry City Georgian architecture. It has many interesting historic buildings. Its 63-acre Templemore Sports complex is among the modern attractions.

Roe Valley Country Park fine riverside landscape and woodlands, with picnic areas, scenic walks, canoeing, angling. There is a visitor centre and restaurant.

Gortin Glen Forrest Park Sperrin Mountains. Signposted walks and a scenic drive, picnic sites etc in superb setting.

Always an encouraging sight to any sea angler – a plentiful supply of fry in the shallows.

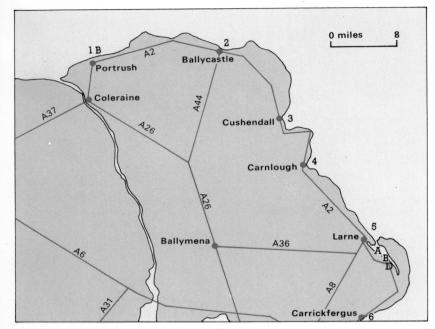

There are rocks to the west of Bushmills, which has a sandy foreshore, then comes the famous Giant's Causeway, steps of basalt rock that tumble to the sea around to Benbane Head. The rocks become less severe eastwards to White Park Bay. The headland around Ballintoy has a rocky shoreline, becoming steep again to Whitehead, opposite Rathlin Island. There is a sandy beach at Ballycastle, then rocks and craggy precipices to Benmore Head, Torr Head, Runabay Head, with the rocks easing again around Cushendun Bay. There is a fair bit of sheer rock south of here, but again mellowing to Red Bay. Sand, rubble, and small outcrops of rock characterise the foreshore round Garron Point. Carnlough Bay is separated from Glenarm Bay by rocky Straidkilly Point, with boulders, rubble and sand becoming more frequent from Glenarm south east to Ballygalley Head. There are just a couple of rocky outcrops between this Head and the sand and mud flats of Lough Larne.

Island Magee has sand on its landward side, rock on its seaward side, with a causeway of sand and rubble separating it from the Isle of Muck. Rubble and sand proliferates on the northern shores of Belfast Lough; the south side, around Holywood, consisting of extensive sand flats.

Charter boats operate out from Ballycastle, Portrush, Waterfoot, Carnlough, Ballylumford, Portmuck, Belfast, and possibly lesser harbours. Trailed craft may be launched from ramps sited at Portballintrae (near Portrush), Ballycastle (the nearest point for a quick run to Scotland), Larne, Whitehead and Carrickfergus. Other sites are available for smaller craft.

The fishing around the Antrim coast is good, though far from over-developed. About the only fish that is scarce here is the bass. Hake are caught in Belfast Lough, though less than in years gone by. Pollution by industry along the shores of this lough is blamed for the decline

The tidal difference from London Bridge is minus $2\frac{3}{4}$ hours and from Dublin, subtract $\frac{1}{2}$ hour for Belfast. Subtract $5\frac{1}{4}$ hours from Dublin times for Portrush. With such extensive variation around this coast, it is essential that tide times are obtained locally.

1 Portrush Inside the harbour there are good conger to be caught. One way to provoke the fish to attack the baits is to toss in weighted carrier bags full of fish slurry. The piers here offer good sport in winter for whiting and shore-sized coalfish. At Ramore head, fish from the rocks under the coastguard station for pollack, wrasse, conger, dogfish and the occasional

ray or winter cod. Other rocks in front of the town provide fishing for conger, flounders, plaice, rays and dogfish. Details from Joe Mullen, 70 Main Street, Portrush.

2 Ballycastle Rathlin Sound, between Ballycastle and Rathlin Island, has deep water and a strong tide race, making boat fishing practicable only on neap tides, and even then preferably at slack water. The wreck of the *Drake* lies here, torpedoed during the First World War, and now is very prolific in the catches of fish it yields. There is some fair general shore fishing here for conger, wrasse and pollack from rocks, coalfish, whiting and codling in winter. To the east, both Fair Head and Torr Head are precipitous, making access difficult. Agile anglers can get down, however, though local guidance is advised to prevent accidents. Pollack, wrasse and conger are the quarry once there. In between the two headlands, Murlough Bay offers fair fishing in winter for small coalfish, codling, whiting and flatfish. Night fishing from this beach is recommended for best results.

3 Cushendall Night fishing around high water inside Red Bay, to the south of the town, produces whiting, coalfish, cod and flatfish in winter. Summer season fishing yields the occasional bass, with some fair plaice, especially early in the summer, while small species are likely to be found at other times. Try also fishing the strand at Cushendun at night.

4 Carnlough To the north, Garron Point should be fished on the sheltered southern side for pollack, wrasse, conger eels and a few red rock cod in summer. Winter fishing produces small conger at times, together with more cod and a few whiting. There is fair offshore boat fishing to be had from this harbour for virtually anything from tope to gurnard. To the south, at Glenarm, there is fishing from the pier and rock marks for mackerel, small pollack, and small conger. In winter codling, flounders and whiting are abundant.

5 Larne For boat fishing take the ferry from Larne to Ballylumford on the eastern side of the inlet – this is where most of the boats leave from. A popular boat mark is the Maiden Rocks, a series of pinnacles crowned by a lighthouse. It is best not to try it alone as tides are confused and and strong around these rocks. From the shore, there is a little rock fishing for pollack, small coalfish, wrasse and conger. The beaches yield the occasional turbot, plaice, flounders, dabs and, at the mouth of the inlet, the occasional tope. Winter fishing produces the usual species mentioned above.

6 Carrickfergus   To the north, off Portmuck, lies a bank of shingle called The Gobbins. It produces fair general boat fishing, but the most interesting has to be the feathering practised around dusk in early June for the herrings, known locally as 'black-gut herrings'. The fishing period is brief, but the catches can be spectacular, with boatloads of anglers enjoying a fiesta atmosphere, smothered in silvery scales, with maybe six to eight stone of fish per angler per boat. Very often big cod are below the herring shoals and a pirk will bring a few aboard.

The pier at Carrickfergus produces fair fishing for most of the species to be found along this section of the coast. There are good mullet there at times, though few anglers bother to catch them.

Out in the lough, fishing from a boat, the occasional large cod or hake is taken even today. Perhaps one day the ravages of mankind will recede sufficiently to allow stocks to build up, thus making this sheltered lough again one of the most prolific small, sheltered fisheries in Ireland. With plenty of tackle dealers in Belfast, further information can be had, among others, from: Joseph Braddell & Son Ltd, 1 North Street (Tel: Belfast (0232) 20525); John Dowds & Sons, 173 Victoria Street (Tel: Belfast (0232) 31091) also, Rod & Tackle, 78 Holywood Road (Tel: Belfast (0232) 652971).

Bait Areas
Obtaining bait should be no problem, especially in the south of the county, with prolific bait beds inside the loughs.
A   Lugworm
B   Ragworm
D   Clam
Crab should be obtainable wherever you can find a suitable patch of rubble inside an estuary or lough and along the low water mark on some beaches.

An impressive catch, the T-shirt says it all!

FOR THE FAMILY

Holiday resorts on the 'Causeway' coat in the north, and Belfast in the south east, provide plenty of entertainments and places to visit. There is the scenic coast road, dramatic coastline near the Giant's Causeway, the beauty of the Antrim glens, and good boating, walking, trekking, etc.

Shanes Castle Railway   ride the lakeside miniature steam train through woodlands. RSPB Reserve, Apr–Sept. Children's playground, Shane Castle. Deer park.

Lough Neagh cruises   Sixmilewater. Enjoy the sights of the Great Lough on a cruiser. Bar, refreshments. May–Sept.

Giant's Causeway   Portrush.

Geological walk. 3-mile walk with a signposted and explanatory guide to the unique and fascinating rock formation.

Rathlin Island   daily sailings from Ballycastle. June–Aug. A peaceful island where Robert the Bruce saw the spider. Birdwatchers can have a field day.

Carrickfergus   the finest Norman castle in Ireland with splendid weapon collection. Carrickfergus has a fine promenade, beach, leisure centre, 2 swimming pools.

Causeway Coast Lion Park Benvarden. Lions and other wildlife in drive-through park. Restaurant and picnic area. Local and African handicrafts.

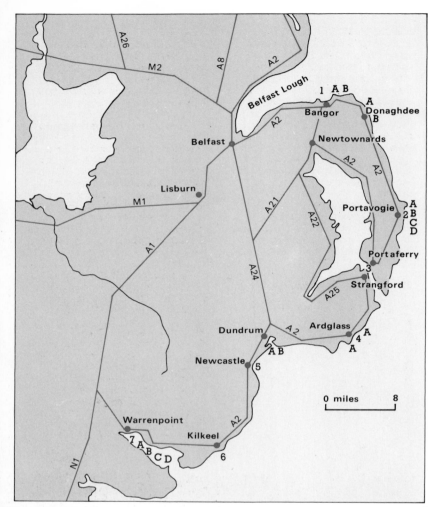

The south side of Belfast Lough is an area of extensive sand flats. From Grey Point, past Bangor to Donaghadee, the shoreline consists largely of sandy coves set among small rocky promontories. Sand becomes the dominating feature, with occasional rocky outcrops and headlands southwards to Ballyquintin Point at the rocky mouth of Strangford Lough, with its multitude of little islands. The shores of this lough are largely of sand with some rocks sticking up here and there.

South of Killard Point, opposite Ballyquintin Point, sand gives way to rock, with cliffs rearing up around Guns Island and flat rock predominating. Ardglass has a rock-girt harbour, while a mile away Killough harbour is extensively sandy both inside and out in the bay.

Rocks then extend south east to St John's Point on the east side of the extensive sands of Dundrum Bay. The western side of the bay, south of Newcastle, is comprised of a foreshore of sand and boulders backed by low hills. This ground extends southwards to Annalong, becoming more sandy towards Carlingford Lough. The lough itself is set among wide sandy beaches with more sands round the peninsula on the southern shore.

Charter boats operate out from Warrenpoint, Kilkeel, Newcastle, Groomsport, Ardglass, Portaferry, Killyleagh, Portavogie, Donaghadee and Bangor. Trailed craft may be launched at ramps at Bangor, Donaghadee, Portaferry, Kircubbin, Quoile, Strangford, Strangford Bay, Killyleagh, Ringhaddy Sound,

Newcastle, Warrenpoint and Carlingford Lough. There are, as elsewhere, other sites where small boats can be dragged down to the sea.

Offshore, the fishing is for dogfish, cod, haddock, conger, plaice, rays, turbot, whiting, gurnard, coalfish, bull huss and spur dogfish, *inter alia*. Strangford Lough is famed for large skate – a depleted resource – very big tope, rays, large spur dogfish and hake, with other species mingled among them.

Shore fishing is for tope, rays, conger, wrasse, pollack, mullet, sea-trout, and the occasional bass among other species.

Tidal difference at Belfast is $2\frac{3}{4}$ hours before London Bridge times, $\frac{1}{2}$ hour before Dublin times. At Dundrum Bay the tidal difference is just 10 minutes earlier than Dublin times.

1 Bangor Dig a supply of lugworm, clam and ragworm from the prolific bait beds inside this lough, and take the results of your labour to one of the piers in this area for coalfish, codling, whiting and flatfish in winter; flatfish and small pollack in summer. Better still, drive out to Orlock Point, 3 miles north of Donaghadee, clamber down to the rocks below the coastguard station and fish for rock cod, small coalfish, lesser spotted dogfish and wrasse. There is also the chance of a ray here, and maybe even a tope, if you have the requisite fish bait and plenty of patience. The boat fishing is fairly good around here. Some anglers go out to Copeland Island and fish from the rocks for cod, mackerel, pollack, conger, wrasse and small coalfish. More details from Trap and Tackle, 6 Seacliff Road, Bangor (Tel: Bangor (0247) 58515). To the south, at Donaghadee, the pier fishing is not very good.

2 Portavogie Fishing from the pier here after dark produces some very fair conger eels. Otherwise, the fishing is for fairly small fish of the more common species found along this shoreline. Not a great deal is known about the shore fishing along this, the Ards Peninsula. Rock marks are likely to produce the standard rock species and open beaches will yield those species that hunt around clean ground.

3 Portaferry The tide runs through the inlet to Strangford Lough quite fiercely, especially during spring tides. Fishing inside the lough, flounders and mullet are abundant, especially round the low tide period when they are grouped together in the channels – some of which are remarkably deep. Indeed, there is a fair chance of tope, that scourge of flatfish, in these channels as the tide floods. Sea-trout are also to be taken in these channels, especially at the mouths of streams flowing into the lough. Around the mouth of the lough, the few outcrops of rock give on to sand, especially around Killard Point, which looks a fair ambush point for better size species. Bait is abundant inside the sheltered lough. Details from Comber Sports Centre, 18 Castle Street, Comber (Tel: Comber (0247) 872 846). This town is at the head of the lough.

4 Ardglass Fish from the pier for small conger, mackerel, coalfish, whiting, codling and flatfish in season. There is fair boat fishing off here, too. Rock marks beyond the golf course yield conger, wrasse and pollack – and golf-balls, especially after bank holidays and strong north westerly winds! Offshore lies a mark that yields specimen short-spined sea scorpions by the hundred. If this species is not on your list, this is the place to remedy the situation. Some are over a foot long.

5 Newcastle Not to be confused with the village of Newcastle to the south, just north of Wicklow. The inlet to the north at Dundrum Bay yields excellent flounders early in the year as they come to the open sea to spawn. Fish in the main channel as the tide starts to flood. Mullet are abundant in this estuary and may be caught on bread after a steady groundbaiting campaign with mashed bread. Otherwise the bay is too shallow to produce much more than small flatfish.

6 Kilkeel The pier produces codling, whiting, plaice, dabs and flounders, with little in the way of larger species to interest the shore angler. Small coalfish become abundant in the autumn here and may be caught from the inner harbour on fly tackle, or strings of feathers.

To the south, the pier at Annalong produces similar pier fishing, with mullet abundant during the summer months, but rarely fished for. The boat fishing can be quite good off here, though the facilities are limited unless you take your own vessel.

7 Warrenpoint Fish from Cranfield Point at the mouth of the Carlingford Lough for dogfish, flounder, a few bass, whiting, codling, small coalfish and so forth. Inside the lough there are plenty of mullet – largely ignored by local anglers – and flounders. Dabs and plaice are also caught here. There is a fair chance, if you have the time and patience, of a tope or two when fishing from Cranfield Point, casting a fish bait out a long way, around dusk on a flooding tide – if the dogfish leave the bait alone for long enough. The sheltered waters inside the lough provide fair boat fishing for tope, rays, spur dogfish, conger, flounders and, when the weather settles down in summer, for mackerel. Details may be had from Frank McAlinden, Quo Vadis Fishing Co., Ballinran, Killowen Road, Rostrevor (Tel: Rostrevor (069 373) 437).

Bait Areas
The sheltered loughs and sandy harbours provide plenty of bait but the fishing is not too hot. It seems to be a general rule that where the fishing is best, the bait beds are poorest!

A   Lugworm
B   Ragworm
C   Crab
D   Clam and possibly razorfish

A king-sized crayfish, sadly a rare catch, even by boat-anglers.

FOR THE FAMILY
Enjoy the beaches along the Ards Peninsula, the Mountains of Mourne, Newcastle (which caters for every holiday activity), Strangford Lough and its islands, and the forests, parks, houses and ancient buildings throughout the county.

Ulster Folk and Transport Museum Cultra. 180 acres of natural landscape with reconstructed farm and domestic buildings, all kinds of vehicles, etc. May–Oct.

Castle Ward House Strangford. 18thC mansion. Palladian and Gothic. In 600 acres of woodlands and gardens beside Strangford Lough. Theatre, craft museum.

Strangford Lough a mecca for sailing, boating and birdwatching enthusiasts.

Tollymore Forest Park Newcastle. an oasis of beauty and tranquility. Not far from the heights of Sleive Donard in the Mourne Mountains, 2796 ft.

Rowallane Garden Saintfield. Outstandingly beautiful gardens. Rare trees, rhododendrons, azaleas, etc. Over 50 acres.

Mount Stewart House an interesting house to visit with 80 acres of varied gardens and a Greek-style temple.

Castlewellan Forest Park lake and arboretum, one of the finest in the British Isles, mountain views. Boating, angling, café, exhibition, etc.

Louth and Meath

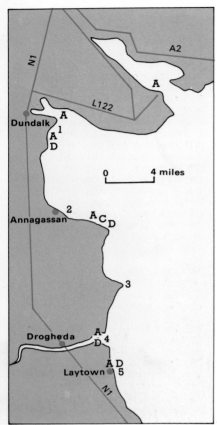

The sands of Carlingford Lough extend southwards from the mouth of the lough to Cooley Point, then westwards to the vast flats of Dundalk Bay. These shallow flats stretch for several miles to Annagassan and on to Dunany Point, then on southwards again to the rocky headland of Clogher Head. The sand continues for several miles to Drogheda, with more to the south as far as Balbriggan where there is a rocky headland.

Briefly, this area is great for paddling, poor for fishing. Charter boats operate out from Port Oriel, but catches are generally of small species. Those with their own trailed craft may launch them from ramps at Osmeath, Carlingford (several), and Greenore – all inside Carlingford Lough – there are others at Mountain Bay, Annagassan, Salterstown, and Clogher Head (several). Other sites exist for small craft that do not require a launching ramp.

The tides here occur about $\frac{1}{4}$ hour earlier than at Dublin. Dublin tides, incidentally, are $3\frac{1}{4}$ hours earlier than London Bridge times.

Although there is not much exciting fishing here, that is not necessarily what sea fishing is all about. Many people are happy to go to a quiet shore for a few hours and find solitude surrounded by the huge expanse of sea, shore and sky. Under these conditions, fish can become an intrusion and the need to check the hooks and rebait an unwelcome chore. However, if you want to apply yourself to more productive fishing, here are some suggestions for where to go.

1 Dundalk Bay The extensive shallows of this bay make it a nursery for a small flatfish. Easily-dug worm baits from the sands can be fished into deeper channels with the hope of catching fair size flounders. Early in the year is best for these, and the best time to try is around low tide when the fish are concentrated inside the channels rather than spread out over the flats.

2 Annagassan The sands are less extensive here. Sometimes school bass can be taken here – along with the ubiquitous flatfish – from the Dee estuary.

3 Clogher Head This is about the only rocky outcrop, certainly the largest, between Dundalk and Balbriggan, a distance of some 30 miles as the seagull flies, further as the shore runs. The small harbour on its northern side, Port Oriel, has a pier wall from which dabs, mackerel and small pollack are taken in summer, codling in the spring, autumn and winter. Dabs and flounders are also caught. From the rocks on the outside of the headland, small pollack, small coalfish and codling may be taken.

4 Drogheda The occasional bass is taken from the estuary mouth of the River Boyne, and from the beaches. This estuary is reckoned to mark the most northerly limit of practical bass fishing on the east coast of Ireland. At low tide, peeler crabs collected from the estuary banks or sand-eels gathered from the sand banks at the mouth can be fished in the river for the bass. Flounders are also common here, and from the beaches to each side of the river mouth.

Mullet – thick-lipped – may be caught from the outflow from the fish meal factory at Mornington. Fish bait, obviously, works best.

5 Laytown Situated at the mouth of the River Nanny, bass and flounders can be caught from the shores on either side of the estuary mouth and from the estuary itself. A sheltered location is in the pool downstream of the railway bridge. Mullet congregate here at low tide. Some sea-trout have been taken while spinning into the estuary as the tide starts to flow.

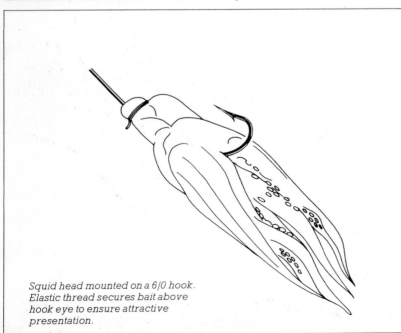

Squid head mounted on a 6/0 hook. Elastic thread secures bait above hook eye to ensure attractive presentation.

Bait Areas

There is plenty of bait hereabouts – but few fish of decent size to offer it to.

Sand-eels can be found on many of the sand bars and flats, with crabs inside some estuaries among rubble, and around Clogher Head. Clams and razorfish can be found inside Dundalk Bay and Carlingford Lough, together with lugworm and some ragworm.

A   Lugworm, ragworm and possibly clam, razorfish etc.
C   Crab
D   Sand-eels

Tired but happy, this angler smilingly acknowledges her day's success to the camera.

FOR THE FAMILY

Louth and Meath cater for every holiday interest – from archaeology to golf. There are good resorts with safe, sandy beaches, heather-covered mountains coming down to the sea. Dundalk, with its May Festival, and Drogheda are excellent centres for entertainment and exploration.

Trim Castle   beautifully situated on the River Boyne, the largest Anglo-Norman fortress in Ireland, with towers and moat.

Rathgory Transport Museum   nr Drogheda. For devotees of vintage cars and motorcycles. See Ireland's first fire engine.

Newgrange   a world famous prehistoric site 2500BC in the Boyne valley. Near the Hill or Tara, once seat of Irish kings.

Ravensdale and Bellurgan   two forest parks near Dundalk. Wonderful walks, nature trail, picnic places, etc.

Book of Kells   in St Columba's church, in Kells, is a facsimile of the original in Dublin. Exhibition and display on the book, and the 5 crosses of Kells.

St John's Castle   Carlingford. In a commanding position overlooking the Lough, a 13thC castle of unusual D-shaped design. The *Slieve Foy* scenic drive has picnic sites overlooking the Lough and the Mountains of Mourne.

Useful Addresses

There are sea angling associations, too numerous to mention here, all over Britain and Ireland. However, listed below are the major sea angling organisations and other bodies who will provide information.

National Federation of Sea Anglers, 26 Downview Crescent, Uckfield, Sussex TN22 1UB (Secretary : Mr R. W. Page).

Central Fisheries Board, Balnagowan, Mobhi Boreen, Glasnevin, Dublin 9. Tel : Dublin (0001 – in UK (01 – in Ireland)) 379206.

Fisheries Branch (Ministry of Agriculture), 2–4 Queen Street, Belfast BT1 6EP. Tel : Belfast (0232) 32417.

Irish Federation of Sea Anglers (Ulster Provincial Council), 15 C Cesnor Park, Carrickfergus, Co. Antrim, N. Ireland. Tel : Carrickfergus (096 03) 65716.

Scottish Federation of Sea Anglers, 8 Frederick Street, Edinburgh EH2 2HB. Tel : Edinburgh (031) 2257611.

Welsh Federation of Sea Anglers, 24 Coveny Street, Splott, Cardiff. Tel : Cardiff (0222) 373730.

European Federation of Sea Anglers, 11 Park Circus, Ayr, Scotland. (Secretary : Mr D. S. Dallas). Tel : Ayr (0292) 67053.

The following tourist boards provide literature and information on sea angling, as well as guidance on accommodation. You will also find the local tourist information office in the area you are visiting very helpful.

British Tourist Authority, 64 St James's Street, London SW1A 3EU. Tel : 01-499 9325.

Irish Tourist Board – Bord Failte, Baggot Street Bridge, Dublin 2. Tel : Dublin (0001 – in UK) (01 – in Ireland) 765871.

Northern Ireland Tourist Board, River House, 48 High Street, Belfast BT1 2DS. Tel : Belfast (0232) 31221 or 36609.

Scottish Tourist Board, 23 Ravelston Terrace, Edinburgh EH4 3EU. Tel : Edinburgh (031) 332 2433.

Wales Tourist Board, Brunel House, 2 Fitzalan Road, Cardiff CF2 1UY. Tel : Cardiff (0222) 499 909.

Acknowledgements

The author and publishers are most grateful for all the assistance they have received in compiling this book and would particularly like to thank all the tackle shops, angling clubs, boat skippers and other individuals who provided invaluable information. We have endeavoured to acknowledge as many as possible in the text, but would also like to thank the following: Charles W. Nevill, Sheerness; E. W. Rodwell, Birchington; David Chamberlain (of the Morning Haze), Kingsdown, nr Deal; H. S. Greenfield & Sons, Canterbury; P. Chidwick, Folkestone; Richard Tunnicliff, Dover – all in Kent; T. Anscombe, The Gunroom Ltd, Henfield; Raycrafts, Selsey – in Sussex; R. Trent, Southampton; Darren Brown (Havant Avenger's AC), Portsmouth, Hants; John Langdon, Truro; Bob Baird, Hayle – in Cornwall; D. R. Clements, Ilfracombe, Devon; Scotts Tackle, Bristol; John Powell, Haverfordwest; I. M. Browning, Milford Haven – in Dyfed; H. P. Hughes, Caernarvon, Gwynedd; John Pouah, Rhyl, Clwyd; Redmayne's Fishing Tackle, Adlington, Lancs; C. E. Howarth, Blackpool; Morton

F. D. Nash, Isle of Whithorn; Innerwell Fishery, Garlieston, Newton Stewart; James McLaughlan, Wishaw, Strathclyde; Alexander MacKay & Son, Tarbert, Strathclyde; Douglas F. McKendrick, Inverness; James S. Taylor, Kirkwall, Orkney; David Waldie Ltd, Stonehaven, Kincardineshire; Captain A. Auld, Peterhead; Bill Treeby, Falkirk, Stirlingshire; Walter M. Laurie, Kirkcaldy, Fife; H. Brown, Pittenweem, Fife; Robert N. Greenwell, Hartlepool, Cleveland; H. Dobson, Scarborough, North Yorks; Jim Blake, Grimsby, Humberside; Sam Kinning, Skegness, Lincs; Jack Codley, Cenit, Kerry; Frank Clarke, Westport, Mayo; Francis Nelson & Son Ltd, Sligo; Charles Bonner, Dungloe, Donegal; C. J. O'Doherty, Donegal; Ivan McCausland, Milford, Donegal; and Smythe Bros, Coleraine, Londonderry.

Thanks also go to all those who worked on the production of the book: **John Bishop** for compiling the 'For the Family' information, **Jackie Fortey** for editorial liaison and research, **Melissa Denny, Hugh Morgan** and **Carole Edwards** for editorial, **Vivienne Webster** for her help with questionnaires, **Clive Sutherland** for production, **Mike Shepley** for reading the manuscript, and **Pete Saag** for design, maps and illustrations.

Index

Index